Martin, James

Learning to pray

Praise for *Learning to Pray*

"A smart, wise, often side-splittingly funny master class in seeking God. Any spiritual seeker—from atheist to professional religious—will cherish this bravura tome from one of our great spiritual guides, in the lineage of C. S. Lewis, Henri Nouwen, Thomas Merton, Gandhi, and Mother Teresa. Hallelujah & amen!"

—Mary Karr, author of *Lit* and *Liars' Club*

"The life of prayer is essential for the believer. And yet so many people feel frightened by prayer. Fear not! James Martin has written a brilliant introduction to prayer, which will help you encounter the Living God, who wants to encounter you!"

—Richard Rohr, OFM, author of *Everything Belongs*

"A trusted teacher, Martin teaches that there is no wrong way to pray, even as he lays out many wonderful ways to pray. This book is for anyone who has avoided prayer for any reason—a strong invitation, a gentle encouragement, a wise masterful guide, and a needed book."

—Ronald Rolheiser, OMI, author of *The Holy Longing*

"This practical and delightful book is truly for everyone. It's reassuring to hear that our moments of pausing, listening, and being grateful are all versions of prayer. This book shows us how to stay with such moments and allow them to change us for the better."

—Kathleen Norris, author of *The Cloister Walk*

"With his customary tact and sureness of tone, Martin presents a gift to a wide variety of readers: those who have never prayed and are curious, those who once prayed and have put prayer aside, those who pray seriously and feel that their prayer life needs a booster shot."

—Mary Gordon, author of *Payback* and *The Company of Women*

"*Learning to Pray* validates your practice and invites you to deepen it. It beckons us to this new and spacious place where we can all rest in the stillness of love and love in the stillness of God. You could not ask for more in a book on prayer."

—Gregory J. Boyle, SJ, author of *Tattoos on the Heart*

"The genius of this book—evident in both its content and its style—is that it speaks, simultaneously, to beginners in prayer and to those experienced in the way of the Spirit. Fr. Martin is a winsome guide to all those who want to deepen their friendship with the Lord."

—Bishop Robert Barron, author of *Catholicism: A Journey to the Heart of the Faith*

"Who else but Fr. Martin can combine the illuminating insights from spiritual giants like St. John Damascene with the likes of Monty Python? A humble, humorous step-by-step guide on the lofty subject of talking to and listening for the Living God."

—Helen Prejean, CSJ, author of *Dead Man Walking*

"What do we need to learn? That prayer changes us—and so changes the world we live in; that God is always there before us; that it's God's action that makes the difference. Practical, comprehensive, and above all God-centered, this book is a deeply valuable companion for growing in faith."

—Rowan Williams, former archbishop of Canterbury

"Drawing on many resources and his own experience, Fr. Martin invites and engages readers so that they can recognize possibilities for prayer in their lives. Everyone will find reliable spiritual riches in this wise, personal, and practical book, as they journey to God."

—Cardinal Blase Cupich, archbishop of Chicago

"Witty, conversational, intimate, and inspiring, James Martin's handbook is the finest, most practical, and comprehensive look at prayer that I have ever read."

—Ron Hansen, author of *Mariette in Ecstasy* and *Atticus*

"A wonderful, attractive, interesting, and very informative book on prayer that only Jim Martin could have written. Because he has discovered the joys of a regular prayer life for himself, he wants everyone to experience the same joy. You will be delighted and enlightened."

—William A. Barry, SJ, author of *The Practice of Spiritual Direction*

"Personal, insightful, honest, practical, expansive, enriching, free-ing, hopeful—these words only begin to describe this excellent book about prayer. *Learning to Pray* deserves to be in the hands and heart of anyone intent on engaging with the unfolding path of prayer."

—Joyce Rupp, author of *Anchors for the Soul*

"Drawing on his broad experience as a leader of prayer as well as one who is committed to deepening his own ongoing conversation with God, Fr. Martin offers a variety of methods and approaches that are accessible and user-friendly—it was a help to me on my own journey."

—John Stowe, OFM Conv., bishop of Lexington

"Never before has a book confronted me with the possibility of learning and re-learning the practice of prayer like *Learning to Pray*. This book had me praying while reading and reading while praying. Martin offers solutions coupled with beauty and oppor-tunity mixed with a wellspring of grace."

—The Rev. Robert W. Lee, author of *A Sin by Any Other Name: Reckoning with Racism and the Heritage of the South*

"James Martin has done it again. He has found a way to make the sublime accessible to everyone. Martin teaches you how to experi-ence God, who has been near you all along."

—Mark E. Thibodeaux, SJ, author of *Armchair Mystic*

Learning *to* Pray

Learning *to* Pray

A GUIDE FOR EVERYONE

JAMES MARTIN, SJ

HarperOne

An Imprint of HarperCollins*Publishers*

Imprimi Potest: Very Rev. John Cecero, SJ

HarperCollins books may be purchased for educational, business, or sales promotional use. For information, please email the Special Markets Department at SPsales@harpercollins.com.

FIRST EDITION

Library of Congress Cataloging-in-Publication Data is available upon request.

ISBN 978-0-06-264323-0

21 22 23 24   LSC   10 9 8 7 6 5 4 3

For William A. Barry, SJ,
whose books, and life,
have helped countless people to pray

CONTENTS

I
—

Everyone Can Pray

AN INTRODUCTION

Everyone can pray.

Let me put that another way. If I can learn how to pray, then so can you.

If you've never prayed before, or have had trouble praying, or think that you're praying "wrong," that opening statement might seem hard to believe. Or too good to be true. But it is true, even though it took me a long time to understand this simple fact: prayer is for everyone.

Until my late twenties I prayed only infrequently and in the most basic way: asking God for help. "Let me get an A on my test," "Let me get a home run in Little League," "Let me get a raise."

There's nothing wrong with asking God for help; it's both human and natural. But until I joined the Jesuits, a Catholic religious order, at age twenty-seven, I didn't realize that prayer could be anything else. When I entered the Jesuit novitiate, however, I learned to pray in new ways. And what I discovered amazed me—there are so many ways, so many practices, so much flexibility.

At the same time, I was encouraged to think *about* prayer in new ways—to imagine prayer as a personal relationship with God, to experience what happens when you pray, to understand that there is no one right way to pray, to know that prayer is something that changes throughout your life, and to see how prayer can change your life. So I learned not only how to pray, but also how to understand prayer.

It was a shock—almost as if someone had said, "Did you know there's another dimension besides the three dimensions you experience?" In fact, that's not a bad analogy. Prayer is like seeing another dimension of life.

My first reaction to this was: "Why didn't I know about this before?" My second was: "Why don't more people know about this?"

The answer to the first question was obvious. I didn't grow up in a very religious family, so I had little religious training. Not having attended religious schools—Catholic or otherwise—meant that I had little exposure to prayer during my elementary-school, junior-high, and high-school years. My family attended church on Sundays and I went to after-school religious education classes for a few years, but we didn't discuss God much at home. We said grace at meals on the big holidays, but didn't pray that much—at least together—on days other than those.

Lest you get the wrong idea, my parents were good and moral people. Still, my family was like many families today: we talked about the spiritual life with neither frequency nor ease. Neither did anyone else I knew. So I didn't pray much, unless to ask for things. Even when I got to college, I didn't meet many overtly religious people, and those I knew I didn't engage in conversations about prayer.

The second question I asked myself was also easy to answer: "Why don't more people know about this?" Or, more generally, "Why don't more people pray?"

To begin with, many do. But when I entered the Jesuits, I didn't know that. For millions of people, prayer is a regular part of life, as natural as breathing. They do it every day, sometimes several times a day. But for just as many people, prayer is foreign. Daunting. Even frightening. Many people, then, just don't pray. I'm not talking about agnostics or atheists. They don't pray for an obvious reason: they either doubt or don't believe in God's existence. I'm talking about believers who don't pray.

So why don't some believers pray? Let's consider a few reasons.

Ten Reasons Believers Don't Pray

1. *They weren't taught.* Many people were never taught how to pray— not by their families, by teachers at school, or by leaders in their church. Consequently, prayer was never part of their world. So naturally they don't do it.

It's like not knowing how to swim because (a) you've never had lessons; (b) you didn't grow up near a pool or a body of water; and (c) you don't know anyone who swims. You don't know how to swim not only because you've never learned, but also because the entire notion of doing it is foreign. Likewise, if you grow up in a prayer-free environment, it's not surprising that you wouldn't know much about prayer.

2. *They consider prayer something reserved for holy people, not them.* "Oh, I can't pray," people sometimes tell me. "I'm no Mother Teresa!" (Ironically, Mother Teresa struggled with prayer, but you get the point.) Perhaps they've read or heard stories about devout people who turn to God in prayer during difficult times, and they think, *That must be nice, but I could never do that, because I'm not that religious.* It's a reluctance based on a degree of humility, a degree of embarrassment, even a degree of shame. Judging themselves "not

holy" means that they shy away from prayer. But if absolute holiness were a prerequisite for prayer, there would be few who would or could try it.

William A. Barry, a Jesuit priest and the author of many books on prayer, writes in *A Friendship Like No Other* that the biggest obstacle to prayer is the belief that the relationship with God depends on us—or on how good or "significant" we are. But God's love does not rely on us and what we do. "God's offer of friendship does not depend on our significance, but solely on God's desire for us."[1]

3. *They've been told that they're praying "wrong."* A man in his twenties once told me, with immense sadness, that he could never become a priest, because a priest he consulted had told him he was praying the "wrong way."

"But I love praying this way," he said. Happily, my friend eventually recognized there is no right way to pray, and a few years later he entered the seminary.

Many report similar experiences. They are told they're praying "wrong," but have no one to tell them that there is no wrong way to pray or to encourage them to continue trying. Often, they just stop. Who can blame them?

Or they believe that their prayers have to be "lofty" and follow certain formulas. People may want to pray but feel that their way of prayer, whatever it is, is wrong. The German theologian Karl Rahner, SJ, writes, "This difficulty may . . . lead serious and thoughtful people to pray infrequently."[2]

4. *They're turned off by religion and are therefore turned off by prayer.* Many people find religion (or a particular church or denomination) distasteful, and because prayer is assumed to be bound up with religion, it too is dismissed. And often when people are raised in a tradition that they later break with, prayer is jettisoned as well. It's no surprise that if people associate prayer with a religious tradition they find boring, stultifying, narrow-minded, misogynistic, racist,

homophobic, or abusive, then the impetus to pray is diminished. Why would they want to engage in a practice associated with an unsavory organization? So they don't pray.

Or perhaps they are, more basically, turned off by God, or by the image of a God they have determined for themselves. Who can pray to a God who "allows" evil to flourish in the world, who "allows" history to be, as Rahner says, "a single stream of stupidity, crudity, and brutality?"[3] Why would anyone want to pray to a God who "allows" those things? The notion that God would want to be with us *during those times* does not yet figure into their consciousness. So they don't pray.

5. *They've never been encouraged to think about what they already do as prayer.* A few years ago, a man with no formal religious background told me that he had never prayed before. But when we talked about his life, he described a profound experience when he suddenly felt connected to something larger than himself and felt an unmistakable sense of encouragement about his path in life. This memorable experience, which he described in detail—what the weather was like, where he was standing, how he felt interiorly—came when he was wondering what profession he should choose. At the time, he took this as confirmation that he was on the "right path."

Before our conversation my friend hadn't considered the possibility that during this incident God might have been communicating with him. So I encouraged him to think about it not simply as an important insight or a confirmation about his path, but as something greater. Eventually this recognition—that this was an experience of God, about whom he had wondered all his life—marked the start of an intentional life of faith.

6. *They've had "bad" experiences with prayer and feel they have failed at it.* Sometimes people find prayer boring. And it's true—prayer can sometimes feel dull. Or they say, "Nothing happens when I pray," or "God didn't answer my prayers." In short, many grow frustrated with

the "results" of prayer. In response, they give up, without allowing themselves the chance to experience the natural ups and downs of prayer and the spiritual life.

Ruth Burrows, a Carmelite sister, sums this up in her book *Essence of Prayer*. She notes that many people think of prayer as akin to playing a musical instrument in which some have a natural aptitude and others do not. "Because of this, some of us are quick to feel we are proficient, others that we are painfully handicapped, are missing out on some secret, or have some lack in our nature which makes prayer difficult if not impossible for us."[4] Thus many people simply say, "I can't do it."

Giving up on prayer is common, but also unfortunate. It's like trying to learn how to ride a bike, falling off on the first few wobbly attempts, and giving up. Without someone to encourage them by saying, "Falling off is natural. It happens to everyone!" they give up before having the chance to enjoy the feeling of sailing down a hill on a bike as the wind blows past their ears.

It's also common for people to move away from prayer if God doesn't seem to answer their prayers during a difficult time. If a woman's father has a life-threatening illness, she prays to God to heal him, and her father dies, then it's natural for her to say about prayer, "What's the point?"

We'll talk more about unanswered prayers later. Still, it's a common reason for people to stop praying.

7. *They don't see the point, since God already knows what they're thinking.* Some people think, *Why bother? I'm just telling God what God already knows.* The possibility that God might want to listen to and accompany them anyway doesn't occur to them.

Imagine that you're grieving the loss of your parent. Obviously, a good friend would already know that you're sad, but would still be interested in listening to you and being with you. And if your friend, who cares for you, wants to be with you, how much more would God, who created you? Father Barry once said to me, "It's not a question of information, but of whether you are willing to tell God what you are feeling. In other words, it's about trust."

Likewise, the objection that God already knows what you're thinking presumes prayer is a one-way street. In this conception, prayer is limited to telling God what you want and feel. "Talking at God," the Jesuit priest and author Mark Thibodeaux calls it. Less appreciated is the possibility that God might want to tell *you* something. Thinking *Why bother?* means that you'll never allow God to bother with you in prayer.

8. *They're too busy.* Many people *want* to pray and like the overall *idea* of prayer, but don't have time for it. Or they don't make the time for it.

But if we think of prayer as a relationship (more about that later), it becomes clear how self-destructive that reasoning is. If you believe in God, why would you not want to nourish yourself by spending time in God's presence? It's like saying you don't have time to eat. Eventually you will starve. In this case, you will starve spiritually.

A more apt question might be: How important do you consider God? Like any meaningful relationship, your relationship with God requires time. Imagine telling a friend, "My brother is the most important person in my life." And your friend asks, "How much time do you spend with him?" And you say, "Not much, to be honest." How important can this relationship be if you never spend any more than a few minutes a month with him?

9. *They're lazy.* From time to time we're all guilty of laziness, including me. A man who sees me for spiritual direction (guidance in one's spiritual life) once told me that he hadn't been praying much.

Was he very busy?

"Not really," he said. "Life's pretty relaxed right now."

So why wasn't he praying?

He shrugged his shoulders eloquently. "Lazy, I guess."

Sometimes probing the circumstances surrounding the time when the prayer stopped reveals an obstacle or a fear standing in the way. Individuals may be afraid of something they might discover about themselves. Sometimes, though, it is simple laziness.

Prayer wasn't a priority for my friend. But although this may be a common reason for not praying, it's also a common reason for the flabbiness of our spiritual lives. Think of it like exercise: there are many valid reasons you do not or cannot exercise (an injury, old age, lack of time, etc.), but if the main reason is laziness, you may need to ask yourself how responsible you yourself are for being out of shape.

10. *They fear change.* Sometimes when people start to pray, they wonder, *What will happen if I keep praying?* They worry that they'll become religious fanatics. (Unlikely, I say.) Or that God will invite them to do something outlandish, like quit their job to work full-time with the poor. (Also unlikely, but then again, who knows?) Finally, they think that perhaps God will invite them to some sort of change. (Likely.)

In that last case, fear of change leads to an avoidance of prayer. Even the *possibility* of change can be frightening. Best for things to stay the way they are, some people feel. They might want things to improve, but changing their lives in any way is daunting. A Jesuit priest liked to say, jokingly, "I'm against change. Even change for the better."[5] We prefer status quo over true engagement with God.

A young woman once told me that she was avoiding going deeper in her spiritual life because she was afraid she would become a "Jesus freak" like some religious people she knew. She found them so "phony" and "annoying" and was worried that God was going to "turn her into that." But her fear was rooted in her image of

God—as someone who would do something bad to her. So I had to ask her if she trusted God, and if she trusted God to change her for the better.

For all these reasons, and for others, some believers don't try prayer, or they pray less than they could, or they give up on prayer after they've started. All these reasons are understandable. But they are also, in their own way, dangerous, because they all draw people away from God.

An Invitation

This book is for anyone who has avoided prayer for any or all those reasons. It's also a response to the second question I asked as a novice: "Why don't more people know about prayer?"

Learning to Pray is written for everyone from the doubter to the devout, from the seeker to the believer. It's an invitation for people who have never prayed. It's designed for people who would like to pray, but are worried they'll do it the wrong way. It's meant for people who have prayed and haven't found it as satisfying as they had hoped. It's also aimed at people who might be afraid of prayer. As I said, prayer can frighten us. It's unfamiliar territory for some and can be frightening even for believers, because God can seem frightening.

Especially if you listen to people talk about prayer, praying can seem daunting, even impossible. Occasionally people who pray are the worst ambassadors for the spiritual life, because they raise such high expectations that they make it look impossible for newcomers.

Sometimes those experienced in prayer talk only about the highlights: "I *love* my hour of prayer in the morning!" "The most *incredible* thing happened in prayer yesterday!" "I went on an *amazing* retreat!"

If you've never prayed before, avoid comparing yourself to a spiritual "pro." To return to the image of a bicycle, imagine never having ridden a bike or having struggled to stay upright, and seeing a professional cycler racing by you on a track. "This is so much fun!" she shouts as she whizzes past. You might think, *I could never do that in a million years.* The bicyclist would probably tell you that it takes time to reach that point, and you might have to fall off a few times before you get the hang of it.

So for all those who have wanted to pray, this book is written for you.

This book is meant for the agnostic too—more specifically, the open-minded and adventurous agnostic. If you are someone who doubts God's existence but are willing to give prayer a try, you might discover that God is more accessible than you thought.

In a way, this book is an invitation to both prayer and faith, because you can't have one without the other. Prayer without faith means you don't believe in the One with whom you're in conversation. Faith without prayer means you're not in conversation with the One in whom you believe.

Finally, this is a book for the person who prays occasionally and wants to learn more as well as the experienced *pray-er* who prays regularly. (Sorry, there's no adequate English word for the person who prays.) Even if you pray every day, see a spiritual director every month, and go on a retreat every year, this book is designed for you too. My hope is that even if you've been praying for decades, you might learn something new. Whenever I read a new book on prayer, I'm always surprised. Everyone's approach to prayer is necessarily personal, which means there's always something new to learn.

As we begin this book, however, I'll assume that you know next to nothing about prayer. That way I'll be able to include everyone, beginners through those with years of experience. But I will also assume that you can come up to speed quickly.

This book is meant for people of all faith traditions and none. Although I write as a Catholic, many people whom I've counseled over the years have not been Catholic. Some were just embarking on their faith journey and could have checked "None" in the column marked "Religious Affiliation." Since this book is meant for everyone, I'll try not to use any terms that might be unfamiliar to the general public. Or if I do use them, I'll explain them.

First, we will consider why people pray. Then we'll look briefly at some common definitions of prayer. Then we'll get to the heart of the book and discuss the different ways to pray. At various points, I'll offer perspectives on why, how, and when people pray and the challenges encountered in prayer. I'll try to anticipate as many questions as I can—and I've heard a lot (and asked a lot) over the last few decades. And I'll share some real-life experiences from my own life and from the lives of others. But don't worry: no confidences will be broken—I'll change the details to ensure anonymity. Basically, I will share with you all I know about prayer (or at least a lot of it) and answer the questions that I'm most commonly asked.

One of the main goals of this book is to focus on what *happens* in prayer, that is, what happens when you close your eyes. Some books on prayer gloss over that topic and speak vaguely about the "gifts of prayer" or the "fruits of prayer," leaving readers in the dark about what is supposed to, or what does, happen during prayer. I want to address that directly because it can be one of the most confusing parts about the spiritual life—but needn't be.

This book will look only at personal, or private, prayer rather than at communal prayer—in other words, the time you spend on your own with God. There are myriad ways of praying in common with others—for example, in the Mass for Catholics or Sunday services for other Christians—but the focus of this book will be on personal prayer. There are already hundreds of fine books on subjects like the Mass, for example, the discussion of which would probably quadruple the length of this book. Also left out will be some devotional practices familiar to Catholics (which I participate in), such as Adoration of the Blessed Sacrament and pilgrimage. This book is primarily concerned with the kind of prayer that you can do anywhere.[6]

A few of these topics were covered in my book *The Jesuit Guide to (Almost) Everything*, which talks about "Ignatian spirituality," the spirituality based on the life and writings of St. Ignatius Loyola, the founder of the Jesuit Order. A few sections of this book appeared in an abbreviated way in that earlier book, but are here greatly expanded. This book is a fuller and more wide-ranging treatment of the topic.

By the end of this book I hope you'll have a better knowledge of prayer. More important, I hope that you will have *started to pray*. Finally, I hope that your prayer will lead you to either begin, explore, or deepen your relationship with God, for prayer isn't an end in itself: God is. The goal of prayer is deepening one's relationship with God.

What Do I Know About Prayer?

If you were reading a book on dieting, wouldn't you want to know what expertise the author has on questions of food, nutrition, and health? So it's fair for you to ask me what I know about prayer.

I'm not an expert on prayer—because no one is. It's not that there aren't many experienced writers and lecturers on the subject, but prayer is not something to be "mastered." It's something to be faced with openness, wonder, and awe, each time you pray. There's never a time when you can say, "Well, now I'm a spiritual master. No need to read any more books on prayer or see a spiritual director or be open to new experiences." It would be like saying you're an expert in love. There's always something new to learn. In fact, just last year, a new form of prayer was suggested to me, which I first resisted, then tried, and then loved—after thirty years as a Jesuit.

On the other hand, I've learned a good deal about prayer over the years. So to answer the question more directly, I've learned about prayer from several sources.

First, I have learned *from practice*. Experience may be the best teacher when it comes to prayer. Since starting to pray in earnest as a Jesuit novice, I've learned what works, what doesn't, and which practices are the most helpful, at least for me. I'll share as much as I can about what I've experienced, to help you in your own spiritual life.

Second, I have *studied and read about prayer*. A good part of Jesuit training is concerned with prayer and the spiritual life. That education begins in the novitiate (the first two years of Jesuit training) and continues through graduate studies in theology and beyond. And to keep up I still read a great deal on the subject. By now I've lost count of the number of books and articles on prayer that I've read. I've been studying prayer for the last thirty years.

Third, I have learned *from my spiritual directors*. "Spiritual direction" is the ministry of helping people notice where God is at work in their prayer and their daily life. A person engaged in this ministry is called a "spiritual director." (The term is somewhat of a misnomer, since it has more to do with listening than directing.) A good spiritual director listens attentively to your experiences of God and tries to "direct" or encourage you to notice things you might have overlooked. He or she will also invite you to try out new practices in your prayer, to challenge things that need challenging, and to affirm things that need affirming.

From the first week of our novitiate, Jesuits are expected to go to (or "have") spiritual direction on a regular basis. My first was with the assistant novice director, David Donovan, who trained for many years as a professional spiritual director. David was the first of many directors—mostly Jesuits and members of Catholic religious orders, but also laymen and -women—whom I've seen faithfully since I entered the Jesuits. In the novitiate, we met weekly; after the novitiate I've met with my directors monthly, as most Jesuits do. I've also benefited immensely from the spiritual directors who have guided my annual eight-day retreats. And twice in my life, as all Jesuits do, I've spent thirty days in silent prayer during the Spiritual Exercises, a retreat designed by St. Ignatius Loyola.

From each of these women and men I've learned about prayer, about the spiritual life, and about how God works in people's lives. I'll share some of their insights here and will try to remember who said what, even though their wisdom is so much a part of my life that I sometimes forget which spiritual director said what.

Fourth, much of what I've learned has come *from studying and practicing spiritual direction myself.* Working as a spiritual director has been one of my greatest joys as a Jesuit. Beginning just a few years after the novitiate, I've directed dozens of people on a regular basis and have seen an equal number on weekend and weeklong retreats, people from all walks of life. I have seen Catholic priests, deacons, sisters, and brothers, of course, but also anyone interested in prayer—mothers, fathers, teachers, lawyers, physicians, writers, students, actors. I've worked with pastors, ministers, and lay leaders from various Christian denominations and with a rabbi. Over the years, I've also taken several courses on the practice of spiritual direction, including a summerlong course at a Jesuit retreat house.

Also, I've learned about prayer from working with another intriguing group, those who came to the weekend retreats I offered over a period of ten years at a Jesuit retreat house in Gloucester, Massachusetts. Almost always on those weekends the participants included several people who had never been on a retreat or who had never prayed before.

What draws the newcomers? Perhaps the picturesque setting on the rocky shores of the Atlantic Ocean, perhaps a friend who encouraged them, or perhaps curiosity. Invariably they would enter the room reserved for spiritual direction—a compact space with a window and two simple chairs facing one another—sit down, look around, smile, and say, "So what am I supposed to talk about?"

I enjoy accompanying newcomers to the spiritual life. Usually, they are open, have fewer preconceptions, and find God quickly. Or rather God finds *them* quickly. Sometimes I think God gives newbies intense experiences at the beginning of their spiritual lives to grab their attention and "hook them." So I'm able to hear about how God works with that group, which has helped me to speak to people who may not have much experience with prayer.

Because of interactions with so many wonderful people from different backgrounds, I've been privileged to see not only how God works in people, but how people respond to God, what they experience in prayer, and what challenges they face in prayer. After years of doing spiritual direction, I've also come to see that many people face similar challenges and have similar joys. At the same time I see how God deals with everyone uniquely, personally, and intimately. God's Spirit is both general and specific. God deals with people in very personal ways, but also in very similar ways.

A Pray-er Like You

As I've mentioned, the most important teacher in the spiritual life may be experience. I've learned about prayer as someone who prays. Someone who prays every day. Someone who has gone to spiritual direction every month for the last thirty years. Someone who makes eight-day silent retreats every year—religiously, if you will. Equally as important, I've learned about prayer as a person who struggles with prayer, whose prayer isn't always rich, and whose prayers aren't always answered. And as someone who didn't pray until well into adulthood.

Let me amend that last sentence. It may be more accurate to say that I wasn't *aware* that I was praying. Looking back, there were several moments that I can now identify as prayer. If a person described these kinds of experiences to me today, I would say, "You're already praying." In fact, I've said those same words to many people.

Even if you're an agnostic or an atheist, you've probably had some of these experiences. But perhaps no one encouraged you to consider them in relation to God.

So before we launch into a discussion of prayer, let me share a few experiences of my own prayer while growing up. I write about them not so you can say, "He was so holy when he was younger," because, frankly, I wasn't all that holy as a boy. Nor am I now. Rather, I offer them so you can see how God can work in the life of an average person.

Let me tell you about my earliest experiences of praying—even though I had no clue that I was praying at the time.

2

Walking to School

CHILDHOOD PRAYER

The students in my elementary school were divided into two categories: walkers and bussers. The walkers lived within easy walking distance of the school. Those living farther away had to take a school bus, so, "bussers." I was a walker.

At the time, walking to school at a young age—I started at four— was unremarkable. Today it may seem unusual, for two reasons.

First, the number of children walking to school in the United States has declined. Parents worry about letting their children out of their sight, because they are concerned about crime. Second, the social milieu that allowed most children to feel safe walking through suburban neighborhoods has also changed. When I was a boy, fewer women worked outside the home. Consequently, parents knew that on weekdays many mothers would be glancing out their windows as children made their way to school. This is not an argument for or against mothers (or fathers) staying at home or for or against mothers (or fathers) working outside of the home, only an observation that American culture has changed since I was a boy.

But the other reason walking to school seems remarkable to me is that it was a surprisingly beautiful experience.

My elementary school was a mile's walk from our home in suburban Philadelphia. The thirty-minute walk wended its way through a neighborhood of modest 1950s-era split-level houses. After a good-bye kiss from my mother, I would cross the street, carrying my schoolbag and lunchbox. I liked walking on that side because it was closer to the woods, which made it easier to watch the tall trees sway in the wind and hear the birds practice their morning songs. Sometimes a deer poked its nose out of the woods, and we would stare at each other until one of us decided he'd be late for homeroom or late for his breakfast of acorns and leaves.

When I was older, I started to ride my bike to school. By the fourth grade, I and a dozen of the other neighborhood kids would congregate in front of the house across the street in the morning and painstakingly arrange our bikes in a row. At a designated time, our bike line began its stately journey to school, carefully maintaining a single-file formation all the way through our neighborhood.

Much of the time, though, I walked to school alone. And I liked being a walker.

You could reach Ridge Park Elementary School in two ways. You began by walking to the end of our street and at the bottom of the hill jumping over a paltry stream that ran through the neighborhood at its lowest topographical point. For an assignment in fifth grade, I knelt on the damp bank of the stream, filled up a small glass with water, and later placed it on a windowsill in the classroom. A few days later I peered at a drop of it on a glass slide under a microscope and was amazed to see tiny organisms swimming around. Who knew they lived in our neighborhood?

After fording the little stream, I would cross a few feet of a friend's wide backyard, climb a steep hill, cross the school's vast baseball fields, walk through the black-topped playground, and arrive at the door to my homeroom. That route shaved ten minutes off the walk.

If I had more time, I would take the path that I preferred. It led past the little stream to another sidewalk, perpendicular to the road, which ran between two houses and ended in a steep set of concrete stairs. To my mind, a sidewalk running *between* two houses, rather than in front of them, seemed odd, almost subversive. The concrete walkway carved a straight line through several lawns, and so was at odds with the other curvy sidewalks that bordered the streets. It was probably placed there by town planners to enable children to walk to school more quickly.

At the top of the stairs was an empty field, the memory of which, even fifty years later, fills me with joy. It was bordered on one side by a concrete sidewalk and a stand of oak trees and on the other by the school's baseball fields. A bumpy dirt path, hardened by the tires of thousands of kids' bicycles, ran diagonally across the meadow.

On the city planner's map, it doubtless looked like an unremarkable empty lot. But in the spring and summer the little field was beautiful, bursting with wild snapdragons, yellow daisies, and Queen Anne's lace. The smell of the flowers and grasses and old leaves underfoot was like perfume. In the fall, you could run your hands over the frost-tipped grasses, squeeze the dried milkweed pods, and crunch your feet over a carpet of whitened leaves.

Most of the time walking to school I thought about school: which tests I needed to study for, whether I would finish my art project on time, whether I had practiced my trumpet enough, and when the highlight of the month would arrive—the shipment our class had ordered from Scholastic Books. Each month we filled out small order forms and gave our dollars to our homeroom teacher, and a few weeks later a box of books materialized. The only thing more enjoyable was the annual book fair, when Scholastic would take over the entire gym with an impressive display of new books.

I thought about all these things walking to school. Occasionally, though, I would pray. As I look back, it seems that my own experience of prayer is a microcosm of the life of prayer for many beginners.

Although I believed in God, was raised in a Catholic family, went to Mass, and attended Sunday school from time to time, I wasn't very religious. And as should be evident by its name, Ridge Park was not a Catholic school. The closest Catholic school was our parish school, a few miles away, and the total number of children I knew who attended was zero. But I believed in God. And I sometimes called upon God on the way to school. *Why not?* I thought. It couldn't hurt.

"God, Please Give Me a Dog!"

My first way of praying was to ask for things. On the day of a big test I would say the Hail Mary, which I had learned in Sunday school. Its opening lines are the greeting of the Angel Gabriel to Mary, the mother of Jesus, as recounted in the Gospel of Luke.[1]

My feet pounded the pavement to the prayer's cadence. The more help I needed, the more prayers I would say, being careful not to step on a sidewalk crack, since, as everyone knew, it didn't count if you stepped on a crack.

> *Hail* Mary,
> *full* of grace. The
> *Lord* is with thee.
> *Blessed* art thou
> *among* women and
> *blessed* is the fruit of
> *thy* womb, Jesus.

The second part of the prayer is a petition to Mary, asking for her prayers.

> *Holy* Mary,
> *Mother* of God,
> *pray* for us sinners,
> *now* and at the hour of our
> *death*. Amen.

The more I wanted something, the more Hail Marys I'd say. I imagined it as a payment to God. The bigger the request, the more I would pay.

Other times I would ask for things *directly*, with no Hail Mary payments. Although requesting things of God, with or without "payments," is a form of petitionary prayer, which we will discuss later, this led to a second kind of prayer.

As with most children, there were many things I wanted—and thought I deserved. During my childhood, the sequence of desires progressed from pup tent, to new bicycle, to dog. Desperately I prayed for a dog, and that desire was almost satisfied. I got as close as identifying a litter of puppies and even naming one, but the plan was ultimately scotched because of my sister's allergies.

When I was around age ten, my most ardent desire was to be chosen for the safety patrol, a children's group sponsored by the American Automobile Association. In the fifth grade you could apply to be a "safety" and help with school safety, assisting younger "walkers" at the outdoor pedestrian crosswalks and ensuring that they walked to their classes quickly and quietly in the hallways, mainly by screaming "Walk!" as loudly as possible.

I wanted to be a safety for two ungenerous reasons. First, I would be singled out as special. Second, safeties wore a cool white strap over the shoulder that was cinched at the waist, with a gleaming silver badge positioned over the chest emblazoned with "AAA" and surmounted by an American eagle.

On the way to school I told God what a great safety I would be. There was some real spiritual subterfuge involved: I wanted to convince God to choose me, so that I could be marked for greatness.

Wanting to be special and coveting a cool badge are not the most exemplary motivations, but it brought me into this second kind of prayer: conversation with God. I tried hard to convince God that I would make a good safety. It was something of a one-sided conversation, however.

As it turned out, God answered that prayer: I eventually became a safety. However, in one of the first reminders that aspirations seldom cease, I discovered there were safety *captains* and *lieutenants* too. They wore even cooler medals etched with special colors. If you are motivated by pride, once you reach your goal, there will always be another goal to tempt you.

In a Meadow

Finally, there was one unusual prayer in childhood, something that could be described as mystical.

Before you think that claim boastful, I want to point out that mysticism is not foreign to most people. Many people, if they dig deep enough, will discover moments that can be fairly described as mystical. But most people aren't encouraged to dig. In the first chapter of her book *Guidelines for Mystical Prayer*, Ruth Burrows, a Carmelite nun, writes that her book is meant "for all."[2]

One warm morning in the late spring, on the way to elementary school, I hoisted my bike to the top of the concrete steps near my school. Then I began to pedal across the bumpy dirt path that ran across the meadow. I can still remember the sweet smell of flowers and grass hanging in the air, with the sun's morning rays slanting over the field and casting long shadows from the flowers. Bees buzzed around the snapdragons, black-eyed Susans, daisies, and Queen Anne's lace; crickets hid in the leaves making their metallic sound; and grasshoppers jumped with an audible snap from the top of one blade of grass to another.

Suddenly the wire basket on the front handlebars of my bike swung to one side. Maybe I had too many books crammed into the metal basket. Maybe I was examining the stickers and decals on my notebooks, which were all the rage that year. Just as likely, I was distracted by the smell of flowers and the sound of crickets.

To right myself, I set my feet down. Then I looked around. All around me was so much life—the sights, the sounds, the smells—and suddenly I had a visceral urge not only to be a part of it, but also to know it and somehow *possess* it. I felt loved, held, understood. The desire for everything, somehow for a full incorporation into the universe, and a desire to understand what I was doing here on this earth filled me.

It wasn't a vision. I was still looking at the meadow. I hadn't "left myself." And as a boy, I don't think I would have been able to describe it as I just did. But I knew something had happened: it was as if my heart had stopped and I was given a conscious inkling of the depths of my own desire for . . . *what?*

I wasn't sure.

Early Openness

Children may be more open than adults to experiencing God, because they are not as burdened with as many expectations about prayer. It may be similar to why my two nephews, when they were still very young, didn't care what clothes they wore. They simply threw on whatever was clean. If something was too small or too large or didn't match, they didn't care. Society hadn't imposed upon them its expectations about the right or fashionable way to dress.

Adults, however, are only too ready to believe that there is a "right way" and a "wrong way" to dress—and to pray. The religious world, with its constellation of expectations, imposes on adults a series of "shoulds" that can frustrate prayer.

Children often relate to God in any way they please. This allows them to be more open with God than adults are. A few years ago, after Mass on Christmas Eve, I brought my then six-year-old nephew Matthew to see the Christmas crib in front of the altar in his parish church. In a little wooden stable Mary and Joseph flanked the Baby Jesus, whose manger was almost buried in banks of red poinsettias. I asked Matthew if he'd like to say something to Jesus. I expected him to pray silently or maybe ask for another toy.

Instead, he said aloud, "Make me a good boy, Jesus."

Perhaps God takes a special interest in children, grabbing their attention early, in the same way that adults often lavish attention on young people and spend more time with them, out of a reverent care for the gift that they are and will be.

As I look back on my ordinary childhood experiences, then, I can distinguish three common ways of prayer: first, petition; second, conversation; and third, moments of mystical experience. Agnostics or atheists might chalk up the first form to superstition (using prayers as an incantation), the second to wish fulfillment (talking to someone who doesn't exist), and the third to ignorance (mistaking a feeling of happiness for something more). I will talk about each kind of prayer, and others, in this book.

Fifty years later, I see how God was trying to reach me. And over the years I've heard about similar experiences from others.

From our earliest days God calls to us in love and invites us to respond in love. Some might dismiss these moments as superstition, wish fulfillment, or puerile ignorance, but others can see them for what they are: encouragements to prayer. Such invitations continue throughout our lives, but if we are closed to them, we may never realize how much God desires to be in relationship with us. If we are open to them, we may begin to pray.

3

Why Pray?

SOME COMMON REASONS

If you've had experiences similar to the ones I described in the previous chapter, you might say, "Come to think of it, I remember when I prayed a while ago, and it felt good. But I'm too busy these days for prayer. Besides, God knows what I'm thinking anyway, so I don't have to bother praying."

Conversely, if you've never had such experiences, you might say, "I've tried praying once or twice, and nothing happened. It was a waste of time. Maybe I'm not cut out for prayer—I'm not holy enough." Or "God's disappointed with me, so God won't talk to me."

Both types of responses bring us to an important question: Why pray?

Let me suggest the first reason for prayer: *God wants to be in a relationship with you.*

How can you know this? Because you want to pray.

And how do I know that? Because you're reading this book.

That may sound sarcastic, but it's not. There's a serious point here: your desire for prayer reveals something about how God created you. Deep within you is a natural desire to communicate with God, to share yourself with God, to have God hear your voice, or, more basically, to encounter God. Deep within you is a longing to be in a relationship with God. So you long to pray.

You may doubt many things when it comes to prayer. You may doubt that you'll be able to pray. You may doubt that God wants to communicate with you. You may even doubt God's existence. But you cannot doubt that you feel a desire for prayer. After all, you're reading this book. So clearly something within you desires prayer.

You might still object to that, saying, "I'm only reading this book because I feel lost," or "I'm curious about what others have told me they experienced." That may be true. But you can't deny that you have at this moment a desire for prayer.

Where does the desire for prayer come from? *From God.* The most common way God draws you closer is by placing within you the desire to be closer, the desire that drove you to think about prayer and to read this book. Strange as it sounds, your reading of these lines at this moment is a sign of God's call.

How else would God draw us closer, other than by planting a longing inside us? Once I saw a ceramic plaque in a retreat house that summed this up: "That which you seek is causing you to seek."[1]

This insight is helpful to those beginning their journey of prayer, because it helps them feel, even before they've started to pray, connected to God. It helps them know that God has taken the initiative, that God is calling to them, that God *desires* them. It helps people take the first tentative steps toward God.

Some people object to this way of thinking, seeing this desire as mere wish fulfillment. But in my experience recognizing this insight is one of the first steps to beginning a spiritual life.

A few years ago, I met a man with little experience in prayer—or so he thought. Yet as we talked about his past, he recalled an incident that had happened years before. When he was thinking about what path he should take in life, he had an important insight. He was walking along the bank of a river when the clouds parted and the sun shone down on him. Suddenly he felt that he knew that he was on the right path. What he was doing professionally was where he was supposed to be: it was enjoyable, satisfying, and a good use of his talents. As he sat with me, he expressed his desire for more. He desired, he thought, a relationship with God.

After he described his experience, I asked, "Did you ever wonder if this was God reaching out to you? If this was God confirming you on your path?" He admitted that he hadn't, but that it made sense. How else would God seek us? Accepting that possibility, which he later came to see as a reality, was the beginning of his intentional pursuit of the spiritual life.

On another level, many of us have felt that there is more to life than what we know. We feel a sense of incompletion. We long to feel complete or, as I did in the meadow that day, to be connected, to be satisfied, to *know*. Inside us are nagging feelings of longing, restlessness, and incompletion that can be fulfilled only in a relationship with God. There is a hole in our hearts that only God can fill. The fourth-century theologian St. Augustine put it best when he wrote, "You have made us for yourself, O Lord. And our hearts are restless until they rest in you."[2]

Your desire to pray is a sign that God desires you. It's an indication God is calling you. And that is perhaps the most important reason to pray. Not simply because you desire it, but because the desire is a sign of something else. You desire to pray because *God* desires it.

A second reason for prayer is a slight reframing of the phenomenon just described. We pray *because we want to be in relationship to God*. That may sound obvious—of course we pray to be closer to God. But it's important to state that the aim of prayer is not simply physical relaxation, mindfulness, knowledge, or a connection to creation, as important as those things are. These are goals that many people mention when speaking about meditation. But the goal of *prayer* is closer union with God.

More basically, we pray because we love God. Father Barry writes, "The primary motive for prayer is love, first the love of God for us and then the arousal of our love for God."[3] We pray to come to *know* God as well. "Who is God?" is an important question in the spiritual life. So are "Who is God for me?" and "Who am I before God?"

Prayer reminds us of our need for God. It reminds us that we are not the center of the universe and that we are not God. Sometimes when things are going well, we can grow arrogant and complacent in our self-sufficiency. Prayer, which places us in the presence of God in an intentional way, reminds us of who is in charge, or rather who is nurturing us. Gerard Hughes, a Scottish Jesuit, writes in *God of Surprises*: "To begin prayer is sufficient to acknowledge that I am not self-sufficient, that I am not the creator of myself and creation. If I can do this, then I acknowledge that there is some power—I may not know whether it is personal or not and may be in complete ignorance of its nature—greater than I."[4]

This inevitably moves us to humility, as we realize more and more our need for God. The Trappist monk and spiritual master Thomas Merton went further, saying that prayer is inseparable from humility. Humility, he said, "makes us realize that the very depths of our being and life are meaningful and real only in so far as they are oriented toward God as their source and their end."[5]

When we realize the awesome nature of that second reason—we pray to be in union with God—it puts everything into perspective. As Joyce Rupp, OSM, a Catholic sister, writes: "False justifications for not praying fall away when we perceive the priceless value of our union with God."[6]

A third reason is that *we have to*. If you're not used to praying, that may sound ridiculous, but once you start, you'll see that it can feel as natural as breathing. Our innate desire for God means we naturally crave a relationship with God. Prayer is an outgrowth of the human longing for the divine. In a sense, we can't *not* pray, because prayer is part of being human.

There are other reasons that prayer feels necessary. In the face of your problems, how can you not ask for help from your Creator? We'll talk more about petitionary prayer later, but for now I'll say that I've never met anyone who felt that his or her life was free of problems. So we pray for a fourth reason: *we are in need*.

A fifth reason is that *prayer helps us*. This may sound selfish, but it's another common motivation, similar to reasons for doing physical exercise. If you never get off the couch, you'll end up out of shape, and that will influence your overall physical condition; less exercise means more pulled muscles, perilous cardiovascular health, and greater stress. Not praying—not spending intentional time with God—means your spiritual life will be out of shape, even flabby, and that will influence the rest of your life. You'll probably be less grateful and thus more irritable, less connected to the deepest part of yourself and thus more scattered, less aware of your reliance on God and thus more frightened. Prayer helps you.

On the rare days that I don't pray I feel off balance. And I always know why. Certainly I feel guilty that I've not spent time with God in an intentional way, but I also feel, to put it bluntly, worse. I'm more irritable, more distracted, less patient, and less able to maintain perspective on life. Even when prayer feels "dry" (more about that later), it helps me feel more connected to the center of my being, which is God. Being centered in that way always means more perspective, because you know where you stand.

Prayer is also a way to *unburden* ourselves when we're feeling sad, angry, stressed, or frustrated. That's a sixth reason. Often, after you have told God your problems, you feel less alone. God is always with you, but praying in this way is a great aid nonetheless. Sometimes I've stood up from prayer and said, "At least I know that God knows how I feel."

A seventh reason for prayer is that it helps us *praise God*. If you're a believer, you may wonder about the best way to express your gratitude. You can do good works, live a moral life, and help your fellow human beings. Those are fine ways to show your love in gratitude. As St. Ignatius Loyola says, "Love ought to show itself in deeds more than words." But it's just as important to say "thank you" to God. Prayer is one way of doing this. Simply resting in things you're grateful for is a way of giving thanks.

In light of your blessings, beginning with the blessing of being alive, how can you not want to thank God? After seeing a tree in autumn, a spectacular sunset, a baby's smile, how can you not want to praise God? We pray because we are grateful.

Prayer, however, is not a solitary act. This leads us to an eighth reason: *solidarity*. When we pray we are, consciously or unconsciously, expressing a connection to our brothers and sisters who also pray—even if they're not physically with us. Although the prayer that we will discuss in this book is private prayer (one-on-one time with God), prayer in common is an essential aspect of the spiritual life. As social animals, we naturally find comfort and support in groups. Praising God in a group makes double sense: we naturally want to do it, and we naturally want to do it with others. Both are part of being human.

Whenever we pray, we are united with believers across the world who are lifting their hearts and minds to God. We are also united with those who have gone before us, who continue their prayers before God. This is one part of what Catholics mean by the "communion of saints."

Not long ago a friend told me that when she prays the Rosary, the series of prayers counted out on beads, she remembers all the people she knows, living and dead. In this way, she says, even when alone, she is praying the Rosary with other people.

That kind of prayer also expands us. If we are more aware of others when we pray, we are enlarged. In their book *Christian Spirituality*, theologians Lawrence S. Cunningham and Keith J. Egan speak of the Christian life as "an attempt to enlarge our circle of human concern in a way that helps us to enter God's circle as well."[7] Prayer can encourage us to move beyond our own narrow concerns.

A ninth reason: we pray *to be transformed*. This is somewhat different from praying to God for help—but it's related. Knowing that we are flawed and imperfect, many of us look to God to help us grow into better people. This is not to say that we are all terrible sinners or irredeemable reprobates. Rather, we are all human beings in need of God's grace.

In my own life, that desire manifests itself especially during prayer. If I do something sinful, I am filled with a remorse that becomes more obvious when I spend time with God. A few years ago, I did something selfish that affected a friend. In my prayer the next day I saw how uncharitable it was and was moved to seek out my friend and apologize. I was also reminded of my need for God's grace and my desire for more charity. We might also become aware not of one particular sin, but of a general pattern in our lives, a place where we are unfree. We may ask for freedom from this in prayer.

There is a kind of petitionary prayer here too, but of a different nature. "Help me to be a better person, God" might be called a prayer of transformation.

Not long ago, I had been praying that God would change me in a particular way, and not much seemed to be happening. Then, suddenly, it was discovered that I would need some minor surgery. Lying in the hospital bed a few weeks later, tethered by tubes to various machines, I started to think about all the things I was hoping to change in my life: my flaws and failings, all the things I hoped God would change or eradicate. As I enumerated them, these things that were distracting me from being the kind of person I wanted to become seemed, in a word, ridiculous. In other words, I saw the emptiness of whatever was moving me away from God.

During those days I felt God saying to me in prayer, "What kind of life do you want to lead?" It was not so much a matter of waiting for God to change me or remove my flaws; God was telling me that the change was largely up to me. It was a transformational moment, as it seemed to offer me freedom and reminded me of my own agency in life. Transformation is another reason for prayer.

That short list of reasons why people pray is by no means complete. There are as many reasons to pray as there are people.

You may still have many questions about, or even objections to, the idea of prayer. "How do I know if God hears me? Why don't I get what I pray for? What does it mean for God to answer me?" We'll get to those questions in time.

For now, let's say that there are many reasons to pray, chief among them that God is calling to you. It's as if God is saying, "Would you like to spend some time with me?"

Why not say yes?

4

Praying Without Knowing It

NINE TYPES OF PRAYER YOU MAY BE UNAWARE OF

The experiences I described from my childhood are not unusual. During childhood most people have had many moments—even if they have a hard time remembering them—when God was inviting them into prayer. Despite this, many people still think that they'll never be able to pray.

How do I know people think this? Because they tell me—frequently. During spiritual direction; in private conversations; in letters, emails, and phone calls; in discussions on the steps of churches after Mass; at question-and-answer sessions after lectures; in line at book signings; and through countless social-media channels, many people share with me their frustrations about prayer.

Some people feel that they're not doing it right. Others feel distracted. Some feel like nothing is happening. Many feel they are missing something. Most believe that other people must be doing it better than they are.

When I speak to groups about prayer, I often invite them to take part in an exercise. To begin, I ask everyone to close their eyes—to avoid embarrassment, since people are often self-conscious about how they pray. Then I pose some questions. The results are almost always the same.

First, I say, "Raise your hand if you pray."

Usually most people raise their hands. Keep in mind that I'm usually speaking to people interested in the spiritual life. The percentage would be lower in a more randomly selected group of people.

Next, I say, "Now, keep your hand up if you pray *regularly*."

Half will keep their hands aloft.

Then I'll ask everyone to put their hands down.

Finally I say, "Now raise your hand if you're happy with your prayer life."

In response, only a handful of people raise their hands.

"Now," I say, "keep your hands up if you think you pray well."

Most hands will go down. Perhaps only one or two will remain.

Why so few? Does this mean that most people aren't praying "well"? Not at all. Rather, it shows that many people *think* they are not praying the way they think they should. When you dig deeper, you find that even people who pray regularly say they imagine that other people must be praying better. A satisfying prayer life, they think, is for someone else—someone holier than they are, someone who prays longer than they do, someone who is gifted in ways that they are not. *It must be wonderful*, people think longingly, *to have a rich prayer life, like other people.* As a result, there is a good deal of frustration and sadness when it comes to prayer.

That makes *me* frustrated and sad, because prayer is for everyone.

Besides, it's something that God does within you, so you don't have to worry so much about your "doing it."

Moreover, many people are already praying unawares. That boy walking to school was praying in several ways, even if he didn't know it. Often when people share with me what's inside their hearts, how they ask God for help during the day, how they try to notice God's presence, and how they sometimes enjoy experiences of awareness, and then say that they wish they knew how to pray, I am reminded of, believe it or not, something I read in high-school French class.

Specifically, I'm reminded of a play by the seventeenth-century French playwright Molière that we read called *Le Bourgeois Gentilhomme*, loosely translated as "The Middle-Class Gentleman." In Molière's satire, a vain man, Monsieur Jourdain, hires a tutor to aid him in his quest to climb higher on the social ladder. At one point his tutor patiently describes the difference between prose and poetry. When Monsieur Jourdain grasps the point, he exclaims delightedly, "By my faith! For more than forty years I have been speaking prose without knowing anything about it, and I am much obliged to you for having taught me that!"

Many people are praying "without knowing anything about it." And they are even more delighted than Monsieur Jourdain when this is revealed, because they realize that they have been in a relationship with God all along.

Prayer is somewhat like speaking prose. Part of beginning to pray is recognizing, like Monsieur Jourdain, that you're already doing it.

Wait a minute, you might be thinking, *I'm already praying? What does that mean?*

If you're an experienced pray-er, you are probably praying in a formal way. You may sit down (or lie, kneel, or walk around) at a certain time each day and enter an intentional conversation with God. You may have set ways of praying. You may go on retreats. You may even know something about spiritual direction. But you also may be, like Monsieur Jourdain, doing it without knowing it.

Nine Ways of Praying, or Starting to Pray, Without Knowing It

Let's consider the most common times of praying unawares.

1. *You spontaneously ask God for help.* Although you don't consider yourself someone who prays formally—taking time to place yourself in God's presence, being aware that you are praying, reflecting on what happened in prayer—you ask God for help from time to time. Short spontaneous prayers come to your mind and sometimes your lips, almost without your realizing it.

This often happens during times of stress: "Help me, God!" Or "God, let me get through this." And sometimes, "God, are you even there?"

That last one is prayer too—because you're in conversation with God.

Likewise, you find yourself wishing that God would help you, especially during times of struggle or sadness. A request for help is an obvious prayer. So is a longing for help, even if not expressed formally. In that case, your heart is praying for you.

2. *You pause to think about something that inspires you.* Perhaps you read an article about a woman who works in a refugee camp and are moved by her generosity as she describes what it means to spend her days among refugees. Or you read about a refugee and are amazed by the drive, courage, and persistence she has shown, as she led her family from a war-torn country to a peaceful nation and built a life for herself and her children. Or a co-worker tells you how he cares for his

special-needs child or a parent with dementia, and you think, *That's beautiful*. Moved, you pause to think about these things, maybe even getting teary-eyed over them.

Or you linger over a magazine, are caught by an image on your computer screen, or think about a friend's comment as you drive home from work. You ponder. You let yourself be inspired. Briefly you wonder if God is part of this somehow. This kind of reflection is both an invitation to prayer and a sort of prayer itself.

Here's another kind of inspiration. During a tough time, you find yourself thinking of a familiar Bible verse, like the beginning of Psalm 23, "Even though I walk through the darkest valley, I fear no evil; for you are with me," or a simple inspirational phrase such as "Let go, let God." You turn this calming phrase over in your mind like a smooth stone in your hand. You wonder why this calms you down. It's more than the message itself. There's a longing for the source of that comfort. *Is God behind these feelings?* you wonder. This too is an inchoate prayer.

3. *You're aware that you feel compassion.* You pass a homeless person on the street and feel a surge of pity much greater than what you normally feel. You wonder where such a strong emotion came from. You're not naturally inclined to help this homeless person—perhaps you think that the poor should take care of themselves—but something about the look on his face touches you. *Does this powerful feeling come from outside of me?* you wonder.

As you pass that person, you remember Jesus saying, "Blessed are the poor." It resonates with you in a surprisingly deep way. You wonder, *What did Jesus mean?* Something dawns on you about those words that you've never considered before. Something has taken root in you. You consider that for a while, but then move on. This consideration is the start of prayer.

4. *You wonder about God.* You may wonder why something bad has happened to you. In response, you start to think about the way God

works. *Does God cause bad things to happen? Is God behind what happened to me? Does God notice what's going on in my life? Does God care?*

Conversely, you see the veins on a new leaf in the spring, the intricate pattern of a rosebud, or a bright new zinnia in your garden, and you think, *How exquisite!* Or you're at the beach watching the rolling waves crashing against the shore, or in the mountains seeing storm clouds moving over the landscape, and you think, *This is so beautiful!* Then you wonder, *What's behind all this? It can't be random!* You pause and wonder for a few minutes about God. Wondering about God is the beginning of prayer.

5. *You wonder if God approves of your actions.* Faced with an ethical dilemma at work or in your private life, you wonder whether you'll be judged for what you are about to do. You start to think about the commandments and rules in the Bible and in your religious tradition.

Or you've done something that you realize is wrong, and you feel awful. You can't sleep. It weighs on you, like a physical thing. You wonder if your conscience is speaking to you. In other words, you're listening to God's voice and paying attention to what it's telling you. You turn over in your mind what you've done and think about how God might judge this. Listening to and reflecting on what your conscience tells you is another form of prayer.

6. *You wonder about the meaning of your life.* Near the end of my time working in corporate America, I started to think that my life was circular: you go to school, so you can go to work, so you can earn a living, so you can go to work. Business is a real vocation for many people, probably for many readers of this book, but it didn't seem to be for me. I used to think: *What's it all about?* If you have a family, you may watch your children grow up and leave the house and then feel sad, lonely, or purposeless.

Sometimes you are almost embarrassed to ask yourself: *What's the point?* Sure, you have loving relationships in your life, a decent job, and maybe children, but you wonder if you're meant for more. You wonder if God has anything to do with this. *What's the meaning of it all? Why am I here? Does God have a plan for me?* The questions overwhelm you at times, and although you try to avoid them, part of you is drawn to considering them. In the morning, while you're showering, or getting the kids' breakfast ready, or driving to work, you ponder this. This pondering of ultimate questions, this contemplation of reality, can be a kind of prayer.

7. *You are aware that you are grateful.* You're moved to say thanks about something wonderful, and your gratitude feels directed somewhere, to something, *someone.* Your gratitude feels as if it needs a place to go. Or you might look at a beautiful sight—a flower in bloom, snow on your porch, a bird that flies by—and say, "I'm so grateful to see that." This is reflexive gratitude, and the natural desire to express it can be the beginning of prayer.

8. *You try to "center" or "connect."* You've heard about people who "center themselves" or try to "connect with the universe" or who practice yoga and find it calming. One day, with the door to your bedroom closed, you try to do that. You try to center. You think you feel it working. And you do find yourself calmer and, yes, centered.

But there's also a sense that the calm is coming from outside you. You wonder where it all comes from and pause to think. That wondering and pausing is an invitation to prayer.

9. *You wish you could pray.* You may be in a church for a wedding or a funeral, see someone kneeling in a pew, and feel a sudden longing. You have a desire for prayer *itself* and wonder what it would be like. This can be the beginning of prayer, if you allow it to be.

Each of these experiences is a kind of prayer, or at least the beginning of prayer. They are moments that sometimes happen reflexively.

Sometimes you're aware that you are praying, and yet you wonder if there's more to prayer than these brief moments. So even if you are not a believer or a person who prays regularly, you are being invited into prayer in these moments.

I love what Joyce Rupp writes about these unexpected moments in her lovely book *Prayer*:

> Praying does not always take place in a contained or predetermined place of reflection. We never know when there might be an interior turning toward the One who dwells within us and among us. Going for a walk or a run, stopping at night to bless sleeping children, driving past a homeless person, looking up to see a bright star in the heavens, receiving a note from a cherished friend, turning toward a spouse in pleasurable love, reading a story in the newspaper, hearing the pain in a colleague's anguish, waiting in a checkout line—at any time and any place we can be surprised and drawn into communion by the unanticipated sense of God's nearness.[1]

All these experiences lead to the question: What is prayer, anyway?

Is There More?

When I entered the Jesuits, I was praying in the scattershot way I had as a boy: asking God for help and complaining to God when things weren't going the way I thought they should. Until my mid-twenties, then, my prayer consisted mainly of memorized prayers that I would recite whenever I wanted something from God. Occasionally I would get down on my knees and pour out my heart to God. If it was especially heartfelt, perhaps I'd shed some tears. Hearing nothing, I'd stand up, sigh, and wonder what was supposed to happen. My idea of prayer was frozen at the level I learned when I was a child.

Many people have the same experience: their knowledge of prayer is frozen at the stage of childhood understanding and practice. There is nothing blameworthy in that. We can know only what we have been taught or have experienced. But imagine translating that practice to any other part of life. Imagine trying to navigate adult life with the emotional maturity of a child. Imagine living a moral life with the wisdom of a ten-year-old. Imagine trying to make it through life with a fourth-grade understanding of math.

Or imagine trying to live an adult life with a child's understanding of language, with its limited knowledge of grammar and vocabulary. At different points in your life, you would be profoundly hindered. You would be unable to express complex emotions; you would be tongue-tied in complicated social situations; you would feel confused when you read books written for adults. You might feel sad when you listened to others talk, not understanding them or being unable to participate in the conversation. You would feel inadequate to the task of living an adult life.

Our prayer life is no different. It's hard to live as adults if we lack an adult spirituality. Imagine facing a difficult situation and relating to God in the same way you did in grammar school or having a profound spiritual experience as an adult and not knowing how to respond.

That's where I found myself at age twenty-five. I understood little about what it meant to pray other than what little I remembered from Sunday school. This is the situation in which many of us find ourselves. The good news is that there's a lot more to prayer, and it's easy to learn.

So let's return to that essential question: What is prayer?

That's the topic of our next chapter.

5

What Is Prayer?

A FEW DEFINITIONS AND INSIGHTS

Open a book on prayer, and you may be overwhelmed by the pro-liferation of terms. There's "prayer" of course, but there's also "meditation" and "contemplation." There's *lectio divina*, "centering prayer," "interior prayer," "devotions," and "infused contempla-tion." If the book is written by a Catholic author, you might read about "adoration" and "intercession." Finally, from a Jesuit author you may hear about "composition of place" and the "colloquy."

The more you read, the more you realize that these terms may also overlap. What one writer means by "contemplation" another one calls "meditation." And they each defend their nomenclature vigorously: "That's not contemplation—that's meditation." Once I read that, for St. Teresa of Ávila, meditation is what we can do and contemplation is what God does within us.[1] A few years later I heard a retreat director say precisely the opposite!

The concept of prayer can be confusing. Certainly it was when I was leafing through books in the Jesuit novitiate library with no real idea what I was looking for other than the fact that I wanted to learn to pray. *Gee, this one has a nice cover. . . . This one looks like it's easy to understand. . . . I like the title on that one. . . . I think our novice director mentioned this author.* At the time, I was desperate to find a book that would answer all my questions about prayer but, in the process, I only grew more confused. It wasn't until I started praying on a regular basis and had a few sessions with my spiritual director that I started to relax and understand more about prayer.

So let's start with the most basic question: *What is prayer?*

There are almost as many answers to that question as there are spiritual writers. We'll begin with the most common ones and those I've found most helpful.

A Raising of the Mind and Heart to God

According to St. John Damascene, an eighth-century Syrian monk and priest:

> Prayer is the raising of one's mind and heart to God or the requesting of good things from God.[2]

The first half of his definition finds its roots in, among other places, the Book of Lamentations, in which the writer exhorts his community, "Let us lift up our hearts as well as our hands to God in heaven."[3] Eventually St. John's definition found its way into the *Catechism of the Catholic Church*, the official compendium of church teaching, and leads off its entry on prayer. It's an excellent starting point for our discussion.

Prayer is a "raising" or, in another translation, a "lifting up." That's a reminder that God is, in a sense, "above us." I don't mean that God is in the sky per se (although God is everywhere, so you could say that God is in the sky too). Rather, we sometimes must remind ourselves that when we pray, we are in communication with the Supreme Being, or, depending on how you like to think of God, the Lord, the Almighty, the Source of All Being. As much as I will write about speaking with God in a familiar way and entering into a friendship with God, it's important to remember who God *is*—the Creator of the universe. It's *God* we're talking about, after all. Prayer is an approach "from below," as some theologians will say.

Sometimes I need to remind myself of this. In my daily prayer, I occasionally catch myself being, for want of a better word, too informal. That doesn't mean that you always need to pray in an overly formal or obsequious way, as the Anglican school chaplain does in a trenchant scene from the Monty Python film *The Meaning of Life*. Dressed in a black cassock and snowy white surplice, he stands in a chapel, in front of the assembled students, and leads them in this marvelously groveling prayer:

> O Lord, oooh, you are so big, so absolutely huge. Gosh, we're all *really* impressed down here, I can tell you. Forgive us, O Lord, for this, our dreadful toadying. But you're so strong, and, well, just so . . . *super*.

Then he leads them in a tuneful hymn that begins, "O Lord, please don't burn us."

I'm not advocating that kind of groveling stance. On the other hand, it's important to remember in prayer that you're not simply talking to a friend. You're talking to God. Reverence and awe are in order, as is an awareness of who's in charge. Hint: not you.

You're aiming for something essential in the spiritual life—balance. Balance between reverence and friendliness, between awe and familiarity, between toadying and arrogance. Remember that God is your friend, but remember that God is far more than any friend.

Prayer is, to return to St. John's definition, a "raising" in another way. When I "raise up" something to someone, it feels like an offering. Imagine finding a wounded baby bird chirping and flapping its tiny wings under a tree. You look in vain for the nest and the mother bird but can find neither. So you decide to bring the bird to a veterinarian. Standing before the vet, you cup the bird in your hands, lifting it up so that she can examine it. There is a plaintive quality here. We lift up something not simply to the one who is "above us" or "over us," but to the one who can help and heal us.

There is always in prayer a lifting. We lift our cares to the One who helps us. We lift our praise to the One who blesses us. We lift our very selves to the One who created us. We lift ourselves up to God.

As St. John says, prayer involves both the mind and the heart. Prayer neglects neither the intellect nor the emotional life. Think of how odd it would be to shut down, or even ignore, either mind or heart when you're trying to deepen your relationship with God. When struggling with any problem, you want to lift up to God both what you're thinking and what you're feeling, as you would in any relationship.

The second part of St. John's definition notes that prayer is a "requesting." As I mentioned earlier, some people find the idea of asking God for help both childish and selfish. It is seen as childish, because it doesn't reflect an "adult" relationship; it supposedly reduces us to the state of children begging for another piece of candy.

It's selfish, so the thinking goes, because who are we to ask for anything from God? "We should be happy with what we have," some people say. "We should be satisfied with whatever God has given us and so never complain. We should trust in God and know that our lives are as complete as they can be."

Although it's admirable to be happy, satisfied, and uncomplaining, it is unhelpful to suggest that we should never ask for anything in prayer. Telling the mother of a seriously ill child that she shouldn't ask God for help is monstrous. That kind of requesting is good, human, and natural. During Daily Mass in my Jesuit community, people will pray aloud for a person in need of help and ask others to do so as well: "Please pray for a friend whose mother is dying of cancer." "Please pray for a man going through a rough spot in his marriage." "Please pray for a cousin who had a miscarriage." Praying for others is a holy act.

It's also good, human, and natural to ask for things for *your-self*. Everyone needs help from time to time. As long as you ask for "good things," as St. John says. "God, make me the meanest person around," and "God, make something terrible happen to my enemy" are prayers, but not very good ones.

Overall, St. John's definition is helpful, but it's also incomplete because it is somewhat one-sided. While you're doing the "raising" and the "asking," what is God doing? It seems to omit God's response. Inadvertently, it may encourage us to see God as a king seated on a throne, waiting for us to raise things up to him and ask him for help. If we're not careful, we can move dangerously close to Monty Python territory: "Gosh, we're all *really* impressed down here."

God is in charge, of course, but again, after you've done all the raising and asking, what's God doing? To answer that, let's look at a few more definitions.

A Surge of the Heart

For me, prayer is a surge of the heart; it is a simple look turned toward heaven, it is a cry of recognition and of love, embracing both trial and joy.[4]

That's from St. Thérèse of Lisieux, one of my favorite saints. Thérèse Martin was a French Carmelite sister who lived from 1873 to 1897, dying at a young age from tuberculosis. During her time in a cloistered convent, the young nun served in several roles, including director of novices. Thérèse also served as a model nun for many in her community. But not all of them—some of her sisters were jealous of her. Aware of Thérèse's holiness, her religious superior asked her to write down her life; contained in her autobiography are not only her vocation story and her reflections on time in the convent, but also her outlook on the spiritual life.

The spirituality of St. Thérèse is often called the "Little Way," for several reasons. Chief among them is its emphasis on doing small things with great love for God. It is beloved by millions of believers, because Thérèse describes a spiritual path that everyone can follow. Thérèse said often that although she couldn't be a great saint like St. Teresa of Ávila, another Carmelite nun, she could do little things.

In her autobiography, *Story of a Soul*, Thérèse meditated at length on St. Paul's vivid image of the church as a "body" and pondered what part of the body she might be. Finally, she realized: "I shall be the heart."

Not surprisingly, for Thérèse, prayer comes primarily from the heart. Her definition is a reminder of the place of *love* in the life of prayer. We pray because we love God and God loves us. Awe, reverence, and duty are part of prayer, but the primary motivation, as Thérèse grasped, is love.

Her own description of prayer—"a surge of the heart"—sounds like something we cannot avoid, an almost unconscious act. Our hearts cry out, reach out, *surge* for God. It rings true for many of us. We *have* to pray. We have to pour out our hearts, our very selves, to God.

Prayer is also directed toward heaven. It is not meditating by yourself or mere navel gazing. It has both an orientation and an object. Thus, as was also clear in St. John Damascene's definition, it is different from some forms of meditation or yoga, for example. It centers on God.

It is a "cry of recognition" in that the soul sees someone it recognizes. This definition alludes to the fact that we have a natural desire for God. Our souls recognize God because they were created by God.

On the front of the annual flyer from the Eastern Point Retreat House in Gloucester, Massachusetts, is a phrase from Psalm 42: "Deep calls to deep." That's how I've always thought of prayer: the deepest part of ourselves calls to the deep. Deep also recognizes deep.

Rarely do you pour yourself out to someone completely unknown. Even if you do so, say, to a physician or nurse during an illness, you may hold back a bit. You're naturally more reticent with someone you don't know well. The more you come to know a person, the more open you will be. Familiarity leads to comfort, which leads to openness. The recognition the soul experiences in encountering God enables it to be open.

The soul also carries itself toward God expressing, as Thérèse says, both "trial and joy," leaving nothing out and holding nothing back. Her friendship with Jesus was the most intimate relationship she had. She told him everything in prayer, both her trials and her joys.

Her lovely description—I don't think she was trying to define prayer as much as describe it—captures a great deal about what motivates prayer. Still, it seems incomplete. Once again, it is we who are doing all the work. What's God doing?

With that in mind, let's look at another definition. Maybe it will tell us more about God.

A Sharing Between Friends

Thérèse's predecessor in the Carmelite order, St. Teresa of Ávila, had a slightly different approach:

> Mental prayer is nothing else than a close sharing between
> friends; it means taking time frequently to be alone with
> him who we know loves us.[5]

Teresa, a sixteenth-century Spanish nun known not only for her spiritual writings but also for reforming her religious order, often spoke of prayer as friendship.

Prayer is intimate, Teresa reminds us. That idea is closer to my own notion of prayer, because it speaks about prayer as an aspect of a relationship. It's a sharing, no longer one-sided, nearer to the kinds of relationships we have with friends. In prayer, we are searching for intimacy with God.

St. Ignatius Loyola often counseled people to speak to God "as one friend speaks to another." This is what St. Teresa's definition helps us to understand. It's also an invitation at times simply to be with God—not to talk, just to be.

Mark Thibodeaux, SJ, who served as a Jesuit novice director in Louisiana for over a decade, breaks down four stages of prayer in his book *Armchair Mystic: Easing into Contemplative Prayer*. "Talking at God" is the first stage. Here you're reciting rote prayers, confident that God hears you. Next comes "talking to God," speaking to God in your own words. Third is "listening to God," being attentive to the ways that God communicates with you, not only in your prayer, but in your daily life. The fourth stage is "being with God." Mark views these stages as a progression, but he also notes that you can pray in different ways at different times.[6]

The last stage, "being with God," is something I've grown more comfortable with over the years. I don't mean simply intellectually, as in, "I agree with that," but experientially as well; as I get older, simply being in God's presence is enough. On this, Teresa, Mark, and I all agree.

A Long, Loving Look at the Real

My apologies for including so many definitions from Jesuits, but this one, from Walter Burghardt, a renowned theologian, preacher, and advocate for social justice, is a favorite:

> Prayer is a long, loving look at the real.[7]

Taken from an essay in *Church* magazine in 1989, it made a lasting impression when I first heard it from David, my spiritual director in the novitiate. It focuses on four important elements in prayer.

First, prayer is *long*. That doesn't mean that you need to do it for hours at a time. Few of us are monks or cloistered nuns with hours of time to pray. (And not even monks and cloistered nuns spend their entire day praying; they're busy with other tasks as well.)

Nonetheless, as in any relationship, it's important not to rush. Imagine scheduling time with a friend you've not seen for many years. Eagerly anticipating your reunion, you spend some time selecting a favorite restaurant for dinner. But as soon as you both sit down, you say to your friend, "Sorry, I only have three minutes! Start talking!" That may sound ridiculous, but this sometimes is how we approach God.

Prayer is long because deepening a relationship with God, noticing God's activity in our daily lives, and settling into God's presence takes time. In a way, prayer can be said to go against human nature, because many of us are impatient people who like to get things done. When we start a regular practice of prayer, if it seems like nothing special is "happening," it may feel like a waste of time, and we might grow antsy. We may feel the temptation to move on to something else—anything but prayer.

It's also long because it takes time to settle down before we can see clearly. Let's return to my fifth-grade biology experiment with the glass of water from the shallow stream that ran through our neighborhood. Before I could see all the microorganisms swimming around in it, I had to leave the glass on the windowsill and wait for the dirt to settle and the water to clear. In prayer, it takes time for things to settle, so that we can see what God wants us to see.

But in another way, prayer is consonant with human nature, because we are designed to be in relationship with God. Once we taste the fruits of prayer, we want to remain in God's presence. Prayer is long because once our souls recognize God, we want to stay with God. Deep calls to deep. It feels like coming home—because it is. As Father Burghardt said, prayer is long—because it must be.

It's *loving* because, as both St. Thérèse of Lisieux and St. Teresa of Ávila pointed out, it's done in the context of love. Everything that happens in prayer needs to be understood from that perspective. God loved you into being, God loves you now, and God will always love you. So when you are with God—even when you are angry with others, with yourself, or with God—you are with the source of love in your life.

Think of a child who is having trouble in a class in school. A good teacher might take the child aside privately and speak with the child about the difficulties. Naturally, the child might be sad, impatient, confused, or even angry. But deep down the child knows that the help is given out of love. That helps the child to listen amid frustration and tears.

Prayer involves a *look* because looking is contemplative in nature. When you truly look at something, you don't analyze it; you gaze upon it. It is an open stance in which you quietly rest before something, allowing what you perceive to enter your being. Father Burghardt said it best in his original essay: "I do not analyze or argue it, describe or define it—I am one with it."[8]

Something similar may happen in prayer. Even during the most stressful times comes a gentle invitation to look at things quietly, in the presence of God's love. This is not to say that strong emotions will not arise. But you are looking at the reality of your situation in a contemplative way.

Why is it a long, loving look at *the real*? Because much of prayer is taken up with the reality of our lives. A good deal of prayer is simply resting in God's presence, without much conscious thought of one's daily life. The "real" may simply be the reality of God. But prayer frequently centers on the stuff of everyday life.

Too often people feel the need to make their prayer more lofty. They approach prayer with the assumption that it should concern elevated theological concepts such as the Trinity. But often prayer focuses on the reality of our lives. Yes, the Trinity is part of that reality, but I'm speaking more about our daily activities: waking up, preparing breakfast for children, going to work, spending time with co-workers, dealing with responsibilities on the job, coming home, cooking dinner, interacting with your family—as well as the other challenges of adult life, like negotiating emotional, physical, and financial issues.

A few years ago I was spending time with my nephew Matthew, then eleven years old, who has a terrific sense of humor. We were playing pool together at my mother's retirement community, and he unexpectedly climbed on top of the pristine pool table and curled himself up to hit a difficult shot. When my eyes registered disapproval, Matthew said, "Uncle Jim, there is nothing in the rules that says you can't be *on* the table!" I laughed. Later, when I was praying about my day, I recalled that moment and thanked God for the gift of my nephew. Matthew was part of the "real" of my life, and I simply spent time "looking" at that lighthearted incident. It was a look at the real.

Burghardt's definition as "a long, loving look at the real" helps us to see that rather than relating to what he terms a "far-off, abstract, intangible God-in-the-sky," we are invited to enjoy God's presence here, among us, in the real.

A Personal Relationship

A definition of prayer that has proven tremendously helpful to me is:

Prayer is a personal relationship with God.

When I was a Jesuit novice, my spiritual director gave me a slim book called *God and You*, by William Barry. The book's subtitle summarizes its overall message: *Prayer as a Personal Relationship*. As it happens, however, in the first chapter Father Barry offers a slight variation. Prayer, he writes, is a "conscious relationship with God."[9]

What might it mean to have a "personal" or "conscious" relationship with God?

First, it means knowing that you are not relating to a far-off, abstract, intangible God who has little interest in the world and even less in your daily life. You are relating to a God who cares about you intensely and whom you can come to know personally.

We can never fully know God, who is far beyond human abilities of comprehension. "For as the heavens are higher than the earth," says the Book of Isaiah, "so are my ways higher than your ways and my thoughts than your thoughts."[10] *Mysterious, ineffable*, and *unknowable* are some of the traditional and highly accurate ways of talking about the mystery of God. In fact, we do not need to understand God in order to believe in God.

The old hymn gets it right:

Immortal, invisible, God only wise,
In light inaccessible hid from our eyes,
Most blessed, most glorious, the Ancient of Days,
Almighty, victorious, Thy great Name we praise.[11]

God is beyond us.

On the other hand, we are invited to come to know God *in part*. We can do this by experiencing God in prayer and daily life, by meditating on Scripture, by reflecting on God's presence in nature, and, well, through as many ways as there are people. God wants to be known by us, even if imperfectly. Christians believe this is one reason the Ancient of Days took on human flesh in Jesus. God desires to be known. Likewise, God desires to know us.

If you're unused to hearing language like that, it may sound strange. Doesn't God know us already? Yes. "You knit me together in my mother's womb," says Psalm 139. "Even before a word is on my tongue, O LORD, you know it completely."[12] So yes, God knows us already, through and through.

At the same time, God desires to enter into a deepening friendship with each of us. How can we know this? As Father Barry says, "Old and New Testaments and the experience of men and women down through the ages testify that he does. The Bible is a record of how God continually tries and tries to awaken human beings to the full reality of who they are, namely, his beloved children."[13]

In this way, God's desire is similar to the desire of loving parents to know their child. And if not parents, then a loving grandparent, aunt, uncle, teacher, or mentor. If you love someone, whether a child, parent, partner, or friend, what happens to them matters to you. You want to know all about them, out of love.

When my two nephews were very young, I wanted to know all

about their lives: what school was like, who their friends were, what they were interested in. In fact, I still want to know that about them. It's part of loving someone. And if I, with all my limitations, feel that way, imagine how God feels toward us.

At this point you might ask: "How can we *know* God desires a relationship with us?" You might also ask: "Who are you to say what God wants or doesn't want?" Father Barry's brief answer indicates the two ways we can know this.

First, it makes sense *theologically*. God is relational, entering into relationships with people throughout what is called "salvation history," the story of the People of God from the beginning of the Hebrew Bible through the New Testament. For Christians, Jesus is the ultimate way that God enters into relationship with us. In fact, God's very *being* is relational. The Trinity—Father, Son, and Holy Spirit—is a kind of community.

Second, we can know it *experientially*. For me personally, God has entered my life in ways both big and small. Big? By calling me through my desires into the Society of Jesus and in this way offering me a path in life. Small? By making me laugh when I'm with my nephew, and in this way showing me love.

But my experiential knowledge is not based solely on my *own* experience. Over the years, I've seen how God works personally in other people's lives. For the past few years, I've gone on annual pilgrimages to the Holy Land with groups of about a hundred people. We visit all the important sites in Jesus's life—Bethlehem, Nazareth, the Sea of Galilee, Cana, Bethany, Jerusalem, and more—and spend a great deal of time praying to, thinking about, and discussing Jesus. At the beginning of the day, there is a spiritual talk to frame the day's visits. At the end of the day, during "faith sharing," we speak about the various ways we met God.

What always delights me on these pilgrimages is how *personal* God is with the pilgrims, meeting them individually, where they are. One woman said that hearing the Gospel passage read during the Daily Mass struck her to the core of her being, moving her to tears; for others the reading prompted nothing out of the ordinary. Another woman found praying in the Garden of Gethsemane nearly life-changing, while a travel mate said about the same place, "Didn't do much for me." A trip to the Church of the Nativity thrilled one man and annoyed another. "Too noisy!" the latter said. God speaks in highly personal ways, suiting the approach to each person.

A few months after one of the trips, a pilgrim who held a position in a New York City museum reported that she was visiting another museum and spied a painting of Judas. She said that before the trip she would have passed it by, but after the pilgrimage it struck her with great force. For someone else viewing that painting it might have been just another work of art. But God reached out to our pilgrim in a most personal way. God speaks to us in ways tailored to the fabric of our individual lives.

Father Barry's insight is not only helpful in understanding what prayer is, but also how to approach it. Looking at our personal relationships can help us get our prayer life in order.

If prayer is a personal relationship with God, then we can use the idea of a personal relationship with others as a helpful analogy. The same practices that make for a good relationship with other people make for a good relationship with God. For example, what kind of relationship would you have if you never spent much time with someone? What kind of relationship would it be if all you did was ask for things? Or if you never listened? We'll look at that in more detail in the next chapter.

Another Jesuit spiritual writer, Thomas Green, who taught for many years in the Philippines, defines prayer slightly differently in *Experiencing God: The Three Stages of Prayer*. He combines the insights of St. John Damascene with those of Father Barry: "Prayer [is] an opening of the mind and heart to God." Note the slight difference from St. John's definition. "Opening" suggests more of a two-way street than "raising." Green also describes it as a "personal encounter with God in love."[14]

Both Barry's and Green's definitions touch upon the essential relational aspect of prayer. But you could also say that a "personal relationship with God" could describe the orientation of a person's whole spiritual life, not simply their prayer. Likewise, being open to God could constitute an entire worldview.

In that case, how do you distinguish prayer from the rest of your spiritual life?

Conscious Conversation

Prayer, at least for me, is slightly different from the relationship itself. Here's the way I like to define prayer:

Prayer is conscious conversation with God.

For me, prayer is intentional one-on-one time with God. It occurs in the context of personal relationship with God but, more specifically, it is what happens when you are intentionally trying to speak with, listen to, or be with God. It's a conversation, as St. Teresa says, and a sharing. And it's more conscious, more intentional, about that conversation than at other times when you are less focused on God. For me, praying means *intending* to pray.

As a Jesuit, I hope everything that I do flows from my personal relationship with God. But not everything I do counts as prayer, at least as I see it. The old adage "My work is my prayer" is both helpful and unhelpful. On the one hand, it's important to live your life prayerfully. I try to do everything prayerfully—though I don't always succeed. At the same time, that doesn't mean that everything you do is necessarily prayer. There's a danger in saying, "My work is my prayer," because it can be an excuse for not praying. If everything you do is a prayer, then why take time out to pray? My novice director used to say, "If your work is your prayer, then you're not doing either of them well."

Imagine a married couple deeply in love. Now suppose you ask one of them, "Do you take time to be affectionate with your spouse?" If the person said, "*Everything* I do is affectionate, so I don't need to do anything special," you might raise an eyebrow. You might wonder if that person ever takes the time to be *consciously* affectionate with his or her partner.

Prayer is similar. In the context of that larger personal relationship you are invited to set aside intentional time, conscious time, to speak to God and to listen to God's voice.

No one definition can fully sum up prayer, but each one captures something important about it. It is a raising up of our minds and hearts; a surge of the heart; a sharing between friends; a long, loving look at the real; and a conscious conversation, all of which happens in the context of a personal relationship with God.

In time, you'll come up with your own definition of prayer. More important, you'll experience prayer. And experiencing it is more important than defining it. As with love, learning to practice it is more important than knowing the right definition.

With that in mind, let's look at, and try, some of the ways to pray. But first, I'd like to share with you the most helpful insight I've ever heard about prayer. It will help to shape and inform the rest of our discussion.

6

Beginning a Friendship with God

FATHER BARRY'S INSIGHT

As I mentioned, when I was a Jesuit novice, struggling with entering into the life of prayer and bursting with questions ("Am I doing it right?" "What's supposed to happen?" "Is this really God speaking to me?"), my first spiritual director gave me *God and You*, by Father Barry. The key premise of this marvelous book, that prayer is a "personal relationship with God" (the book's subtitle), allows us to mine what we know about human relationships for ways to understand our relationship with God. No one insight has more deeply affected my spiritual life than this one.

Obviously, however, it's an imperfect analogy. After all, none of our friends have created the universe *ex nihilo*. And prayer is not simply the relationship itself, but also the way the relationship is expressed. As I said in the last chapter, prayer might be described as a conscious conversation with God—with whom, of course, you are in relationship.

But Father Barry's general point was revelatory: the way you think about friendships can help you think about, and deepen, your relationship with God. And it's important to look at this insight near the beginning of our book, because it will make a difference in how you read the chapters to come.

As we look at healthy friendships, you'll see some of the same traits that make for good friendships with others also make for a good relationship with God. And when you are wondering about your relationship with God, this comparison can be a helpful tool.

So what kinds of things are required for a good relationship— with a friend and with God?

Time

Friendships flourish when you spend time with friends. So does a relationship with God. You wouldn't say that you were someone's friend if the two of you never spent any time together. What about with God? Some people say, "God is the most important thing in my life!" But when you ask how much time they spend with God in an intentional way, they sheepishly admit that it's not that much.

What kind of relationship would you have if you never carved out time for your friend? It would be superficial and unsatisfying for both parties. That's why intentional time with God is so important.

That's not to say that the only way to spend time with God is through private prayer. One hallmark of Jesuit spirituality is "finding God in all things." You can find God through worship services, reading, work, family, social relationships—almost everything. But, as with any friendship, sometimes you need to spend time *one-on-one* with God. Just as sometimes you need to block out time for a good friend, you need to do the same for God, and to let God do this with you—assuming you want to sustain and deepen your relationship. As

the Old Testament's Book of Amos says, "Do two walk together unless they have made an appointment?"[1]

Time also lets a friendship deepen. This is one reason it can be
so difficult for people to move from one city or country to another.
Besides leaving family, they are leaving friends with whom they have
developed deep relationships, which can only happen over time.
Friendships that develop in the new locale will take time before
their depth matches that of the friendships in the former place.

Something like that happens with God. It takes time before you
feel comfortable with God and can tolerate the ups and downs of the
spiritual life. If you "get to know" God, you will know what God is
like in prayer. That is, sometimes things will feel uplifting, and other
times things may feel dry.

Again, something similar happens in friendships. One of my very
closest friends hates using the telephone. When we are together,
conversation flows naturally and freely. But when we are apart, I
hear from him only sporadically. Even his text messages are taciturn.

"Hey, how's it going?"

"Fine. You?"

"I'm fine. What's new?"

"Busy."

Sometimes it's almost comical, but that's the way he is. I've even
asked him, and he's said, "I feel funny talking on the phone for long
periods of time. Self-conscious. I have to use the phone for work,
but even then it's just short and sweet." If I didn't know him better,
I might think from his texts that something was wrong, that he was
depressed or even angry at me. But knowing him helps me understand the silences. That's just the way he is.

This particular example is a reminder that simply because we
don't feel as though we're "hearing from" God in our prayer doesn't
mean that God has abandoned us. The longer we know God, the
more we become comfortable with God's ways of relating to us.

Likewise, seeing friends on the fly or in groups is great, but from time to time you need to give a friend your undivided attention. You also need to spend time with God. Prayer involves being attentive to God. How much time are you willing to spend with God? How much time are you willing to commit to deepening your friendship with God?

Learning

In any close relationship you're naturally interested in learning about your friend. One of the most enjoyable parts of a new friendship is finding out about a friend's background—discovering hobbies and interests, hearing funny childhood stories, and getting to know your friend's joys and hopes. When two people fall in love, there is an even more intense desire to know the other person, which is an important way of being intimate.

The same holds true in your relationship with God. Particularly in the early stages you may feel a powerful, almost overwhelming, desire to learn as much about God as possible. You find yourself thinking about God and wondering: *What is God like? How can I learn about God?* Just a taste of God in prayer can awaken a powerful sense of wonder. This is another, subtle way that God has of drawing us closer.

One of the easiest ways to discover answers to these questions is to listen to *other people* talk about their experiences of God.

Over twenty years ago, when I edited a book called *How Can I Find God?* I mailed letters to a variety of believers asking them for advice. What would they tell someone who asked them that question?[2]

Sister Helen Prejean, CSJ, who works with inmates on death row and is the author of *Dead Man Walking* and the memoir *River of Fire*, said, "The most direct road that I have found to God is in the faces

of poor and struggling people." Sister Helen talked about how working with the poor, specifically men and women on death row, had led
her to places "*beyond* the part of us that wants to be safe and secure
and with the comfortable and the familiar."[3]

Later in her essay, Sister Helen offered the analogy of a boat on a
river. When you begin to seek God, your sails fill up with wind and
your boat is taken to places that you may not expect. Prayer is an
essential part of that journey. Your boat, she says, needs not only
sails, but a rudder too. God gives us both energy and direction. Sister Helen's answer reminded me how much there is to learn about
God through other people.

Each essay taught me something new about God—for instance,
I had never thought of God as a rudder. Letting others tell us about
their experiences of God is like being introduced to a friend's friend
or like discovering something new about a friend you already know.

The practice known as "faith sharing" (which we will discuss later)
is another way of coming to know God through the experiences of
other people. Briefly put, in faith sharing people share with others
their experiences of God in their prayer and daily life. Whether it
is done in a small or large group, one of the main benefits is seeing
how God works so uniquely, personally, and individually with people, often revealing characteristics of God that might not have been
evident in your own prayer life. For example, if someone says that
they were moved to tears by holding a newborn baby, you may get an
insight into how God "is" in a new way.

Another way of learning about God is through *Scripture*. One of
the most moving essays in that same book is by Daniel J. Harrington,
SJ, who for many years taught New Testament at Boston College and
was one of my favorite professors during my theology studies. In his
essay he told a moving story about coming to know God.

When Harrington was a little boy, he stuttered. At age ten, he read
in a newspaper that Moses stuttered too. He looked it up in the Book

of Exodus and, sure enough, Moses says to God, "I am slow of speech and slow of tongue."[4] Dan read the rest of the story in Exodus, which tells how God promised to be with Moses and ultimately liberated the people of Israel. "I read that story over and over," wrote Harrington, "and it gradually worked upon me so that it has shaped my religious consciousness to this day. As a boy of ten or eleven years of age I found God in the Bible, and I have continued to do so ever since."[5]

But there was more to his story. As a Scripture scholar, Harrington spent a great deal of time studying and teaching the Bible. As a priest, he preached on the Bible. And sometimes, he says, "in the midst of these wonderful activities (which are my greatest joy) I occasionally stutter."[6] Then he makes this connection:

> And this brings me back to where my spiritual journey with the Bible began. Though I am slow of speech and tongue like Moses, I still hear the words of Exodus 4:11–12: "Who gives speech to mortals? Who makes them mute or deaf, seeing or blind? Is it not I, the LORD? Now go, and I will be with your mouth and teach you what you are to speak."[7]

Scripture is an ancient path to knowledge of God. First, reading Scripture helps inspire us—in the literal sense of the word, that is, placing God's Spirit into us. Second, Scripture tells us about the history of God's relationship with humanity, and in doing so it tells us something about God. Third, it recounts the ways that people throughout that history—from the Old Testament prophets, to Jesus, to the apostles, to St. Paul—related to God. In Scripture you see God relating to individuals and to humanity. In all these ways Scripture helps you to know God better.

For Christians, knowing God also means knowing a particular person: if you want to know more about God, learn more about *Jesus*. One reason God became human was to show us more clearly what

God was like. Jesus literally embodied God, and so anything you can say about Jesus you can say about God.

Here's another way of looking at Jesus's ministry—through the lens of the parable, a story from everyday life that opens our minds to new ways of thinking about God. The parable form was one of the primary ways in which Jesus of Nazareth invited his listeners to reflect on elusive but important concepts. In Luke's Gospel, for example, Jesus tells the crowd that one should treat one's neighbor as oneself. But when he is asked, "Who is my neighbor?" Jesus offers not a precise definition, but instead the parable of the Good Samaritan, in which a Samaritan helps a "neighbor" in distress.[8] When asked to explain what he means by the "reign of God," the central message of his preaching, Jesus offers short stories about mustard plants, wheat and weeds, and seeds falling on rocky ground.[9]

Where a strictly worded definition can be shallow and closes down thought, a story opens hearers' minds and is endlessly deep. Stories carry meaning without having to convert it into rigid statements. Parables also go against the normal expectations of the audience, as when a Samaritan, someone who hails from a hated ethnic group (at least from the standpoint of Jesus's crowd) and so is seen as the "other," is ultimately revealed as the good guy who cares for the stranger.

In a sense, Jesus of Nazareth was a parable told by God. If Jesus communicated spiritual truths through parables, you might say the same about God the Father. In order to communicate an essential truth, God offered us a kind of parable in Jesus. When the Son of God was asked, "What is the reign of God like?" he told stories of sheep and coins, fishes and nets, birds and flowers, wayward sons and forgiving fathers.[10] When God is asked, "What are *you* like?" he gives us Jesus and his story.

Now, Jesus was (and is) real of course, but you get the idea. His life is a story that reveals what God is like. So, for Christians, if you want to learn about God, get to know Jesus, the parable of God.

You can also learn about God through the *lives of holy men and women* and the ways God leads them to fulfill God's dreams for the world. For me, few things are more enjoyable than reading the lives of the saints. When I read stories of how much they loved God, how they experienced God's love in their own lives, and how they expressed that love to others, I learn more about the source of that love.

For example, Pierre Teilhard de Chardin, a French Jesuit and paleontologist who lived from 1881 to 1955, found God not simply in the celebration of the Mass and in the other, more obvious duties of a priest, but also in his work as a scientist and naturalist, work that took him around the globe. Teilhard wrote extensively about the interplay between science and religion. (For a time, his works were considered too controversial by the Vatican, which was suspicious of his new ways of speaking about God.)

Teilhard encountered God through many avenues, including the contemplation of nature. "There is a communion with God," he wrote, "and a communion with earth, and a communion with God through earth."[11] When I first read that, it helped me to understand the experience I had on my bike on the way to elementary school. Teilhard understood that you can learn a great deal about God through the natural world, in seeing how God reveals beauty and order in the universe and how God is forever creating and renewing the physical world.

We can learn about God by reading about such holy men and women as well as through *contact with holy men and women themselves*, if you're fortunate enough to know them. Through them we can glimpse the divine. Not that they are divine. Rather, they are like a clean window through which the light of God can shine.

Closer to home than Teilhard de Chardin for me was a Jesuit named Joe. When I first met Joe, a priest in his late sixties, he was living with us in the novitiate as what we called a "spiritual father," a living resource and example for the younger men.

Joe was one of the freest people I've ever met. Once, while heading out on a trip to visit some Jesuits in Kingston, Jamaica, his plane was delayed for five hours in Boston. Ultimately, the flight was canceled, and Joe returned home. That night I ran into Joe in the living room of the novitiate calmly reading a book.

"You're back!" I said. "What happened?"

"The funniest thing!" he said. "We were supposed to take off, and then we were delayed for an hour, and then waited another hour until they delayed us again." Joe chuckled as he recounted the delays that led to his trip's eventual cancellation. Afterward, he tracked down his luggage and took a long ride on the subway (the "T" in Boston) to get home. "So here I am!" he laughed.

Had that happened to me, I probably would have been boiling over in frustration. "Weren't you angry?" I said.

"Angry? Why?" he said. "There was nothing I could do about it. Why get upset over something you can't change?"

Equanimity in the face of stress does not make you holy. Much less does it make you a saint. But it's a start. Detachment, freedom, openness, and a sense of humor are signposts on the road to holiness. Joe knew that a healthy spirituality requires these things. Often when you would ask this elderly priest if he wanted to do something new—say, see a new movie, go to a newly opened restaurant, or check out a Mass at a faraway parish—he would answer, "Why not?"

Why not, indeed? People like Joe show the fruits of friendship with God: spontaneity, openness, generosity, freedom, love. Time with Joe taught me not simply about this particular person, but also the way God acts in the lives of men and women. Holy people teach you something about how God works—and so they teach you about God. Time with Joe taught me about God, because Joe had himself spent so much time with God.

Overall, learning about God—through other people's experiences of God, through Scripture, through Jesus, through the lives of the saints, and through encounters with holy men and women—is part of nourishing your spiritual life, because learning about God is part of being in relationship with God.

Honesty

"O LORD, you have searched me and known me," says Psalm 139. Letting God come to know *you* is essential in your relationship with God. Letting yourself be known in this relationship means more or less the same as it does in any relationship: you must speak about your life, share your feelings, and reveal yourself openly.

Honesty is an important part of this process. In *God and You*, Father Barry suggests thinking about what happens when you are not honest in a relationship. Usually, the relationship begins to grow cold, distant, or formal. If you're avoiding something unpleasant, the relationship devolves into one defined by nothing more than social niceties. Eventually the relationship dies.

It's the same with prayer. If you are saying what you think you *should* say to God rather than what you want to say, then your relationship will grow cold, distant, and formal. Honesty in prayer, as in life, is important.

About twenty years ago, I became friendly with a Jesuit whom I really admired. He seemed to lead a charmed life: he was happy, optimistic, hardworking, friendly, and prayerful. For a long time I tried to figure out what his secret was. What enabled him to lead this seemingly carefree life?

A few years later, this same friend went through a wrenching personal crisis and turned to me for help. In a series of conversations he poured out his pain and showed a part of himself that I had previously not seen. Fortunately, the crisis passed. But after he had opened up to me, I felt closer to him, and he told me that he felt closer to me. Both of us were grateful for our friendship. Though I now knew he didn't lead the perfect life, I liked him even more. Honesty had changed our relationship, making it deeper and more real.

How can you be honest with God in prayer? The easiest way may be to imagine God in front of you. You might picture God or Jesus sitting across from you in a chair, sitting beside you on a couch, or whatever feels comfortable. Then just speak in a familiar way, in silence or out loud, about your life.

God already knows what's going on in your life. Still, your openness and intentional sharing are an important part of the spiritual life. Once again, comparing it to a human friendship is instructive. Let's say your father has died. Good friends *already* know how sad you are and probably don't need to be told the extent of your loss. But you tell them anyway, right? And they listen.

Not too long ago I had lunch with a friend who lost his brother at a young age to cancer. My friend is a warm and generous person, and I knew that he was devastated by this loss. But it was still a privilege for me to hear him talk about what had happened, to see his tears, and to hear him recount funny stories about his brother.

Telling a friend about your loss, even if he or she already knows about it, may help make the loss more concrete for you. It gives you the opportunity to accept your friend's consolation, and it reminds you that you are *known* by another person in an intimate way.

Honesty with God means sharing everything with God, not simply gratitude and praise and not just things you think are appropriate for prayer. Honesty means sharing things you might consider inappropriate for conversation with God.

Being honest can be difficult. The spiritual writer Margaret Silf, in *Wayfaring: A Gospel Journey in Everyday Life*, tells a marvelous story about holding back. Once on retreat her spiritual director described to her three kinds of people in prayer. The first uses rote prayers. Silf thinks, "a touch self-righteously," that she has moved past that. "No, that's not me."

Those of the second kind really pray from the heart, enter deeply into Scripture, and open themselves up to God, speaking as a friend speaks to a friend. Silf was inwardly pleased by that description.

"But," said her director, "they pray about everything *except* the one burning issue in their lives—the one thing that they don't want to look at." Silf realized with a sinking feeling that she was that second type of person.

People who constitute the third type, by contrast, bring their whole selves to God, "just as they are" and talk about "whatever comes up." They are, he said, "willing to take off the censorship filters, and let God be God in their lives."[12]

We're all called to that kind of honesty, but often feel blocked. What kinds of things would we not want to bring up before God?

Anger is a good example of something we might avoid bringing up in prayer. Disappointment, which is part of the human condition, often leads to anger. So anger is a sign that you're alive. And all of us can get angry for any number of reasons: a frightening medical diagnosis, the loss of a job, a family conflict, a terrible financial blow, the rupture of a relationship.

God can handle your anger, no matter how hot it burns. God has been handling anger as long as humans have been praying. Just read the Book of Job in the Old Testament—there Job rails against God for causing his painful situation. Usually Job is seen as a patient man, and at the beginning of that book he is. But eventually even Job loses his patience and begins to curse the day he was born. "I loathe my life," he says. "I will give free utterance to my complaint; I will speak in the bitterness of my soul."[13]

"The great tradition of prayer in the Old Testament in the Psalms, in Job, in the lamentation of the prophets," the German theologian Johann Baptist Metz wrote in *The Courage to Pray*, "makes it clear that the language of prayer does not exclude or shut itself off from the experience of suffering and desolation."[14]

Anger, sadness, frustration, disappointment, and bitterness in prayer have a long history. Why shouldn't you allow yourself to express those feelings too? Father Barry frankly acknowledges these situations and offers this advice, "All I can do is encourage you to speak directly to God if you have questions about God's ways, as one friend to another, even if anger is the only emotion you can voice."[15]

A few years ago, I told my spiritual director that I was so angry at God that I used an obscenity in prayer. I was so frustrated that God didn't seem to be doing anything to help me that, one night, I clenched my fists and shouted aloud, "How about some @#$% help, God!" Some readers might be shocked that a priest would use language like that, especially in prayer. I thought my spiritual director, a wise and gentle Jesuit priest named Damian, would reproach me. Instead he said, "That's a good prayer!"

I thought Damian was kidding. But he continued, "That's a good prayer because it's honest. God wants your honesty, Jim."

Being honest also made me feel that God now knew exactly how I felt. Have you ever had the experience of confiding something to a friend and feeling relief? I felt God could now better accompany me, just as a good friend might. More accurately, I would now be able to allow God to accompany me.

Saying it aloud also brought me face-to-face with something else: my ingratitude. Sure, there was a big problem in my life, but there were some wonderful things going on at the same time. I was like an adolescent saying to his parent, "I hate you!" because he's asked to go to bed at a reasonable time, turn off his video games, or take out the trash. Hearing myself talk like that—out loud—revealed a childish aspect of my relationship with God, one I very much wanted to move beyond. Finally, it was a reminder of how often we push God away when we need God most.

So it *was* a good prayer!

William Barry and William Connolly note in their book *The Practice of Spiritual Direction* that one should also not fear expressing the same emotion repeatedly in prayer. People often find that one airing of a strong feeling such as anger (especially anger toward God) "does not eliminate the necessity for repeated expression of it." Often in spiritual direction a person needs to be encouraged to continue to be honest with God, to "keep at it." The problem is not that God has not heard us or that we have not adequately expressed ourselves. Rather, "the development of transparency in our relationship with [God] requires repeated expressions of a particular feeling."[16]

Sadness is another emotion that some people feel reluctant to share with God. Someone once told me a story about going to a movie with a close friend. Because the subject material intersected with his life, he began to sob at the end of the movie and was embarrassed. Later on, as the two sat together in a car in the parking lot, his friend sat silently and let him cry.

His silent friend wasn't the only one showing love. The person weeping gave the gift of intimacy by allowing another to enter his life. Can you give God the intimate gift of your true self, your true emotions, even when you are grieving?

But when it comes to prayer, the *most* inappropriate emotion, at least in many minds, may be sexual desire. In one of the best contemporary books on prayer, *God, I Have Issues: 50 Ways to Pray No Matter How You Feel* by Mark Thibodeaux, SJ, each chapter addresses prayer during a different mood. The moods are organized alphabetically, so that you can thumb through the book when you are *afraid, angry, despairing, doubting, jealous, joyful, sad, weary,* and so on. One chapter is entitled "Sexually Aroused." Mark begins bluntly: "Good Christian people often worry about their sexual feelings. They are embarrassed and ashamed of them."[17]

Mark reminds us that sexuality and sexual activity are gifts from

God to be celebrated. On a natural level they draw people together for the sake of love and creating new life. On a spiritual level those feelings can remind us of the love that God has for us. Many spiritual writers use erotic love as a metaphor for God's love for humanity. (Check out the Song of Songs if you have any doubts.)

But like any gift, sexuality must be used wisely. If motivated by selfishness, it can turn into a desire for possessiveness. On a more benign level, sexual thoughts during prayer can simply be a distraction. So what do we do with those feelings in prayer?

Again, the solution is honesty. "Instead of hiding these experiences, we should share them with God," says Mark, "and use them to remind ourselves how great it is to be alive, how great it is to be a creature of God, and how wondrously we are created."[18] If that doesn't work, or if those feelings are troublesome because they are directed at a person with whom you cannot have a relationship, just be honest with God about your struggles. Be honest with God about everything.

Listening

Friendship requires listening. You would scarcely consider yourself a good friend if all you did was talk and talk and talk. But that's what happens for many of us in our relationship with God. Prayer becomes just a recitation of things we need (too much petitionary prayer) or an endless stream of letting God know how we are (too much talking). As in any friendship, we need to listen.

But what does it mean to "listen" to God? This idea baffled me when I was in the novitiate. Does that mean hearing voices?

Few people have "heard" God's voice in a physical way (that is, few sane people). But it does happen. Mysterious notations in St. Ignatius's personal diaries when he is speaking about his prayer refer to *loquela*, loosely translated as "speech," "discourse," or "talking."

One recent example comes from St. Teresa of Calcutta, who said that in 1946 she heard God ask her to work with the poorest of the poor in the slums. Earlier, Mother Teresa made a promise to God to never refuse anything that God asked of her. Then, years later, as she told her spiritual director, she heard God's voice asking her to leave her work in a girls' school. Not surprisingly, she was reluctant to leave that work for something new and, it seemed, dangerous.

She reported that God, as if recalling her earlier promise, said to her, "Wilt thou refuse?" Mother Teresa accepted God's invitation. By the way, she could have said no. Our relationship with God does not obliterate free will.

But the kind of experience reported by Mother Teresa is exceedingly rare—and many experts, including some of her most ardent admirers, wonder whether hers was an aural hearing or more of an interior hearing. So it's probably best for the rest of us to set aside our pious hopes—or unwarranted fears—that we're going to "hear voices" in a literal way. As Katherine Marie Dyckman, Mary Garvin, and Elizabeth Liebert write in *The Spiritual Exercises Reclaimed*, "Often communication is 'felt' or intuited, rather than heard as ordinary conversation."[19]

During my time as a Jesuit I've met only a few people who have told me they have literally heard God speak to them. One was Maddy, a joyful and prayerful woman who was a member of the Sisters of St. Joseph in Springfield, Massachusetts. Maddy and I first got to know each other when we were both working in East Africa in the 1990s. Later, she worked for many years at the Jesuit retreat house in Gloucester, Massachusetts, where we often directed weekend retreats together.

Since we were longtime friends, I figured that I knew Maddy well. But this no-nonsense woman surprised me during one of these weekends when, in an afternoon talk to the retreatants, she said that when she was young and considering entering a religious order, she heard God's voice saying, "I have chosen you to be with me. You will find your way."

Before entering the Jesuits, I would have thought that Maddy was imagining things or that she was even a bit unbalanced. But now I believe that those moments—while exceedingly rare—can be privileged moments of God's presence. Still, we must weigh these moments carefully, ruling out any psychological illness, comparing them to what we know about God, and submitting them to experienced spiritual guides.

Many people say that during peak prayer experiences, even though they don't physically hear God's voice, they feel *as if* God were speaking with them. This can happen in ways both subtle and not so subtle. For example, someone may ask a question or say something so insightful that it is almost as if a window into your soul had just been opened.

My mother once told me that she was looking out the window and said to God, "Do you love me?" And the words "More than you know!" instantly came to mind. "It wasn't a voice; it just popped into my head." My mother wasn't seeking that answer; it came spontaneously. Of course God *does* love her more than she can know.

Are there other ways to "listen" to God? Absolutely. And these are much more common.

Sometimes when imagining yourself speaking with God, you might also try imagining what God would say in return. That's a popular way of prayer for many Christians, and something that Ignatius suggests as one technique in the Spiritual Exercises.

Praying in that particular way is a challenge for me, but for some people it's not difficult at all. When they picture themselves speaking with God, they can easily and naturally imagine God speaking to them. Sometimes it helps to imagine listening to Jesus in a familiar place from Scripture—by the Sea of Galilee or in his house at

Nazareth. However, the words that you imagine he is saying must be tested against what you know about God, what you know about yourself, and what your faith community believes about God. Does it lead you to be more loving and compassionate? Does it sound authentic? "God's words," as Vinita Hampton Wright says in *Days of Deepening Friendship*, "have the ring of truth."[20]

If that kind of prayer is too difficult, you might try something that I stumbled upon recently: try imagining what God *would* say based on what you know about God.

Here again the friendship model is helpful. Let's say you have an elderly friend who is known for giving good advice. She's wise, experienced, and compassionate. Over the years, you have come to know her outlook on life. When you tell her a problem, sometimes you don't even have to wait for her to respond—you *know* what she's going to say.

Because it's often hard for me to imagine God speaking to me, I sometimes ask myself, "Given what I know about God through Scripture, through experience, and through tradition, what would God *probably* say about this?" Usually it's not hard to imagine.

Most people, however, are still unsure about listening to God in prayer. So how does God *most often* communicate in prayer? That is one of the central questions of this book: What happens when you close your eyes? Later on I'll look at emotions, insights, memories, desires, images, words, feelings, and mystical experiences, all ways that we can hear God's voice in prayer.

Change

Another aspect of healthy relationships is change. Friendships that began in childhood and adolescence can be among the richest of all. Yet if we don't allow each other to change over time, a friendship will not mature. Still, change can feel threatening in your relationship with God.

Many believers assume that their relationship with God will remain the same—or *should* remain the same—as it was when they were children. Some people feel, for instance, that they cannot be angry at or disappointed in God, because they did not harbor those sentiments when they were young. Or, more likely, they were told that those feelings were wrong.

An elderly woman once sent me a copy of some questions from the *Baltimore Catechism*, the religious instruction book used by many Catholic children between the end of the nineteenth century and the late 1960s. At the end of the chapter on sin, there were questions to help children better understand their faith. Some of them sound like questions from a law school exam. She marked one with the ironic notation "a personal favorite":

> Giles is murdered by a Communist just as he leaves the church after his confession. Giles had been away from the church for 28 years. He just about satisfied the requirements for a good confession, having only imperfect contrition, aroused during this week's mission. The Communist demanded to know if Giles was a Catholic, threatening to kill him if he was. Fearlessly, Giles said: "Yes, thank God!" Did Giles go immediately to heaven, or did he go to purgatory for a while? Give a reason for your answer.

Pity poor Giles! And pity the poor third-grader who had to puzzle out the answers. Religious rules and regulations have been around since (at least) the Ten Commandments. Most religions have their own share of rules. (Check out the Catholic church's code of canon law if you want a good example.) So do religious orders. Even Jesus of Nazareth, during his public ministry, offered his own set of rules to his disciples.

Rules are an essential part of any community, because they enable us to bring order to the group, so that we can live in relative harmony with others. They also help order our personal lives. Ironically, some of the critics who dismiss rules in religious organizations, rules that are designed to lead to spiritual health, follow an even stricter set of rules designed to lead to physical health. Diet plans and exercise programs are often as draconian as any canon law.

But an overreliance on a rule-based religion can lead to an image of God as a stern traffic cop concerned only with enforcing the law or, as one friend memorably remarked, a parole officer. How many children who memorized the *Baltimore Catechism* concluded that the spiritual life was not an invitation from a loving God, but a series of complicated rules issued by a tyrant God?

This style of instruction was thought to be necessary to educate young children at one time, but if that teaching is never deepened, it can hinder their ability to relate to God as adults. People taught this way as children are often stuck relating to God as they did when they were eight-year-olds.

An unwillingness or inability to move past any rigid images of God from your childhood may also mean that you continue to fear God—and not in a good way. By the same token, you might also fear any change to which God might lead you.

When you start to be intentional about the spiritual life, prayer is usually delightful. Like any relationship, the initial period is one of infatuation. Reading Scripture and spiritual books is fun, talking with fellow believers about your spirituality is enjoyable, and church services are rich. Everything is natural, easy, and joyful, just as in the start of a love affair. *Hooray*, you think, *I love being spiritual!*

But soon you are invited—through prayer, reading, conversation, the voice of your conscience—to amend your ways, to turn away from sinful behaviors, to a conversion of life. In a word, to change. You may see that selfishness is inconsistent with your newfound beliefs. You may feel called to forgive someone against whom you've held a grudge for many years. You might feel drawn to living a simpler life based on the Scriptures. That's when the fear comes.

It's natural. Change is frightening. But this fear is different: it's a fear of where *God is leading you.* It's the fear that God is sneakily inviting you to something unpleasant or dangerous. You think, *Even though I feel called to forgive this person, I'm sure it will be a disaster for me. God is going to trick me!* One man who was thinking about joining the Jesuits feared that by following God's invitation, he would end up miserable.

That's when people may again need to revisit their image of God. In these situations it's helpful to dig deeper and ask, "Who is God for me?" Often that image of God is stuck in the third grade. Or the image is not life-giving: it's the stern judge, the distant father, or the unforgiving parent. "The particular image we have of God will depend very much on the nature of our upbringing and how we have reacted to it," writes Gerard Hughes, "because our ideas and our felt knowledge derive from our experience."[21]

Religion itself may be a hindrance to developing a healthy image of God. In his book *God's Mechanics*, the Jesuit astrophysicist Guy Consolmagno speaks of a scientist's faith in God and notes, "One obvious way we can let a religion limit our view of the universe is by insisting that its doctrines are a complete and final description of nature and God."[22] God is bigger than religion.

So your childhood image of God may need to evolve. When you're a child, you may see God as I did, as the Great Problem Solver. Later on, you might relate to God as parent. As you mature, you might relate to God in still different ways, as Creator, Spirit, or Love. Christians might find themselves looking at Jesus in a different way too—not only as Savior and Messiah, but perhaps as brother and friend.

The way you relate to God often mirrors relationships in other parts of your life, particularly with parents or authority figures. But remember, although the image of parent is helpful (for some people), God is not your mother or father. This is especially important for anyone who has suffered physical, emotional, or mental abuse from parents. The Australian Jesuit author Richard Leonard often says that when we relate to God as parent, we're relating to the best father or mother possible, one who relates to us in only positive ways.

Even if you feel drawn to the image of God as parent, remember that adults relate to their parents in ways that differ from those of a child. Although the parent-child relationship may be the first one that comes to mind and is usually the one used by preachers, Father Barry believes that the "relationship between an adult child and his or her parent is a better image of the relationship God wants with us as adults."[23]

You also may be surprised to discover fresh images of God buried within ancient traditions. In her book *She Who Is*, Elizabeth Johnson, CSJ, a Catholic sister and theologian, meditates on the feminine imagery that is used of God throughout the Jewish and Christian Scriptures.[24] In one example from her groundbreaking work, she points out that the Hebrew word for "spirit," *ruah*, is feminine. In another she notes that one image for God is personified Wisdom (from the Greek feminine noun *sophia*, "wisdom"), a traditionally female image. About Wisdom, the Wisdom of Solomon says, "She reaches mightily from one end of the earth to the other, and she orders all things well."[25] From Muslim traditions, the Prophet Muhammad speaks of the ninety-nine names of God, each of which highlights an attribute of the divine, including the Gentle One, the Restorer to Life, and the Guide. Each is an invitation to imagine God in new ways.

Our image of God changes over time. C. S. Lewis goes even further. He says it *must* change. In *A Grief Observed* he writes, "My idea of God is not a divine idea. It has to be shattered time after time. He has to shatter it himself. He is the great iconoclast. Could we not almost say that this shattering is one of the marks of His presence?"[26]

One of my favorite images can be found in the Book of Jeremiah, which is especially useful for those who fear that God may be the evil trickster inviting them to change, only to trap them in a miserable life. This fear is surprisingly common. Jeremiah's God says otherwise. "For surely I know the plans I have for you, says the LORD, plans for your welfare and not for harm, to give you a future with hope."[27] God wants only the best for us, says Jeremiah.

You may also discover other, more modern images. Gerard Hughes speaks of a "God of surprises," who astonishes you with new and unexpected invitations to grow.[28] Or perhaps you'll come up with images of your own. One friend on a long cross-country trip ended up stranded in an unfamiliar airport, with his flight canceled. A cheery travel agent patiently helped him sort everything out, so that he could book a new flight. It was a striking image of God, he said—someone who helps you find your way home.

Change may also be part of your growing relationship with organized religion. Some of us were born into a strongly religious family. Some remain rooted in their original religious tradition and develop a mature faith that nourishes them. Others discard old religious beliefs, because they no longer work for them as adults, and begin the search for a new religious tradition. Also common are those who separate themselves from religion and find their way back to the same tradition, on their own terms, developing a more adult faith that works for them.

Finally, you may fear what change might mean in your own life. As Mark Thibodeaux points out, this is one reason people often fear going "deeper" with God in prayer: "They are afraid of what he might say." Yet this is a loss for those avoiding God like this. If you're on a trip and get lost, says Mark, would you avoid listening to the person who knows the right way? "God knows the way to true happiness, and he wants [us] to know about it too."[29]

In each case the relationship with God will change as well. Carlos Valles, a Spanish Jesuit, writes in his book *Sketches of God*: "If you always imagine God in the same way, no matter how true and beautiful it may be, you will not be able to receive the gift of the new ways he had ready for you."[30]

And, as Valles implies, both your relationship and your image of God may change. Barry and Connolly sum this up nicely: "Since God is *semper maior*—always greater—one can expect that relating to him will mean being open to continuous novelty and thus continuous change of images. Spiritual idolatry could be seen as unwillingness to let God be other than one's present image."[31]

Silence

Are you open to silence in your spiritual life? Sometimes God seems distant, and sometimes nothing at all seems to be happening in your prayer life. But silence is part of any relationship.

Think about taking a long car trip with an old friend. Do the two of you have to say something every minute? Think about two lovers walking side by side along the beach without saying a word. Sometimes silence can indicate a painful or confusing moment in conversation between friends, but sometimes a companionable silence can be consoling.

Sister Maddy, my friend at the retreat house in Gloucester, saw another similarity between silence in prayer and silence in friendship. "Sometimes I don't hear from friends for a time," she once told me. "But whether I hear from them or not, I know they're still my friends. It's the same in prayer. Whether or not I feel God's presence, I know he's there."

When I was a novice, silence in prayer bothered me. One day I told David, my spiritual director in the novitiate, "This is ridiculous. Nothing's happening in my prayer. It's a waste of time."

David said, "What do you mean?"

"Well," I said. "I sit down to pray, and not a thing happens. I just sit with God for an hour. It's a waste of time."

David laughed. "Being with God is a waste of time?"

Despite myself I had to laugh. It's never a waste of time to be in the presence of God—even if it doesn't feel like much is happening.

You can delight in someone's company wordlessly. Margaret Silf once remarked to me that you can be silent together, trusting that silence does not mean that God has left you. Or you may simply enjoy being in God's presence.

Another way of understanding this comes from Aristotle, who believed that we become like the object of our contemplation. Have you ever met an elderly couple who have taken on each other's attributes? United in love, they share the same interests, they finish each other's sentences, and they sometimes even *look* alike. It's the same with God: the more time you spend with God, even in complete silence when it feels that nothing is happening, the more you will grow, because being in the divine presence is always transformative. Think of Moses coming down from Mt. Sinai, his face radiant. "Wasting time with God," one of David's favorite definitions of prayer, even during silent moments, turns out not to be a waste at all.

But there is another reason we may have trouble with silence in prayer—today we no longer value silence *at all*. Electronic gadgets—cell phones, laptops, and so on—have created a world of constant stimulation. Most of this is good, efficient, and even fun. Why not have all our favorite tunes or podcasts ready for when we're stuck in a traffic jam? Why not have the TV, radio, and internet to stay up-to-date on the world around us? Those are the sweet fruits of the digital age.

The bitter fruit is our addiction to digital devices. The amount of media we consume each day continues to grow, and our ability to be detached from our devices diminishes. Sometimes our involvement with them becomes intense.

A few years ago, a film executive called me from her cell phone in the car to ask about a music selection she was hoping to use in a new movie about the Catholic Church. What would be the most appropriate Catholic hymn to use?

When I started making a few suggestions, she said, "Wait, I have to text this to someone as we're talking."

I said, "You're driving the car, talking to me on the phone, and texting someone all at once?"

Because our devices are constantly available to us, we often fill every spare moment with them. In fact, many of us wouldn't know what to do without them. We are gradually losing the art of silence. Of walking down the street lost in our own thoughts, of closing the door to our room and being quiet, of sitting on a park bench and just *thinking*.

We may fear silence, because we fear what we might hear from the deepest parts of ourselves. Anthony de Mello, an Indian Jesuit, writes: "There is only one way for people to confront themselves and that is through silence." He says:

> In a sense, silence is God. I love music passionately, but when I am in the mood for silence, even music is too jarring. I want only silence to be present. A person could say that silence is a harmony more beautiful than any other harmony.[32]

We may be afraid to hear that silence, that "still, small voice."[33] What might it say? Might it ask us to change?

You may have to disconnect in order to connect, to disconnect from the world of noise to connect with silence, in which God can speak to you in a different way. You cannot change our noisy world, but you can disconnect from it sometimes, to give yourself the gift of silence.

Silence is one of the best ways to listen to God, not because God is not speaking to you during your noisy day, but because silence makes it easier for you to hear what God is saying. To use the analogy of that glass of water drawn from a stream, sometimes you need to let your soul quiet down, so that things will float up to the surface of your thinking and feeling. To use the friendship analogy, sometimes you need to listen carefully when your friend is trying to make a point. As my sister tells her children, "You have two ears and one mouth for a reason: listening is more important than talking."

If your environment (inside and outside) is too noisy, it might be hard to hear what God, your friend, is trying to say.

Just recently, I was visiting my mother at her retirement community outside of Philadelphia. Early in the morning, I was sitting in the complex's guest apartment, looking out the window. It was a cold, rainy, blustery day, and the trees outside were swaying in the wind. As I sat in an easy chair, I simply enjoyed the silence. I couldn't hear the trees—the windows were closed on account of the chill—but I could see them clearly. It seemed that God was speaking to me through the silence, saying, "Be still."

The New Ways God Has Ready

Although friendship is a terrific analogy for a relationship with God, it is not perfect. As I mentioned, none of our friends created the universe. And God, unlike any other friend, always remains constant.

Nonetheless, thinking about prayer using Father Barry's rich insight—that prayer is a personal relationship with God—can help clarify it for you. If you're dissatisfied with that relationship, think about it as a friendship—think about ways you might be neglecting that friendship and how you can nourish it. That model also makes the spiritual life less daunting and makes a relationship with God more understandable, something you can incorporate into your life, rather than something reserved only for saints and mystics.

It also provides you with a handy way of diagnosing problems in your spiritual life. Father Barry's model has provided me with one of the handiest tools in my toolbelt as a spiritual director. For example, someone might confess a sense of distance from God. If we dig deep, we find that they are resisting speaking about something difficult in their life. In other words, they are not being honest. So their prayer life has become blocked. Usually all it takes for them to confront the perceived distance is to be honest with God about what is really going on.

Progress in the spiritual life even mirrors the progress of a relationship. At the beginning of any relationship, you experience a period of infatuation and an almost insatiable desire to spend time with the other. But the relationship has to move beyond that superficial level and into something deeper and more complex. It will also move into places that you couldn't have imagined when you first fell in love. It will have its ups and downs, its times of silence, its times of frustration. Just like your relationship with God.

Your relationship with God will change over your lifetime. Sometimes it will come naturally, almost easily, and feel rich and deep; at other times it may feel difficult, almost a chore, yielding seemingly little by way of "results." But the important thing—as in *any* friendship—is to keep at it and, ultimately, to come to know and love the other more deeply. And to let the other come to know and love you more deeply.

7

Everyone Needs Help

PETITIONARY PRAYER

Last year I was having lunch with a friend who was in great emotional turmoil. I will keep the details obscure, but my friend was passing through a difficult time. It also seemed that she was feeling alone, so after a long conversation, I asked if she had brought her struggles to prayer.

She looked down at her empty plate and admitted that she hadn't.

"Why not?" I asked.

"I don't know," she said. "I guess I feel guilty about doing that. As if I would only turn to God in crisis. It seems . . . hypocritical."

"Do you turn to God only when you are in crisis?" I asked.

"No," she admitted. She said she prayed frequently.

"So why won't you ask God for help?"

"It just seems so childish," she replied.

That opinion is shared by many believers. Petitionary prayer can seem like the most elementary prayer and therefore not only childish, but almost an insult to God. Some books on spirituality avoid it entirely or talk about it with faint embarrassment. I have been in numerous settings where it was mocked, where learned people chuckled about someone who prays for good weather for a wedding, help in an upcoming exam, or a positive medical diagnosis. Karl Rahner acknowledges this in *The Need and the Blessing of Prayer*: "It is a difficult task to assume the defense of the prayer of petition."[1]

Why do so many of us have a difficult time with petitionary prayer? Perhaps we don't want to ask God for help because it's what we did as children. Or perhaps we were told—by a priest, a spiritual director, an author, a friend (who got it from some theologian)—that it's wrong or selfish to ask for things in prayer. To which I say, "Baloney."

A Very Short History of Petitionary Prayer

The notion that one couldn't ask God for help would have surprised most people in the Bible. Petitionary prayer has a long history in both the Jewish and Christian traditions.

The Old Testament is virtually a record of requests for God's help. In the Book of Genesis, when God decides to punish the city of Sodom for its sins, Abraham bargains with God: "Will you indeed sweep away the righteous with the wicked?" he asks. "Suppose there are fifty righteous within the city?" Yes, says God, if there are fifty good people in the city, he will spare it. Abraham then lowers the number. What about forty? Thirty? Twenty? Abraham continues until he reaches ten, whereupon God says that if there are ten virtuous people in the city, he will not destroy it. Abraham's prayer spares the city (at least temporarily) and stands as one of the earliest examples of petitionary prayer in the Bible.[2]

In the Book of Numbers, Moses also begs God to be merciful to his people: "Forgive the iniquity of this people according to the greatness of your steadfast love," he says.[3] Later in the Old Testament, in

the First Book of Samuel, Hannah begs God for a child: "O LORD of
hosts," she prays, "if only you will look on the misery of your servant,
and remember me, and not forget your servant, but will give to your
servant a male child, then I will set him before you as a nazirite until
the day of his death."[4] Later, she gives birth to Samuel.

After God has established a covenant with King David, the second monarch God asked Samuel to anoint, the king asks the Lord
to remain faithful: "And now, O LORD, as for the word that you have
spoken concerning your servant and concerning his house, let it be
established forever, and do as you have promised."[5] In the Book of
Kings, which recounts the story of Israel during the period after King
David's death, Elijah asks God to restore life to a boy, the son of a
widow: "O LORD my God, let this child's life come into him again."
His prayer is granted, and the boy lives.[6]

Throughout the Old Testament, men and women regularly request God's help, calling on God for the birth of a child, for deliverance from enemies, for relief from suffering, for rain, and simply for
God's presence. Anyone who reads the Psalms, even cursorily, will
see that they are crammed with requests for God's help. In fact, an
entire category called "lament psalms" vividly portray the plight of
the psalmist (or the Hebrew people) and cry out for God's help.

Some familiar examples include: "Incline your ear, O LORD, and
answer me, for I am poor and needy," says Psalm 86. "Hear my prayer,
O LORD; give ear to my supplications in your faithfulness; answer me
in your righteousness," says Psalm 143. And my favorite, a cry to God
in the face of suffering, is Psalm 13. It begins "How long, O LORD?"
and asks, "Consider and answer me, O LORD my God! Give light to
my eyes, or I will sleep the sleep of death." Psalm 65 in fact identifies
God as "you who answer prayer," which makes little sense if nothing
is being asked for.[7]

Prayer in the New Testament relies just as heavily on supplication.
When the disciples ask Jesus to teach them how to pray, he responds

with the Our Father (the Lord's Prayer). It begins with praise to God, but also includes a specific request: "Give us this day our daily bread." This is petitionary prayer. Likewise, "Forgive us our trespasses as we forgive those who trespass against us" is a request for mercy.

Jesus offers several parables to illustrate the need for petitionary prayer. In one, he tells the story of a widow who continually asks a judge to hear her case, as an example of the need to be persistent in prayer.[8] In another, Jesus speaks of a man who wakes a friend at night and asks him for some bread because he has unexpected guests. Jesus says, "I tell you, even though he will not get up and give him anything because he is his friend, at least because of his persistence he will get up and give him whatever he needs." Then he immediately tells his followers, "Ask, and it will be given you; search, and you will find; knock, and the door will be opened for you."[9]

And Jesus *himself* utters an anguished prayer of petition in the Garden of Gethsemane, when he says to the Father, "Remove this cup from me"; that is, let this impending suffering pass from me. Although Jesus eventually says, "Yet, not my will but yours be done,"[10] he initially is asking God for something. He is praying a prayer of petition.

Praying for one's needs continues into the Acts of the Apostles, which recounts the history of the early church. One of the earliest events mentioned in Acts is the disciples' need to find someone to replace the deceased Judas. So they pray, "Show us which one of these two you have chosen to take the place in this ministry and apostleship from which Judas turned aside to go to his own place."[11] Christians might be so used to hearing stories like this that they overlook what is going on: the disciples are asking God for help. This is petitionary prayer.

The Acts of the Apostles takes pains to depict St. Paul as a man of supplication. Paul's own letters often give voice to his requests to God. He asks God to reunite him with his friends: "Night and day

we pray most earnestly that we may see you face to face."[12] He asks
others to pray for him: "Join me in earnest prayer to God on my behalf, that I may be rescued from the unbelievers in Judea."[13] He even
describes a prayer of petition that wasn't answered: "Three times I
appealed to the Lord about this [thorn in the flesh], that it would
leave me, but he said to me, 'My grace is sufficient for you, for power
is made perfect in weakness.'"[14] (Scholars disagree over what Paul
was asking to be freed from—an illness, a psychological problem,
memories of his past, or persecution.) Overall, Paul prays frequently
for a variety of wants and needs, for himself and for others.

Thus, petitionary prayer enjoys ancient Hebrew roots, is pro-
moted by Jesus, and is enacted by the early church. At this point I
could also provide a long list of petitionary prayers from the saints,
theologians, and believers of almost every Christian denomination,
all asking for God's help. But I think you get the point. In an essay on
prayer, Dennis Olkhom, an Anglican priest and theologian, writes
simply, "Christian prayer has always been essentially petitionary."[15]

Why emphasize this? To rebut the common belief that we
shouldn't ask God for help, or that asking for help is childish, or
that it is a lesser form of prayer, or that it is wrong. As a thought
experiment, imagine Jesus telling his disciples to pray for their daily
bread, and Peter saying, "Really, Lord? Isn't that a bit childish?" Jesus might say, as he did elsewhere, "Unless you change and become
like children, you will never enter the kingdom of heaven."[16]

Perhaps you're already convinced. After this brief review of its
biblical antecedents, you may now think petitionary prayer is okay.
But you may still lodge a common qualification: that you should ask
for help only when things are truly dire. A college student once said
to me, "I shouldn't ask for help in school, should I? There are starving people who need more help!"

He's right. There are millions of starving people who need more
help than you. If they come to mind when you are thinking about

your own needs, you might consider this an invitation from God to gain perspective on your life and a goad to help the people you're thinking about—by donating to a soup kitchen, working in a shelter, or advocating for them. Let that pang of compassion move you to action. How else would God move you?

But you can still ask for help for yourself. After all, "Give us this day our daily bread" means bread for all of us. It's a communal prayer. And that includes you.

That others suffer does not mean that your own needs are unimportant, but you must keep your suffering in perspective. Many of us have a natural inclination to focus on our own suffering—after all, we're closer to it than we are to the suffering of others. The spiritual challenge is maintaining perspective—recognizing others' needs but not ignoring your own legitimate needs in your petitions to God.

Let's say a friend has just lost a loved one. At the same time, you are worried about not getting a nice hotel room for your next vacation. If you're praying for your vacation plans to work out and not thinking about your friend's suffering at all, something is awry. By the same token, if a friend calls you and says her hotel room is too small, and you have been diagnosed with a life-threatening illness, not praying for yourself because you think it's "selfish" and instead praying that your friend gets a bigger room is also lopsided.

You can be concerned with others, pray for others, and want to help others and still approach God with your own legitimate needs. With that in mind, what should you pray for?

Praying for Yourself

My answer to the question of what you should pray for, like the answer to many spiritual questions, is a personal one. Indeed, a good deal of spiritual writing is personal.

To begin with, there shouldn't be too many *should*s when it comes to prayer. If prayer is about a relationship between an individual and God, a good deal of what defines that relationship will naturally be personal. What works for one person may not work for another. The most helpful theological discussions about prayer, as we've seen from the various definitions, are framed as practices and preferences rather than rules and regulations.

To return to our question: What should you pray for? Or better put, what *can* you pray for?

In my opinion, you can pray for anything manifestly good. In other words, you clearly don't pray for something bad—like a horrible injury to befall someone you dislike.

There is, however, a history of prayers asking for bad things to befall an enemy. "Curse psalms," or "imprecatory psalms," form an entire category of psalms. During our morning prayer in the Jesuit novitiate, we used a spiral-bound book called *Psalms Anew*, a contemporary translation of the Psalms. As a fresh-faced novice, new to the religious world and certainly to the Psalms, I was appalled to come across so many violent, even bloodthirsty, ones.

One of my favorite psalms, 139, which begins with a beautiful hymn to the God who "knit me together in my mother's womb," takes a malevolent turn toward the end:

> O that you would kill the wicked, O God,
>   and that the bloodthirsty would depart from me . . .

Imagine starting your day at 7 a.m. with that. Or with the most shocking psalm verse of all, in my opinion:

> Happy shall they be who take your little ones
>   and dash them against the rock![17]

There are many ways of looking at curse psalms such as these. First, given the times in which the Psalms were composed, we must accept the possibility that the psalmist did literally want the babies of his enemies dashed against rocks and sincerely prayed for the deaths of all those he considered wicked—gruesome as it sounds to us.

Some scholars, however, say that these images are better understood as metaphors and were understood metaphorically even when they were written. According to one commentary, that last verse does not mean that infants should be dashed against rocks, but that in the invasion of an enemy city its inhabitants should be crushed at any cost.[18] Curse psalms can also be interpreted in a more "spiritual" way. When the psalmist writes, "O that you would kill the wicked, O God," this may not mean that the writer wants God to kill anyone. Rather, it may be a way of praying for God's ways to triumph or for God to prevent the writer from doing evil.

A retreat director once suggested that one way to use that line in prayer was to see it as asking God to free you of sinful patterns in your life, thus "killing the wicked" within you. St. Augustine advanced a similar idea regarding Psalm 137. "For when we were born, the confusion of this world found us and choked us while yet infants with the empty notions of various errors."[19] In other words, for Augustine, the "little ones" in the metaphor are our immature failures to recognize sin, which we hope will be done away with. That's far less disturbing than imagining babies being dashed against rocks.

Lest you get the impression that the Hebrew people were the only ones to curse others with prayers, remember that those same psalms have been prayed by Christians throughout the ages. In a practice that might alarm us today, some monasteries in medieval France used formal religious ceremonies to curse their enemies, a practice known as "clamors" or "maledictions." From roughly the tenth to the thirteenth century, monks used imprecations in liturgies to ask God to defend their possessions and properties when appeals to secular authorities had failed.

So the monks (mainly but not exclusively Benedictines) took their pleas to God, praying, in one case, "May they be cursed in town and cursed in the fields. May their barns be cursed and may their bones be cursed. May the fruit of their loins be cursed as well as the fruit of their lands." You can read more about this tradition in the marvelously named book *Benedictine Maledictions: Liturgical Cursing in Romanesque France.*[20]

A Jesuit told me the story of visiting his elderly mother in her home and finding this tradition updated. He walked into his mother's room and saw her praying the Rosary. "What are you praying for, Mom?" he asked.

"I'm praying the Rosary against your cousin Timmy," she answered.

Apparently, Timmy was supposed to visit her and help her with some chores, but he never showed up.

The Jesuit was aghast. "Mom, you can't pray the Rosary *against* someone!"

"You wanna bet?"

I would advise you *not* to pray to have your enemies killed, maimed, or in any way harmed; some evil befall a friend; or some misfortune be visited upon an opponent. Why? First of all, Jesus asks us to pray for our enemies, not against them. Such prayers and intentions also end up poisoning the heart of the one praying. Consider the corrosive influence of spending time thinking of how your enemies will suffer. So even though I have been occasionally tempted to pray in this way, I have resisted.

It is also absurd to ask the God of mercy to be unmerciful. It goes against all that we know about God. Remember the friendship analogy. Would you ever ask a friend to murder someone? It goes against all that you know about your friend and would damage your whole relationship.

In addition to not praying for something bad to happen to someone, I also never pray for suffering for myself, although I am aware that this is a time-honored tradition among many saints. In fact, many Christians feel the desire to participate in the sufferings that Jesus underwent and so ask for suffering. This is part of the desire to be close to Christ in every way, even suffering.

But as I see it, life naturally will send challenges, and so there's not much need to seek them. Your crosses will find you. Once a young person told me he felt that there wasn't enough suffering in his charmed life. I was tempted to say, "Just wait." In those sufferings we are invited to join in the sufferings of Christ. But we don't have to ask for them. They will come.

So what *do* we pray for?

To my mind, we can pray for anything good that we might need. Let's remember that one reason we pray is because we need to. How could we not ask for help in the face of life's misfortunes? When we imagine ourselves standing before God, we become acutely aware of our limitations. Approaching God, the source of all good things, we come face-to-face with our unmet needs. Overall, in the divine presence we experience the human condition, which is finite, limited, needful. The obvious and appropriate response is to pray for what we need.

Here are the gifts for which I pray most frequently. I offer them not as prescriptions, but just as examples to make our discussion more concrete.

1. *Wisdom.* Even those of us with the tiniest level of self-awareness realize that we're not God, and so we need help in discerning the right course of action: "How do I deal with children who don't listen to me?" "What job should I accept?" "How can I confront a

long-term illness?" For me, this is not praying for an answer, but for help in arriving at the answer.

2. *Humility.* St. Ignatius Loyola, the founder of the Jesuits, asked Jesuits to pray for humility often. In his early life, he struggled with "vainglory," and in his later life he saw the corrupting influence of vanity and ambition, especially among the clergy and members of religious orders. Plus, it's easy to get a big head. So I pray for humility frequently. At the same time, I am reminded of the spiritual master who was asked if he prayed for humility. He responded that life humbled him enough!

But humility often comes in a way that we won't like. My current spiritual director says, "No humility without humiliation." What humbles us usually doesn't make us happy. At least at first.

Not long ago a young Jesuit told me of a difficult interaction that had happened in his community, which made him recognize his own sinfulness as never before. It was "compunction," as spiritual writers used to say, an awareness of one's own limitation. It also led him to realize that he was being called to true humility, the kind that he had prayed for during the Spiritual Exercises. "I didn't think humility would hurt so much," he said. But that initial hurt leads ultimately to greater freedom.

3. *Freedom.* Many days, the lion's share of my prayer is asking for freedom from unhealthy patterns of behavior. For example, freedom from the need to be loved, liked, or approved of; or freedom from selfishness or an excessive focus on self. One favorite image of Jesus is Christ the Liberator, the one who frees us.

The freeing, however, may not happen all at once. In Gerard Manley Hopkins's epic poem "The Wreck of the Deutschland," the narrator asks God to change him "Whether at once, as once at a crash Paul, / Or as Austin, a lingering-out swéet skíll"; in other words, all at once, like St. Paul's conversion, or gradually, like St. Augustine's. In my own life freedom most often comes gradually.

4. *Perspective.* Sometimes I get so wrapped up in a problem, person, or situation, I lose perspective. Spending too much time online can be one way to ensure that. I need to pray for a sense of what's important and what's not. Sometimes it's healthy to find the grace to be able to say, "Who cares?" and to be reminded that there are other good things going on around me. Again, we need the perspective of knowing that we're not God, nor are we the center of God's universe.

5. *Courage.* Like anyone, I get frightened. Standing up for an unpopular cause can bring opposition. Being charitable in a sea of uncharity can bring contempt. Advocating for the marginalized among the privileged can bring rejection. So we need the courage that only God can give. Smaller events also require courage: a visit to a doctor to hear a diagnosis, a confrontation with a difficult person, or turbulence on an airplane. As the saying goes, there are no atheists in foxholes. It's okay to pray for courage. We all need it.

6. *Patience.* The ancient Greeks had two notions of time: *chronos* and *kairos.* *Chronos* is the tick-tock time of everyday life. "What time is it?" is a *chronos* question. *Kairos* is more nuanced. It's the right or opportune time. If someone tells you to "strike while the iron is hot," they're not talking about the time of day, but the opportune moment. In the Gospels, when Jesus speaks about the "time" for something to happen, especially as it relates to the coming of the reign of God, the word used is *kairos.*

Finding the patience to wait for God's time, not mine, is hard. For those who like to get things done quickly and efficiently, this is a struggle. The desire to get things done is healthy; it enables us to accomplish many tasks. But its shadow side is the inability to be patient. Thus, I pray for the gift of patience.

7. *Hope.* Sometimes life can seem bleak. Our personal problems can build to the point that we have a hard time falling asleep at night, or eating, or even getting out of bed. The bleakness of our world, and

of our churches, can cause people to lose hope. When things seem overwhelming or I'm close to despairing, it's always good to pray for hope.

8. *Inspiration.* Particularly when writing (like now) or preparing a homily, I ask God to inspire me. In these times I simply say, "What do you want me to say?" A teacher about to counsel a troubled student, a parent about to speak with an upset child, or a businessperson about to meet a difficult client might utter the same prayer.

9. *Success.* By success I don't mean something like "I want to triumph!" or even something worldly like "I want to become pope!" After all, Jesuits make a promise at the end of training not to "strive" or "have ambition" for things like this. A Jesuit became pope, of course, but we're not supposed to have any ambition for such things. And, for the record, Pope Francis did not seek the papacy, but accepted it after being elected.

Rather, by success I mean simpler things in my ministry: help me get this book finished on time. Help me be a good confessor. Give me the grace to help this grieving family. Help me do a good job in the homily. Let me be a good spiritual director.

It's natural to pray for things to go well in your own life, work, and ministry; in your family; for your friends. As with anything else, we need to keep success in perspective. If all you do is pray for success for yourself, something is out of place.

10. *Deliverance.* A few years ago I served as a consultant for Martin Scorsese's film *Silence*, about seventeenth-century Jesuits in Japan. The whole creative team, including the director, wanted every aspect of the film to be accurate, including substantial sections about Jesuit history, ministry, and spirituality. At one point, while they were filming in Taiwan, I got a phone call from Mr. Scorsese's assistant. "Marty wants to know something about the scene where one of the Jesuits is drowning—what would he say? Is there some special prayer?"

I suppressed the urge to make a glib remark like "There's no Jesuit prayer for drowning." But it was a sincere question. I thought of all the prayers from the Psalms, like "Though the waters overtake me . . ." But then I realized that the most accurate answer was probably the simplest. The Jesuit, I told her, would probably pray, "Help me, God."

Sometimes the easiest prayer in a difficult situation is "Please get me out of this."

We pray for more specific things as well—healing from a major illness, relief from a stressful family situation, help with challenges on the job. All these things are struggles for which we would naturally want God's aid. How can we *not* ask for help?

Then there are more quotidian requests. When you're sick with the flu, you probably pray to get better. When your train, bus, or plane is running late, you pray for it to come quickly. When it's raining on the day of a big outdoor event, you pray for it to stop. To me, those are legitimate things to pray for. Why not?

But there must be limits. Think again of the relationship model of prayer. Is your relationship with God characterized *only* by asking? What kind of friendship would that be? Imagine having a friend with whom your only interactions were requests—even for the smallest things. You would start to see your friend as simply a dispenser of favors. That's how we might look at God if all we did was ask for help.

Likewise, do you want to pray every moment of the day for favors? "God, let that parking space open up! God, let that store have those shoes that I want. And in the right size! Thanks! And let them be on sale." Soon your spiritual life will become a litany of minor requests.

I think it's okay to ask for help for small things. If your son or daughter is getting married, why not ask God for good weather? Yet sometimes I wonder if we pester God for too many little things. I often think of a scene from an off-Broadway play called

The 25th Annual Putnam County Spelling Bee, a lighthearted musical comedy about a spelling bee for children. One earnest young girl, named Marcy, desperate to win, receives a surprise visit from Jesus, who appears onstage bathed in a heavenly light.

> MARCY: Would you be disappointed with me if I lost?
> JESUS: Of course not. But Marcy, I also won't be disappointed with you if you win.
> MARCY: You're saying it's up to me then?
> JESUS: Yes. And also, this isn't the kind of thing I care very much about.

On balance, though, I still go to God for any good need.

How to Pray for Help

If you're new to prayer, you might ask: How do you ask for help?

You might opt for a simple method. Imagine yourself in the presence of God or Jesus, and then ask for help silently, in your own words. Sometimes I say my requests aloud. Other people find it helpful to write God a letter. I mean that literally. "Dear God," you might begin. "I need your help . . ." I usually suggest writing this longhand, but sometimes people write it on a computer or phone, print it out, and pray with it. See what works best.

If it's a prayer for something big, you might make the prayer more "formal." For big requests, I sometimes wait until I'm in a new church, on a pilgrimage, or at some other holy site.

What happens after you've prayed for help? Sometimes you'll feel nothing. Other times you'll feel a sense of relief, because you've gotten it off your chest. Other times you'll feel heard.

What happens when God seems to answer your prayer exactly as you had hoped? This is usually not a problem for people, but it's important to cover the joys of the spiritual life as well as the sorrows. Sometimes having your prayers answered is overwhelming. When my first nephew was born, after nine months of my family's praying for his safe delivery, I was so happy that I could barely contain myself. In fact, it was hard to know *what* to do. After I first saw him at the hospital, I wept for joy. But then I thought, *Now what? How do I thank God adequately?*

Perhaps you've had this experience. Your prayer seems to have been answered, and all you can do is be stunned. So here are some suggestions:

Savor it. Allow yourself to be happy. Often when our prayers have been answered, we may think, *Thank God that turned out okay! On to the next thing!* We don't give ourselves time to rejoice, to feel joy. If you've just gotten a good diagnosis from the doctor, or you've just found out that you've been accepted by your top choice for a college, or your company just gave you a bonus, take the time to be happy.

To that end, don't rush. Sit down, lie down, or take a walk and let it sink in. Better yet, give yourself the rest of the day to savor it. Allow yourself that pleasure of basking in the grace God has given you. Often we see receiving what we prayed for as a transaction rather than a gift. As with any gift, we need to take time to appreciate it.

Thank God. Spend time in prayer thanking God. Especially if it is something you've long been waiting for, take the time or make a special visit to a favorite place to pray and thank God explicitly. This too is part of being in relationship with God. What kind of relationship would it be if you never said,

"Thanks"? This may sound obvious, but sometimes when a prayer is answered, we are grateful, but only in a vague, general, and confused way. Your gratitude should have a focus, and that focus is God. Say thanks.

Show God your gratitude. Needless to say, I can't speak for God, but I would imagine that God would be happy if you "paid it forward." Show gratitude by doing something kind for someone else. Call a lonely friend. Send your mom some flowers. Send your dad some flowers, for that matter. Spend time with someone who you know feels lonely or unloved. Donate to a good cause. Buy the homeless man in your neighborhood a meal. "Love shows itself more in deeds than in words," St. Ignatius wrote. So does gratitude.

Share your joy. Sometimes it's hard to share good news. It might evoke jealousy or envy in people you wouldn't expect to act that way. But when it comes to answered prayers, it can help to share it with good friends. "I wanted to let you know that I had a prayer of mine answered: it's not cancer." A real friend will rejoice. It can also strengthen the faith of your friend. Just be careful not to gloat.

In the end, answered prayers are an invitation to see God's care for you. But what happens when it seems God has *not* answered your prayer? More about that later.

Praying for Others

Praying for yourself all the time is like talking about yourself all the time. It not only demonstrates your selfishness, but also increases it. Others need your prayers as well.

In high school, I thought that I was the only one who had prob-

lems. My body was the only one that was imperfect. My emotional
life was the only one that was unsteady. My family was the only one
that was (mildly) dysfunctional. Intellectually, I understood that
others suffered. But in high school my friends and I didn't share too
much of our lives with one another, except for the surface worries
about tests, small conflicts with friends, and confusion over which
colleges to apply to.

But in college, as I listened to friends speak more deeply about
their lives, I saw how each person struggled with many things:
family problems, health problems, psychological problems. It was
a marvel to me, in fact an important life lesson: just scratch the
surface and the problems would be revealed. How could I not have
known that? Everyone has problems. I love the old saying, "Be
kind, for everyone is fighting a hard battle."

Many of those you know have need of prayers. I'm sure I don't
have to encourage you to recall the many needs your friends and
family have.

It's also important to pray for people we don't know. When I
worked with the Jesuit Refugee Service in Nairobi in the 1990s, I
asked my friends in the United States to pray for the refugees. Over
the course of two years I met hundreds of people struggling simply
to survive in the midst of terrible poverty. I had to ask myself, with
great shame: *Before I came to Kenya, did I care about these people?* Sadly,
the answer was no. It was a reminder to pray for people I don't know,
particularly those who are poor or marginalized in any way.

You might be moved by reading a story about a refugee family—
men and women in a war-torn country, or people devastated by
drought and hunger. Sometimes reading about these situations can
feel overwhelming. That is not such a bad thing. Feelings of being
overwhelmed, saddened, or angry over injustice may be invitations
to unite ourselves with God in prayer. It's also one way that God has

of working *through* us. To quote C. S. Lewis about prayer, "It doesn't change God. It changes me." I believe that we are feeling God's feelings in these moments.

This is not the time to enter a theological dispute about whether God changes (classical theology says no, because God is perfect, whereas process theology suggests that, since part of perfection is change, God can change) or whether God's intervention in our lives constitutes "change" for God.

But there is a key insight in Lewis's comment. Quite apart from any help others receive from prayers on their behalf, it is we who are changed. Lewis's point is that prayer transforms *us*. If we are praying for a sick friend, it may be time to visit her. If we are praying for someone who is struggling with money, it may be time to offer him a loan. If we are praying for someone who is lonely, it may be time for a phone call. In these ways, prayer can soften our hearts and spur us to action.

Even though I am aware of my own responsibility to act, I still believe in praying for someone else. I believe in asking *God* to help someone. How could you not, knowing of someone in need? That impulse is also well attested in the Old and New Testaments, with numerous examples. One of the most poignant examples is the story of the father who brings his epileptic son to Jesus for healing:

> "Teacher, I brought you my son; he has a spirit that makes him unable to speak; and whenever it seizes him, it dashes him down; and he foams and grinds his teeth and becomes rigid; and I asked your disciples to cast it out, but they could not do so." . . . And they brought the boy to him. When the spirit saw him, immediately it convulsed the boy, and he fell on the ground and rolled about, foaming at the mouth. Jesus asked the father, "How long has this been happening to him?" And he said, "From childhood. It has

often cast him into the fire and into the water, to destroy him; but if you are able to do anything, have pity on us and help us."[21]

More than two thousand years later, the father's love for his son and his own desperation leap off the page: "If you are able to do anything, have pity on us and help us." He is asking Jesus to help his son. In the same way, we go to God for help for others.

Perhaps the more basic question for the beginner is: How do I pray for someone? For me, this is where I like to use St. John Damascene's idea of prayer as a "raising" or "lifting." I often imagine lifting up a person's face to God. Sometimes I imagine accompanying the person to God, that is, walking with them toward God, hand in hand, and then asking God to help them. Others picture placing the person's hand in Jesus's hand.

Alternately, you can pray for someone by offering a standard prayer like the Our Father or Hail Mary and thinking of the person as you pray. This may sound suspiciously close to the idea of a "payment" to God, as I used to do in my youth. On the other hand, in my own life I offer prayers for people as a sign to God of how much I care for them.

There is no rule for how to pray for others. Be flexible. One exercise I heard about on a retreat was to imagine Jesus sitting in a chair in a room; you open the door to that room for a friend in need and invite the friend to sit beside Jesus. In another example, a Benedictine friend told me that he asks for help for others with these words: "Lord, look not on my many sins, but on the faith of the church and of the one asking for my prayers."

And again, we have to be open to the possibility that, as Margaret Silf writes, the answer to our prayers is *us*. If you're asking for someone to be helped, you might need to do the helping. If you keep praying for a friend who is lonely, but never call them or visit them, what's the point of your prayer? "If we ask God to act on behalf of others, we must be willing to become the implements of that action," Silf writes. "Perhaps our reluctance to do so is the reason that many of our intercessions seem to remain unanswered."[22]

Unanswered Prayers

One of the most important questions in the spiritual life is: What happens when we don't get what we pray for? It is also one of the most neglected topics in books on prayer. And it is another reason people are sometimes opposed to petitionary prayer—not because they think it's childish or selfish, but because they have tried it and it hasn't "worked."

In his essay on petitionary prayer, Karl Rahner writes sympathetically in the voice of those whose prayers did not work: "We prayed, and God did not answer. We cried, and he remained mute."[23] Why don't we get what we ask for?

This question is a special concern for Christians because of one passage in the Gospels:

> Ask, and it will be given you; search, and you will find;
> knock, and the door will be opened for you. For everyone
> who asks receives, and everyone who searches finds, and
> for everyone who knocks, the door will be opened. Is there
> anyone among you who, if your child asks for bread, will give
> a stone? Or if the child asks for a fish, will give a snake? If
> you then, who are evil, know how to give good gifts to your
> children, how much more will your Father in heaven give
> good things to those who ask him![24]

In that passage, Jesus seems to be saying explicitly that Christians will receive what they ask for. So why does that not seem to be the case?

Before answering that question, we have to ask other questions: How does prayer work? That is, how does God hear our prayers and how does God answer them?

The short answer is that we have no idea. None of us know how prayer works, for the simple reason that none of us are God.

Yet Christians and Jews have always believed that God hears our prayers. The Psalms speak of God as the "one who answers prayers," and Jesus asks us to express our prayers to God. This is a constitutive part of the Jewish and Christian traditions. And to use some simple theology, if God is the all-powerful, all-knowing, all-loving Creator of the universe, it is surely not beyond God's capacity to hear our prayers—all of them. Our human minds, however, cannot comprehend how this can be or what this means.

We may be tempted to think of movies in which God is hearing billions of voices crying out from the earth at once. In the 2003 film *Bruce Almighty*, an average man, played by Jim Carrey, becomes God. Upon assuming his divinity, his ears are filled with voices—millions of prayers from earth. In response, Bruce decides to organize things and wishes that all the prayers were in file cabinets. Instantly hundreds of file cabinets fill his room, to his consternation. So he opts for prayer Post-Its and is immediately covered with a blizzard of small yellow notes. Finally, he selects something more efficient (and, in 2003, still relatively new): emails. Immediately he has 1,527,503 messages in his in-box. It's a humorous depiction of the dilemma that our human minds cannot comprehend: how God hears all our prayers. Nonetheless, I believe that God, who loves us, does hear our prayers.

How do we know *when* God answers our prayers? This too is mysterious. But not only do I believe that God does answer prayers, I have experienced this to be true. When I have prayed for courage, I have received it. When I have prayed for insight, I have received it. And when I have prayed for spiritual healing, I have received it. Many times.

Sometimes prayers are *clearly* answered. A few years after my father's death, my mother decided to move out of our family home. Having investigated the options, she was inclined to move into a nearby retirement community. After visiting the place, which was clean, comfortable, and filled with friendly people, we checked the price. We were not wealthy but found that it would be almost within our means after we sold our family house. Still, my mother was undecided. Was this the right place?

Around that time, I went on a weeklong pilgrimage to the Holy Land with a friend, as part of the research for a book I was writing on Jesus. Toward the end of our trip, we visited the Church of the Holy Sepulchre, the place of Jesus's tomb, where he rose from the dead, traditionally the holiest place in the Christian world.[25] At one point I entered the tomb itself, located inside a kind of church within the church—a little building called the Aedicule.

Awaiting entrance, I realized that thus far on my pilgrimage I hadn't prayed for anything. My friend and I prayed every day about what we had seen and how we had been moved, but I hadn't really prayed *for* anything.

Entering the Aedicule, I decided I was going to offer the entire pilgrimage as a prayer for my mother's move. Eventually, I entered the tomb's tiny space, no bigger than a closet, which contained the marble slab under which Jesus was very likely buried. I knelt next to the four or five other pilgrims who had squeezed into the space and prepared to kiss the tomb. As I kissed the cold stone, I thought of my mother's situation and prayed, "Make this happen."

Exiting the tomb, I felt as if I had fully left my prayer behind. Probably more than at any other time in my life, for some reason— perhaps the holiness of the site, perhaps the distance I had traveled, perhaps my mother's needs—I felt that I had made myself clear to God. Afterward I thought happily: *God certainly knows what I want.*

One day later I returned to New York. That night, after unpacking and doing laundry, I called my mother, who was still in our family home. After listening to me recount some highlights of our pilgrimage, she said, "I have some good news about the new place."

"What's that?" I asked.

"They're having a 40 percent off sale, since the demand is low right now. And if I sign up before Christmas there's an even bigger savings. Isn't that great?"

I leaned back in my chair and shouted out, "Thank you, God!" It seemed a direct answer to my prayer. Could it have been any clearer?

I told my mother the story of my fervent prayer at the Church of the Holy Sepulchre and how I felt that God had heard me. "I'm still not sure if I want to take the place," she said.

"*I* am!" I said.

A few months later she took it and has been happy there ever since.

Not every prayer seems to have such a direct result. In fact, most of the answers to my own prayers are neither so direct nor so immediate. How do we understand that?

With difficulty. I will not sugarcoat this aspect of the spiritual life. We will probably never understand why it seems that some prayers are answered and others are not. But I don't have to understand God to believe in God. I trust that God hears our prayers and answers them, in some way. This is an essential element of prayer: trusting that God both hears and listens. Karl Rahner writes that God listens to us "patiently, even blissfully, an entire life long until we are through talking, until we have spoken out our entire life."[26]

Why some prayers seem answered in ways that we would like and others are not is beyond our powers of comprehension—certainly my power and beyond that of even the best theologians. But we all must confront this difficult question. Over the years, I've heard many suggestions. Here are the most common explanations, with my responses.

God answers our prayers, but God does so with what is best for us. In other words, we might not get what we asked for, but whatever we get is what's best for us. The idea is appealing. If we ask for a particular job and it doesn't pan out, perhaps God has a better plan in mind for us. In this understanding, God is like a wise parent who does not give her child the extra piece of candy because, even though the child asks for it, she knows that candy is not the best thing; she has something more nutritious in mind and gives the child an apple instead. So even though the child is disappointed, it's really all for the best.

Just recently a friend told me that he and his wife had placed a bid on a new house. It seemed perfect. But the owner sold it to someone else. We both uttered the pious Christian thought, "God has something better in store." Sure enough, in a few weeks another house came on the market, and they put in their bid and purchased it. They say it's perfect.

Here's a subtler example. For several years, I lived in a Jesuit community with a man who hated me—and that's not too strong a word. For about ten years he more or less refused to talk to me. No matter how I tried to reconcile with him (apologize for whatever I might have done wrong, be kind to him in community, seek him out for conversation), he refused to speak with me. A wise older Jesuit told me that these things were mysterious and that all I could do was be "cordial." The other Jesuit never warmed to me; we never reconciled, and it was a source of considerable angst. Times spent with him in community—especially over meals—were, to say the least, difficult. Needless to say, I prayed for a turnabout every day that we lived together. Eventually he moved out, and I was left wondering what it was all about.

In time, I was able to see that living with someone who disliked me helped free me of the desire to be liked by everyone. It enabled me to see that not everyone, not even every Jesuit, was going to love me or even like me. Later on, when I faced opposition for a book I had written, I was able to maintain a healthy distance. So perhaps God had answered my prayers in another way, which ended up being more beneficial to me than simply reconciling with that one Jesuit.

But the idea that God always answers your prayers with something better has far less appeal in more serious situations—for example, when you ask for a child to be cured of cancer, and the child isn't cured. This explanation, then, can cause misery for people. Imagine telling someone that their child's cancer is, in the end, what's "best" for them, or that many years later they will see that it was "all for the best." Such explanations fail in the face of the reality of the situation. They also make God in this case not only a trickster (you have to "figure out" what good has come of the child's illness), but a sadist (God is "using" the illness to give you or your child something better). So, overall, that approach fails.

God answers our prayers, but sometimes the answer is no. This explanation is closely related to the first one, though harsher. But this explanation appeals to me because it's brutally honest. I pray for something. It doesn't happen. Using the candy analogy, it would be as if the parent were simply saying no to the request for more candy.

This explanation, however, is confusing. Why would God not want something good to happen? Why wouldn't God help? Doesn't this go against the idea of God as the one who answers our prayers, to say nothing of Jesus's saying, "Ask, and you shall receive"? What about the child with cancer? The argument again falls short.

God answers our prayers, but we can't see how. In this conception, God hears our prayers, but gives us something that is hard to see. I pray for healing and instead am given courage. Indeed, it is often incumbent upon us to look for the "answer," which may not be as obvious as we had hoped.

Let's say you are lonely and pray for a friend. For several days, nothing happens. Weeks pass, and you lose hope and grow angry at God. Months later you unexpectedly strike up a friendship, but you may not relate this to your prayer. In this view, God answers our prayers all the time in ways that are concealed from us or in ways we're too slow to understand. Overall, we trust God as a loving child would trust a loving parent, even if, as a child, we don't fully understand all the parent's reasons.

But this argument is also incomplete, because it again can lead people to think of God as a trickster. God has given or will give you an answer, but you must figure it out, like a puzzle. Sometimes this can frustrate people's relationships with God. And people could pray for a close friend—or, as with many of my friends, a spouse—and never see any discernible results.

God doesn't answer our prayers in the way that we would like, and why remains a mystery. In the end, why some prayers seem answered and others don't is a mystery. To me, this is the most honest response and the one that I rely on most. God's ways are far beyond our ways.

I often ask God for help. Sometimes it seems that God answers as I would like (as with my mother's retirement community). Sometimes it seems that the answer is more mysterious (as with the Jesuit who disliked me). But always I believe God hears me, is with me, and helps me. The key is still trusting and believing in a God whose ways may remain mysterious.

For me this is not only the most intellectually and spiritually honest answer, but also the one that squares with experience. It's honest because it admits that we sometimes have a hard time understanding God, who is a mystery. It squares with experience because all of us will admit that at times it seems that God does not answer our prayers, at least in the way that we would like.

Jesus, the Model Pray-er

The most common time that people turn to God is when they are in distress. This is true certainly for believers, but even those estranged from religion often find themselves on their knees begging for help (and when nothing seems to happen, they may turn even more firmly away from God). But in those times, I invite any and all to trust in God as they would a beloved parent, a dedicated mentor, or a talented doctor on whom they rely but at times do not understand.

At the beginning of the book, we reflected on the kind of prayer that we often use first as children, petitionary prayer. But, as we saw, this childhood prayer contains the seed of the hardest and most adult question about prayer: Why doesn't God answer all our prayers? We don't know. So the question we are left with is: Can we believe in a God we don't understand? To me, that is the invitation of a lifetime.

At the end of his essay "The Prayer of Need," Karl Rahner points to Jesus as the perfect model of the one who prays.[27] He looks at three prayers uttered by Jesus in the Gospels, which beautifully sum up the stance of the one who prays. Rahner's insight has changed the way I see petitionary prayer, because he links it so clearly with Jesus.

Jesus's prayer includes "realistic petition," "heavenly confidence," and "unconditional submission." The first can be seen in his prayer in the Garden of Gethsemane, when, faced with a fate he does not want, he prays, "Remove this cup from me." Heavenly confidence is evident when, standing outside Lazarus's tomb before raising him from the dead, he prays to his Father in front of the crowd, "I knew that you always hear me." And in the Garden again, after he intuits that the Crucifixion is coming, we see unconditional submission when he prays, "Yet, not my will but yours be done."[28]

Can we pray for what we need? Yes. Will we always receive what we think we need? No. Does that mean that we never pray again or trust in God? No.

I can't improve on what Rahner wrote, so I end our chapter on petitionary prayer with his insight:

Jesus wrestles with the will of God until he bleeds but is always totally devoted to him. He shouts his need to heaven and is always certain of being heard. He knows that he will be heard always and in everything and wants to do nothing but the incomprehensible will of God. . . .

How mysterious is this unity of the most contradictory in Jesus's prayer of petitions! Who can thoroughly interpret this mystery? But the mystery of the true Christian prayer of petition, of the God-man prayer of petition, of the true prayer of petition of *every* Christian, is contained in this mystery in which, if we may be allowed to say it, as in Christ himself, the most godly and the most human are united and permeate each other while being unadulterated and unseparated. Truly Christian prayer of petition is totally human.[29]

8

Now I Lay Me Down to Sleep

ROTE AND OTHER FORMAL PRAYERS

The prayer I have said most often in my life is the Hail Mary. This is not because I am somehow opposed to the Our Father or any other prayer. Nor is it that my devotion to Mary exceeds my love of Jesus. Rather, as a Catholic, I was taught it in Sunday school, and it's always been on my mind, in my heart, and on my lips ever since. I have prayed it on the way to school as a boy, when I was getting ready for tests in high school, when I was searching for a job after college, and when I was waiting to enter the Jesuits—and in almost any situation of need.

Sometimes this lifelong affinity for the prayer makes me smile. Once I knelt before a statue of Jesus in a church and wanted to ask him for something. Out of habit, I started to pray, "Hail Mary, full of grace . . ." Then I looked up at the statue, into Jesus's face, which seemed to say, "Hey, what about praying to me and not my mother for a change?"

My Catholic predilection for the Hail Mary reflects many people's affinity for what are known as rote prayers. Rote prayers are ones that have already been written. They are among the most familiar of prayers, often the kind of prayer many of us learned when first taught how to pray. "Did you say your prayers?" often means not "Did you speak with God today in your own words?" but "Did you recite your rote prayers?"

"Our Father, who art in heaven . . . ," "Hail Mary, full of grace . . . ," "Hear O Israel: the LORD is our God . . . ," and "Now I lay me down to sleep . . ." are all rote prayers. These include the Psalms, various petitionary prayers, mealtime blessings, and short prayers such as the "Jesus prayer" ("Lord Jesus Christ, have mercy on me, a sinner"). For many of us, rote prayers are an essential part of our spiritual treasury, formulas that have been with us since childhood and upon which we call frequently.

Consequently, you might think that rote prayers would hold an exalted position in the spiritual world. But often spiritual teachers can intentionally or unintentionally denigrate rote prayers. Supposedly overused, formulaic, unoriginal, hackneyed, and impersonal, they are sometimes portrayed as inferior to the kinds of prayer that adult believers should pray. (There's that baneful word "should" again.) The temptation is to think that a rote prayer is not as good as, say, a spontaneous or more imaginative kind of prayer. But rote prayers are valuable in many ways.

Using Rote Prayers

We pray rote prayers for a number of reasons.

First, *we know them.* In times of struggle or when words fail us, it's helpful to have a "premade" prayer. Having them memorized is of even greater help. If you're in the middle of a frightening moment—aboard a plane in turbulence, waiting for a diagnosis from a physician, getting the news about whether you'll be laid off—you might recite, even in part, Psalm 23, to calm yourself:

> The LORD is my shepherd, I shall not want.
>   He makes me lie down in green pastures;
> he leads me beside still waters;
>   he restores my soul.

And not simply to calm yourself. That prayer can remind you of a consoling image of God—the loving shepherd—which invites you into a relationship with God during the moment of crisis. When we are frightened, it can be difficult to think clearly, and we can forget that God is with us. Simply reciting Psalm 23 can "restore" us to ourselves, reminding us of God's presence.

Charles Healey, SJ, makes this point in *The Ignatian Way*: "Prayers that have been deeply assimilated and internalized can sustain a person and make prayer possible in more difficult external circumstances, such as illness, fatigue, or a noisy or distracting atmosphere."[1]

Second, *they have distinguished history*. Many rote prayers come from significant religious figures. The most obvious example is the Our Father, which came from the lips of Jesus himself after the disciples said to him, "Teach us to pray." That alone should recommend the Our Father. Praying it not only gives us words and enables us to fulfill Jesus's command to "pray in this way," but it also connects us to Jesus. The prayer itself brings us into connection with its author.

Prayers written by other religious figures can connect us to their spirituality and remind us of their distinctive lives. They are not precisely rote prayers, but are nonetheless already written for us. One of my favorites, by Thomas Merton, is one that almost anyone can pray:

> My Lord God,
> I have no idea where I am going.

I do not see the road ahead of me.
I cannot know for certain where it will end.
Nor do I really know myself,
and the fact that I think I am following your will
does not mean that I am actually doing so.
But I believe that the desire to please you
does in fact please you.
And I hope I have that desire in all that I am doing.
I hope that I will never do anything apart from that desire.
And I know that if I do this you will lead me
by the right road,
though I may know nothing about it.
Therefore will I trust you always,
though I may seem to be lost and in the shadow of death.
I will not fear, for you are ever with me,
and you will never leave me to face my perils alone.[2]

The prayer is nearly universal in its appeal. Who hasn't felt in some way lost? But it's not just a wonderful prayer on its own—because of what it says—it also connects you with the spirituality of its author. Whenever I pray it, I imagine Thomas Merton composing it at his desk at the Abbey of Gethsemani, and I'm reminded of the monastic life. The prayer itself is an entrée into the contemplative life because it was written by a contemplative.

Third, when we pray them, *we unite ourselves with believers throughout the world and down through time.* Have you ever wondered how many people are praying the Our Father at the same time you are? The prayer connects you to believers around the world in a way that is mysterious (you can't see them) but real (you know that people are surely praying the prayer). Thus, when you pray the Our Father, you are engaging in a communal act of worship.

By that same token, have you ever wondered how many people

have prayed the Our Father throughout history? It was prayed first by Jesus, then by the apostles, then by the early Christians, all the way up to today. Imagine the millions—billions—who have uttered it.

St. Peter prayed the prayer Jesus taught him until his martyrdom. It may have been the last prayer Peter uttered on his own cross. Any of the disciples who heard Jesus teach them in person would never have forgotten it. The early Christians facing severe persecution would have treasured it. St. Augustine, St. Jerome, St. Teresa of Ávila, and St. Thérèse of Lisieux all knew and said that prayer. So did Martin Luther, Dietrich Bonhoeffer, and Nelson Mandela. Dorothy Day prayed it. So did Martin Luther King.

That kind of timelessness makes the prayer even richer. And Catholics who believe in the "communion of saints," the idea that the faithful in heaven are praying with us, believe that they are praying the Our Father with us now. "Those who pray are not alone," the theologian Johann Baptist Metz wrote. "Prayer is a matter of historical solidarity."[3]

Fourth, *they often express how we feel better than we can.* This goes against the belief, popular in some spiritual circles, that it's *always* best to pray in our own words: "Oh, you're still doing *just* rote prayer?" Sometimes rote prayers express what we are feeling with more clarity than we can muster. They are often admirably concise. It's hard to improve on "Lord Jesus Christ, have mercy on me, a sinner." The sheer poetry of a rote prayer—the words, the cadence, even the rhymes—may make it more appealing to us than our own choice of words. We might like the feel of the prayer, the way the words sound, or even the memories associated with it.

There are some superb collections of rote prayers, many of which have been compiled over the centuries. The Book of Common Prayer, for example, used in the Anglican and Episcopal traditions, is a wonderful compendium of prayers that cover a variety of topics. The Liturgy of the Hours, the daily prayers used by many

Catholics, especially priests and deacons, which lean heavily on the Psalms, also includes a great many beautiful prayers.[4]

A lovely prayer that I often use is one that asks for Mary's help. As an aside, this is a good time to mention that when Catholics pray to the saints, they are asking for the saints' prayers, much the way that you would ask others in your community to pray for you or for a person in need. When someone says, "I'm praying to Mary," it doesn't mean that Mary has the ability to answer the prayers herself, in effect taking the place of God. It means they're asking for *her* prayers to God on their behalf.

The prayer is known as the Memorare (from the first word in Latin):

> Remember, O most gracious Virgin Mary,
> that never was it known that anyone who
> fled to thy protection,
> implored thy help, or sought thine intercession,
> was left unaided.
> Inspired by this confidence,
> I fly unto thee, O Virgin of virgins, my Mother;
> to thee do I come, before thee I stand, sinful and sorrowful.
> O Mother of the Word Incarnate,
> despise not my petitions,
> but in thy mercy, hear and answer me.
> Amen.

Sometimes I balk at the beginning of this traditional prayer. Why start with a near command, especially to Mary? "*Remember,* O most gracious Virgin Mary." Lest you say that it's a prayer for *us* to remember, it's clearly directed toward Mary, since we talk about "thy protection," "thy help," and "thine intercession." It would be like saying to someone who has done a favor for you, "Don't forget, you always give me what I want." It also presumes that Mary would somehow forget her former prayers on your behalf. It is praise of course, as we praise her constancy, but I often wonder if the prayer wouldn't be better begun, "We remember, O most gracious Virgin Mary, that never . . ."

Even with those minor cavils about the first line, I find the rest of the prayer extremely powerful. The idea of standing before Mary asking for her prayers always moves me. I could never come up with something so poignant. This formalized prayer expresses what I want to say better than I could myself.

Fifth, *they challenge us.* Sometimes rote prayers go beyond expressing what we feel and remind us of something we hadn't considered. As in the Memorare, the reminder that we are coming to Mary (or Jesus, or the Father) "sinful and sorrowful" is a needed addition to our spiritual life. Often when we pray, especially when we ask for things, we tend simply to ask, without considering our own situation. Yes, we are all sinful; of course none of us is perfect; and of course we don't have to focus on our sins to pray, but as the Memorare points out, it's important to call to mind our sinfulness before asking God for yet another favor.

In rote prayers comes a wisdom that we often need to hear.

Limitations

Rote prayers aren't perfect. No form of prayer is. No one kind of prayer can fully satisfy our desires to relate to God.

Think again of prayer as a personal relationship. No one means of communication is sufficient for any relationship. Take the example of a marriage. There are many ways of communicating in a marriage: talking one-on-one over the dinner table, conversing while driving, "pillow talk" in bed, chatting on the phone or via emails and texts, making opinions known in a family discussion with children, walking silently hand in hand, and so on. Each is valid, but a marriage would founder if it relied on a single form of communication. The way two people communicate in a marriage may also change as the relationship deepens. An elderly couple after a lifetime together may feel little need to say much to one another, yet they still communicate through actions, expressions, and gestures, and even companionable silences.

It's the same with prayer. No one form of prayer can satisfy everyone's needs to connect with God. With that in mind, let's look at the occasional limitations of rote prayer. (These may not be limitations for you, but can be for others.)

To begin with, the repetitiveness of rote prayers, the very attribute that makes them so comforting for so many, can occasionally render them meaningless. Rote prayer is helpful in giving you the words you need and as a kind of mantra to lead you into a deeper connection with God, but if you're not careful, you can simply mumble the words with little awareness of what you're saying.

Lawrence Cunningham and Keith Egan point out in *Christian Spirituality* that, as we noted earlier, rote prayers "have a history" and we, in using those prayers, "enter into the tradition of praise, thanksgiving, penitence, and petition, which has gone on before us." But they follow that with a wise caution: "We must be alert not to allow the language of prayer to become a rote exercise or an automatic mouthing of phrases," pointing out that Jesus himself warned against the "heaping up of empty phrases" in the Gospel of Matthew.[5]

Sometimes when I pray the Our Father, I accidentally glide over the words so fast that I realize I'm not paying attention. When that happens, I ask myself: "Is that how Jesus intended for his followers to pray that beautiful prayer? Is it right that I am inattentive to the very words that Jesus taught the disciples? Can this be the way that he meant for us to pray it?"

One guard against this danger is saying the prayers more slowly and more meditatively. If you're saying the Our Father, you might even pause a few seconds between the phrases to let the meaning sink in. Slowing down in that way can be helpful. Things might come up that you hadn't thought of. Here's a fictional example of what might happen interiorly—based on conversations I've had with many directees about this prayer:

Our Father . . .

I never heard the "Our" before. Usually I think of this prayer as going to God on my own. It feels different to think of approaching God with others, together, in a community. It's as if we're asking God for something together. Or worshipping God together. I wonder what that means about my relationship with other believers, and with the church. Jesus told his disciples to call God "our Father," not just "my Father." I wonder if Jesus said it that way so that we would know to come together as a community, as a group, rather than everyone being on his or her own.

Who art in heaven . . .

Where is God? In heaven? What does that mean? Whenever I pray the Our Father I think of God in the sky, on a throne. That's probably not the way it is. Then again, who knows? In my mind, I like to think of God not in the sky, but everywhere. But I like the idea of God caring for me. Even though I know God's everywhere, there's something about God looking down at me from heaven that's comforting. Like God can see all that I'm doing and is keeping an eye on it.

Hallowed be thy name.

Boy, I take the name of God in vain a lot. I say, "Oh my God" way too often, and "God damn it," which is probably worse. Maybe I should think more about God's name as something holy. Jesus is telling us that. Maybe I should treat it with more reverence. What would it mean for me to "hallow" God's name?

Thy kingdom come . . .

Once I heard a priest talk in his homily about God's "reign" instead of his "kingdom." I think I like that better. "Kingdom" makes me think of God wearing a crown and sitting on a throne in some castle. "Reign" is more open-ended. Not just a place, but the whole idea of God looking over everything. I wonder what God's "reign" would be like. Certainly less suffering and poverty than there is now. I wonder how I could help bring about God's reign. Is it going to "come" by itself or am I supposed to help?

Thy will be done . . .

Whenever I hear this, it feels as if I'm supposed to be okay with everything God wants to happen. God's will and all that. But I'm not there yet. In fact, this phrase sometimes bothers me. I'm a little afraid of what God's will for me is going to be. Sometimes I feel like praying, "Thy will be done, if it's my will!" But maybe Jesus is asking me to let go a little bit. Maybe God's kingdom isn't so bad after all, or God's reign.

On earth as it is in heaven.

I'm not sure what that means either. Maybe that means that Jesus wants his Father's reign not to be far away, but where I am too. Of course this prayer is Jesus's telling his disciples how to pray. So maybe he wants the disciples to make earth more like heaven. More just, more fair. But since I'm one of his disciples, that must mean me too.

Give us this day our daily bread . . .

Boy, I never realized that we're asking for something specific. I just zipped through that line. Jesus is asking us to ask for something. And bread? Maybe he means just food, but I never thought of people who might need that from day to day. Me? I try to skip bread because of all the carbs, but I bet there are a lot of people who really mean that prayer, who need their bread daily. Maybe I should do something about that. Could I?

And forgive us our trespasses . . .

Yes, please forgive me, God. Whenever I hear the word "trespasses," I think of someone stepping into someone else's yard and ruining their lawn or the flowers in their garden. It makes me think how easily we can damage someone's soul when we "trespass" against it. I'm sometimes careless in my sinning against people, like a kid running through a lawn or stepping on the flowers. My sins are not simply something bad that I do, but something I do *against someone*. Trespassing. And yet God always forgives. Which is amazing. That's why I like going to confession with the priest. Other people find it hard, but I don't. I love going to confession. In a homily a priest once said that confession is not about how bad you are, but about how good God is.

As we forgive those who trespass against us.

That's always been hard for me. Maybe it is for everyone, but when someone is mean to me, I get angry, and it festers. Sometimes I wonder if you have to wait till the other person wants to be forgiven or asks for forgiveness. But now I know that's crazy, because sometimes you'd wait forever. Better just to forgive. Let go of all that. Be unburdened. In fact, there are a few people I need to forgive right now.

And lead us not into temptation . . .

I'm glad I have God's help in that because I need it. "Lead us" is a great phrase because sometimes it feels like I'm being "led" into temptation. I think about sin, but I also think about temptation. Lots of things that tempt me, and I need to be careful about setting boundaries and making sure I don't put myself in situations where something is bound to happen that's not what I want for myself. So I need God's help in figuring out how to avoid those situations and, if I find myself in them, how to get out of them. When I was a kid I heard the term "near occasion of sin" and thought it was a kind of partial sinning, but now I know it means being brought so close to sin that it's almost impossible to avoid it. My friend was telling me how he cheated on his wife with someone who lives down the street, and since he arranges ways to see her a lot, he said it was a "near occasion of sin." Meaning that there wasn't any sin in seeing her, but he's putting himself in a position where the more he did it, the easier it would be for him to sin. He told me that if you put yourself in a certain position nature will just take over. So I pray not to be led into temptations like that.

But deliver us from evil.

It's easy to do the wrong thing, and I seem to do it a lot. Or more than I would want. Almost against my will. I like that line from St. Paul where he says something like, "I don't do the good I want to do, but instead the evil that I don't want to do." That's why I need help from God. So I hope you're listening, God!

Amen.

In addition to slowing down and meditating, as this (fictional) person does above, you might find yourself not just pausing, but resting on a few words. A friend told me that she likes to take just one piece of the Our Father each time she prays. For example, why not simply meditate on the words "Our Father"? What does that mean to you? What does it mean that Jesus said, "Our Father" and not "My Father"? Remember that Jesus was teaching the prayer to a group of disciples, not just one person. What does that tell you about how he understood the communal aspect of faith? And how does your image of God caring for everyone influence your own desire for help?

Your reactions to this prayer will depend on your own history. If you did not grow up with a father or if you had a cold, uncaring, or abusive one, these experiences may color your reaction to the prayer and may even hamper your ability to pray with it. What would it mean for you to call God your "father"? Can God be the father that you hoped you would have? Or because God has no gender, do you ever feel called to pray "Our Mother"?

Often the way we relate to God is heavily conditioned by the way we relate to our parents, guardians, or other authority figures. If we have had parents who are judgmental, we tend to think of God as just as, or more, judgmental. A friend once told me that he has a hard time praying because he's "embarrassed to be honest with God." It turned out that his parents were uncomfortable with my friend's expressing his feelings. Not surprisingly, he had imagined God as someone who was also uncomfortable with hearing his feelings. This is an extremely common—almost universal—problem in the spiritual life.

God, the ideal parent, is beyond what we can imagine: all-loving, all-kind, all-generous. Can you move beyond your own negative experiences with a human father to embrace God the Father and let God the Father, Our Father, embrace you?

Another technique that helps people pray rote prayers is to alter the prayer slightly. One woman told me that she found the Hail Mary boring until she hit upon a new technique. One line in this popular prayer says, "Pray for us sinners, now and at the hour of our death." Rather than using the words "us sinners" (that is, everyone), she inserts the names of people who need help. So, "Pray for my mom, now and at the hour of her death." This has helped her slow down and increased her appreciation for the prayer.

Rote prayers can also sometimes be a barrier to a new kind of relationship with God. A few years ago, during a retreat, I asked a woman if she was interested in learning about Ignatian contemplation, which we'll discuss later in the book.

"No," she said firmly, "I have the Rosary."

I knew enough not to assume that her prayer was inadequate. Still, I wondered if she might be interested in learning about other ways to relate to God.

"No, thank you," she said.

So most of her retreat consisted of rote prayer. It was fine for her, but again, who knew what God might have had in store for her if she had been willing to try something new? Your relationship with God may grow stale if you use only one kind of prayer.

Rote prayer can sometimes be a barrier to greater intimacy with God, especially for those who may be reluctant to open themselves up to God fully. Because of their formality, rote prayers may keep God at arm's length and prevent people from expressing themselves in more personal ways. This can preclude deeper intimacy.

It can. But it doesn't have to. Many people who use rote prayers enjoy great intimacy with God. But rote prayer cannot be the sole way of praying—no prayer can.

Try It

Rote prayer needs its defenders, as it's often unfairly denigrated in spiritual circles. But, as we've seen, rote prayers have a long history among believers and are comforting in their familiarity; they provide a lifeline in times of struggle and an aid to union with God.

If you've never prayed rote prayers, why not learn a few and try to pray them? For Christians, the Our Father and Psalm 23 are good places to start. Catholics might add the Hail Mary, the Memorare, and the Rosary. Jewish people might use Psalm 23 and the Shema prayer ("Hear O Israel, the LORD is our God . . ."). Muslims are probably already familiar with rote prayers, as they pray five times daily. Seekers might try the Serenity Prayer ("God, grant me the serenity . . .") or Thomas Merton's "My Lord God." Soon you'll know them by heart, and they will become part of your spiritual treasury.

If you've already been praying rote prayers, you might ask yourself a few questions to help deepen this practice.

First, *what happens when you pray them?* Do you experience any noticeable feelings: a sense of comfort, of being heard, of being less alone? Can you see this as God's response?

Second, *have you thought of varying your rote prayers or tried other forms of prayer?* If you pray the Rosary regularly, you might think about setting your beads down for a while and praying some of the Psalms. You might try some of the more free-form prayers mentioned in this book. It's good to vary your spiritual life. God might want to meet you in a new way.

Finally, *what does God "feel like" while you're praying the rote prayers?* A friend's mother once summarized prayer as "God looks at me, and I look at God." What is God *like* when God looks at you? Does it feel as though God is being patient with you? Is it a comforting presence? A loving one?

A young man told me that most of his prayer was sitting in God's presence and praying rote prayers. To describe how they made him feel, he used an image from his own life. "Sometimes when I go fishing," he said, "I see the little fish swim between my feet in the ocean. And I smile because it's so funny, seeing them wriggle and go all sorts of crazy ways. And I think God is like that when I pray my prayers. Smiling at me even in the midst of the craziness in my life." If you think about what God is "like" in your rote prayer, you may find that these familiar prayers become prayers of surprises.

Rote prayers are a wonderful way to encounter God. Enjoy rote prayers—but don't let your spiritual life become rote.

9

I Am Here

THE DAILY EXAMEN

Almost twenty years ago I met the Labyrinth Theater Company, a free-spirited and boundlessly creative acting troupe based in New York City. Initially I was asked to help with a play called *The Last Days of Judas Iscariot*, written by Stephen Adly Guirgis, who later won a Pulitzer Prize, and directed by Philip Seymour Hoffman, the Oscar-winning actor who died a few years after the play debuted.

As part of my affiliation, I joined the company for a weeklong "summer intensive" workshop at Bennington College in Vermont. Summer intensives were a series of workshops providing a space for company members to write new plays, hone their acting skills, bond with one another, try out new parts, and have fun. And smoke. I had never seen so many cigarette smokers in one place before.

During the day, the playwrights, actors, and directors from "Lab," as it's known, worked on unfinished plays that were performed in the evenings and participated in seminars on skills like movement, fight choreography, and Shakespearean drama. I'm no actor (at all), but I was invited to attend any of the workshops. One made a lasting impression on me.

It was a class on voice taught by Andrea Haring, a gifted voice teacher who has a marvelous voice—deep, resonant, and expressive. When I read the list of workshops being offered that weekend I thought, *Well, I preach and give talks, so maybe I can learn something useful in this one.* Andrea's workshop, I surmised, would focus on diaphragms as well as breathing, projecting, and other techniques I had heard about from my actor friends. Instead, it was about something else.

In a ragged circle, we sat on the floor of a large Bennington classroom as Andrea explained that the exercise we were about to do was originated by Kristin Linklater, a distinguished voice teacher. Then Andrea asked us to stand, one at a time, in the middle of the circle and recite a simple sentence. She invited me to go first. I stood up in front of the group of thirty actors and said: "I am here, in this room, with all of you, at Bennington College today." One by one, everyone stood and repeated the same bland declaration.

I expected Andrea would now talk about enunciation or maybe speaking from the diaphragm, which I had heard about but was never sure how to do. Instead, she surprised us by asking, "How did it feel to say that?"

We looked at one another. Shoulders were shrugged.

"It felt okay," someone said tentatively.

Andrea smiled. Then she led us in an exercise.

First, we were given a large sheet of white paper, which we placed on the floor. With a magic marker we traced a curvy line and were asked to think about the course of our lives. "Start from the beginning," said Andrea. "Mark special moments on the line to denote significant events in your life. How have you come to be who you are? How does your story affect who you are now?"

I wasn't sure what we were doing, but by this point in my relationship with Lab I knew that actors did things differently from Jesuits! So I gave myself to the exercise. There is a way of participating in unfamiliar exercises grudgingly and not fully giving yourself. (It's the same with unfamiliar forms of prayer, by the way.) But I had decided not to hold back.

Next, Andrea asked us to look at the room. We were to wander around and notice the space we were occupying, to study the walls, the floors, the ceiling, the lights, and the windows. So we did.

Then she said, "Now look at everyone in the room. Approach each person, look carefully at their faces, consider who they are and what relationship you have with them." Some of the actors stood mere inches away from me, as if I were an insect specimen on a slide, and peered into my eyes. Although I found this uncomfortable, the actors didn't. They were used to this kind of free-form experiential learning. Good actors are fearless.

Next, she asked us to peer out the windows of the classroom. At the height of the summer, the campus looked spectacular—vast lush lawns, tall evergreen trees, handsome red brick buildings, all under a clear cerulean sky. "Get a feel for where you are," said Andrea.

Finally, Andrea asked us to think about our day. "What was it like so far? What would you do for the rest of the day? How do you feel? Consider the day itself."

Frankly, I still didn't know what we were doing. What did this have to do with *voice*?

After about thirty minutes, Andrea asked us to call to mind all we had been thinking about: our lives, this room, one another, the college, and this day.

Then she asked us to say the same sentence that we had started with. She asked me to go first. So I stood up, and out of my mouth came the same words: "I am here, in this room, with all of you, at Bennington College today."

I couldn't believe it. My voice sounded completely different—

deeper, calmer, more resonant. It even felt different. *I* felt different. That previously bland sentence was now invested with meaning. Because of the way I had spent the last half hour, considering who I was, where I was, and who I was with, each word and phrase *meant* something: *I am here, in this room, with all of you, at Bennington College today.* Without intending to, I also said each word more slowly and deliberately. It was like speaking from the bottom of a deep well. If you had told me this would happen, I wouldn't have believed you.

Everyone stood up and repeated the same words. To a person, everyone's voice sounded different from before. A few people cried. Why? Perhaps because they felt grounded in a new way, perhaps because they had a fuller appreciation for who they were, where they were, and who they were with. It was a remarkable experience.

How could a simple exercise influence how we spoke? How we sounded? And how could we be taught so much about something we had taken for granted—speaking?

After we had all spoken, Andrea explained that the exercise was about "being present." Once you are present to what you are saying, you express it differently, and as a result it sounds different. This was, she believed, even more important than breathing or projecting for actors in a play, because it would help make their voices be grounded and, therefore, heard.

After the session ended, I promised myself that I would use that exercise at every Mass and every lecture.

Two Lessons from Andrea

This story from the acting world illustrates two insights about prayer. First, it's important to *be aware of what you're already doing.*

At the beginning of that exercise, we unthinkingly recited, "I am here, in this room, with all of you, at Bennington College today." We might have been reading instructions for cooking pasta. Few of us, it seemed, were focused on the meaning of the words or the act of speaking. We weren't really aware of what we were doing. At least I wasn't.

That's a good reminder, particularly when it comes to the subject of our previous chapter—rote prayer. Sometimes we glide through prayer without paying attention to the fact that we are doing something meaningful, something profound, something holy. Occasionally during prayer, when I catch myself daydreaming, I say to myself, "You're speaking with God! Pay attention!"

More broadly, prayer itself is often about noticing—specifically, noticing where God *already* is. All of us were in that room that day, but we weren't aware. We weren't appreciating our blessings: of being an individual with a complicated history ("I am here"); of being in a specific place ("in this room") with one another ("with all of you"); of being on a beautiful campus ("at Bennington College"); or of being given the gift of another day ("today"). Sometimes prayer is simply about noticing where, when, and how you are already. And how God already is with you.

A second insight from Andrea's exercise is that even if you've been praying for many years, *you can always learn something new.* All of us at Bennington knew how to speak. We all knew how to pronounce the words and, especially the actors, express them with fluency. But on that day all the actors, whose craft is deeply concerned with speech, and I—a writer, preacher, and occasional public speaker—learned something new. Looking at it from a different perspective helped each of us.

Likewise, you can always try a new way of praying. If you are too wedded to one form of prayer, no matter how much you enjoy it, you might miss out on new ways of encountering God.

The Examen

My friends at Lab asked me to lead a seminar that week. But I had a hard time figuring out what I could teach them. I've never acted (unless you count my turn in the 1978 Plymouth-Whitemarsh Senior High School production of *Bye Bye Birdie*), so I couldn't teach them anything about their craft. In fact, they used to tease me about my appalling lack of theater knowledge. When the actors were preparing for *The Last Days of Judas Iscariot*, I said, "How many practices will you have before the play starts?" One of them laughed and said, "You mean how many *rehearsals* before *opening night*, Father Jim?"

Eventually it dawned on me that I could teach the group a prayer popularized by St. Ignatius Loyola called the "examen." Essentially a review of the day, it helps you see where God is active in your daily life. It's the most helpful prayer I know for people starting out in the spiritual life.

The prayer goes by several names. In the *Spiritual Exercises* it is called the "examination of conscience." St. Ignatius did not invent the technique of examining your conscience—the practice reaches back as far as the Greek philosophers and was used in the early Christian church.[1] In the latter case it was used (and still is) as a way to recall your sins in preparation for confession. What St. Ignatius and the early Jesuits did was shift the emphasis away from sin to seeing where God was present. Sin was still to be considered, but so were joy, grace, and fulfillment.

Examen is a Latin word meaning "examination." "Conscience" in Latin is *conscientia*, but *conscientia* also means "consciousness." This led to another name for the prayer, popularized by the Jesuit writer George Aschenbrenner: the "examination of consciousness" or "consciousness examen." His nomenclature reminds us, as Andrea's workshop demonstrated, the importance of being conscious of what's going on around us. Being conscious helps us notice God and "discern," which means making good decisions in a prayerful way. Also, as Father Aschenbrenner writes in his book *Consciousness Examen*:

> Examen of conscience has narrow moralistic overtones. Its prime concern was with the good or bad actions we had done each day. Whereas in discernment the prime concern . . . is with the way God is affecting and moving us . . . deep in our own affective consciousness.[2]

The purpose of the examination of consciousness is to help us see where God is "affecting and moving us." But as much as I like Father Aschenbrenner's insight, I'll stick to "examen" (which is, conveniently, pronounced "examine"). It's the name that most practitioners use today. But we'll bear in mind his important insight about being conscious of God's activity.

Another purpose is to learn to continually see God in the present—that is, not simply in the day that has passed, but in the one to come. Thomas Green writes, "The purpose is so that tomorrow I will be more spontaneously sensitive when important things happen."[3]

For many people, the examen is one of the easiest of prayers, because it is essentially a review of the day in God's presence. That's something that most people, even newcomers to prayer, feel they can do. It's also one of the most powerful of prayers, because people are often surprised when they recognize the ways God is present in their lives. For that reason the examen can be life-changing.

Let's look at one way to pray the examen. Although there are many versions, each includes the same elements, all of them centered around the daily review. Find one that suits you. Besides, as Jim Manney points out in *The Prayer That Changes Everything*, the examen is "an attitude more than a method."[4]

Here are the steps in the version I use:

1. Presence
2. Gratitude
3. Review
4. Sorrow
5. Grace

Let's look at those steps one by one.

1. Presence

As with all prayers, it's important to begin by placing yourself in God's presence in a conscious way. We're always in God's presence, but there is a temptation in many prayers, especially the examen, to forget this.

In the examen we review our day, so the temptation is to say, "Time for my review!" and recall the day on our own without any sense that this is happening *in God's presence*. It's the difference between looking at photos on your own and going through them slowly with another person. Like all prayer, it is a conversation.

In his book *Reimagining the Ignatian Examen*, which offers multiple ways to pray this prayer, Mark Thibodeaux reminds us that the examen "needs to be God-centered." This means that you ask God to take the lead in the prayer, talk to God instead of yourself, and listen for God's voice. In other words, remember that this is a dialogue. This does not necessarily lead to an overflow of feelings in the examen, Mark notes. "For it to be a prayer . . . we don't have to feel God's presence all the time; we simply have to be oriented toward God."[5]

How do you place yourself in God's presence? The simplest way is consciously to remember it, to say, "I am in the presence of God." Or you might invite God to be with you: "Be with me, God." Yes,

God is always with you, but this conscious inviting is often a help-ful way to remind you that you're with someone else. Or in this case Someone Else.

Another way is to use a creative technique taken directly from St. Ignatius's *Spiritual Exercises*: imagining God looking at you. In this practice, you spend a few seconds looking at the place where you're going to pray. And Ignatius meant that in a literal way. If you pray sitting in a chair, then you stand apart from it and look at it, imagining God looking at you from that same vantage point. Then, when you sit in the chair, you're reminded, often in a surprising way, that God is gazing upon you and is with you in your prayer.

2. Gratitude

St. Ignatius asks us to begin the examen with gratitude. Indeed, his *Spiritual Exercises* concludes with an exercise in which we meditate on the ways God has blessed us. Ignatius asks us to consider "how all good things come from above . . . like rays from the sun, or the rains from their source." Gratitude was at the heart of Ignatius's spiritu-ality. In fact, he termed *in*gratitude "the most abominable of sins."[6]

That's a standard notion. But why did Ignatius place gratitude at the beginning of the examen? Why not review the day and then be grateful for what you remember?

There are (at least) two reasons for starting off with thanksgiving. First, it combats the common tendency to focus on the negative. If asked to summarize your day, you might be tempted to jump to what didn't go well, because that is what often stands out. "Oh, I had the worst meeting today at work. It went on for three hours!" Ignatius invites us *not* to start with our problems. The examen can even invite us to find grace amid the negatives.

Second, starting with the positives goes against the propensity to problem-solve. Some of us look at our days, even our lives, as a series of problems to be solved. Thus, if I asked you about the past twenty-four hours on the day that your car broke down, you'd tell me how you had to call the garage and get your car taken in for service. If you failed a test in school that day, you'd tell me what mistakes you made and how you should have studied more. If you've had a fight with your spouse, you'd tell me what happened in the argument, how upset you were, and how you want to reconcile.

We need to address the problems that come before us. Cars need to be repaired. Tests need to be passed. Relationships need to be healed. Life presents us with challenges to be met. In fact, a friend recently told me that she structures her own examen as "Blessings and Challenges."

But when taken to the extreme, our day becomes nothing more than a series of problems. As a result, our minds are drawn more to challenges than to blessings. Yes, your car broke down, but did you see that beautiful tree filled with autumn leaves? Yes, you did poorly on that test, but did you enjoy that night out with your roommate? Yes, you had a fight with your spouse, but did you feel satisfaction finishing that project at work?

Beginning the examen with gratitude forces us to move away from problem-solving and recognize the blessings as well as the challenges. It also works against our built-in psychological tendency to attend to the negative. Thomas G. Plante, a psychologist at Santa Clara University and director of the Applied Spirituality Institute there, recently explained it to me this way:

> In order to survive and thrive over so many centuries, we humans have had to adapt to our ever-changing and often threatening environment by being hypervigilant to dangers and often ignoring peaceful times. Research in evolutionary psychology and behavior suggests that these adaptive tendencies for survival in nature remain with us, and so we find ourselves putting much more emphasis on what *could* go

wrong rather than what is going right for us, making many of us "negatrons," or people who tend to see the glass as half empty rather than half full.

For other reasons, Ignatius knew that gratitude was important. Giving thanks reminds us of the source of our blessings and therefore our inherent reliance on God. It's also part of a healthy relationship. Imagine someone mailing you a gift for your birthday: a book, a sweater, a necklace. The first thing you would want to say to your friend would be, "Thanks!" It's the same with God. You've just been given the gift of another day. How could you not say thanks?

Also, as George Aschenbrenner notes, this step reminds us not to "either begin to make demands for what we think we deserve . . . (often leading to angry frustration) or blandly take for granted *all* that comes our way." It's a bulwark against "entitlement." Gratitude comes from a stance of poverty and humility before God. "The more deeply we live in faith, the more we become aware of how poor we are and how gifted; life itself becomes humble, joyful thanksgiving."[7]

How do you "do" gratitude? Why not start by asking God to help you become aware of the things you are grateful for? Then simply call them to mind. If it's some great news—getting into that college you've dreamed of, receiving that promotion you've always wanted, hearing that your son or daughter is engaged, and so on—it won't be hard to remember it. But don't forget the simpler gifts. The smell of the flowers as you pass a rosebush. The sight of an unexpected butterfly on a city street. A sunset that makes you stare.

What else? A friend who made you laugh. A scene in a movie that made you cry. A line in a book that made you think. Also, things that you had been praying for. You passed that test. The garage finished with your car early. Your girlfriend reconciled with you. Anything that gives you joy.

For many people, gratitude is the heart of the examen. As Jim Manney writes, "Gratitude isn't preliminary to the real meat of the examen. It's actually the other way around: the examen instills gratitude."[8] Often when people are struggling, I suggest that their entire examen consist simply of gratitude.

After you've called these things to mind, you "savor" them. In other words, you don't simply recount them to yourself as if you are going over a shopping list. Spend a moment appreciating them, as you would appreciate a delicious meal.

3. Review

The third step constitutes the bulk of the prayer. Here you review your day from start to finish. The aim is to notice moments when God was active in your life during the past twenty-four hours. We know that God is active in every moment, but the examen asks you to examine that in a contemplative way, to be more aware of this reality. The main question is: How has God spoken to you through the events of the day?

The review of the day, by the way, is not meant to be an exercise in picking at your sins or failings, but an invitation to review your day in the light of God's mercy. There is a subsequent step that includes looking at where you have failed, but the examen should not be focused on sin. This phase of the prayer is especially useful when life is hard. Looking over your entire day (rather than just the stressful parts) can give you perspective and invite you to see things that you might otherwise overlook in your sadness or distress.

All this reminds me of an insight from Damian, one of my spiritual directors. At the time, I was upset about some problem, which I cannot even remember now. After I complained about it, he asked me a helpful question: "Are you being honest with God in prayer?"

"Of course!" I said. "I talk to God all the time about how angry it makes me."

Damian said, "Well, that's not being honest, is it? If you're focusing only on one part of your life, then you're not bringing to God the whole picture. In a sense, you're not being as honest as you could be. There are a lot of other things going on in your life besides that one problem. Can you give God the whole picture?"

He wasn't asking me to ignore my problems. Rather, he was asking me to consider the entirety of my life, to look at it in greater context. When I did so, my perspective changed; things seemed better and indeed more real. My life was more than that one problem. The examen helps you to look at the whole picture.

How do you do the review? Recall your day from the moment you woke up right up to the time you are doing the examen. Most people pray the examen at the end of the day, so the time from waking up to going to sleep is the most common time frame. But some people have a hard time staying awake at the end of a long day, especially when they quiet themselves down, so they pray the examen in the early morning (in that case, they review the previous day) or the middle of the day (in that case they review the period from lunchtime to lunchtime).

Simply recall the day. If you like, you might ask yourself a few questions: "Where did I experience God? Where did I see God's invitation? Whom did I love? Who showed me love?" You don't have to remember every second of your day, but you should try to remember it with as much specificity as you can.

Let me give you an example of what your examen might be like if you were, say, a college student. (This is based on conversations not with just one student, but with many of them.) I'll also include the kinds of distractions that can pop up during the examen:

Okay, God, here I am. Please help me in my examen.
What happened when I woke up this morning? Hmm . . .
I was tired from staying out so late last night, but happy I

didn't oversleep. Guess I should thank God for waking me up! Breakfast was grim: a cold slice of that leftover pizza. Maybe I should take better care of myself. I remember that homily from Mass a few weeks ago. Was that last week or the week before? Let's see, two weeks ago, I was at that party and met that girl . . . and, oh yeah, it was last Sunday. The priest talked about reverencing your body, like you reverence other things in life. I like that idea: as if your body is something holy, to be taken care of. Maybe less pizza and more fruit or something.

The morning was crazy. I was late to my English lit class, but I was glad that I finished that paper in time. I got a lot out of that book too. I didn't think I'd like Jane Austen, but she has a good sense of human nature. When did I see that movie based on that book? Did I see that with my girlfriend? Or was that before we started to go out? Maybe it was with . . . Oh, I'm getting distracted. Yeah, and it was funny before class when my friend kept teasing me about getting my paper in on time. He's a great guy. I'm happy we met freshman year. Wow, we've been friends for two years now. I'm really grateful for his friendship, and I guess I never prayed about that before. Maybe I should tell him. Nah, maybe not now, but at least I can be thankful for him.

Thank God we didn't get too much reading for the weekend from that theology class! The professor is great, giving me that extension a few weeks ago. It's awesome when people go out of their way to be kind. That's something I don't appreciate as much as I could. People just being nice. Kind. Thank you, God.

Lots of people in my life are nice to me like that, for no reason—my mom sent that care package of cookies the other day even though she was busy, my grandma sent me that card with $50 in it, my resident adviser who told me what courses to sign up for—and she was right! It's wonderful to have those people in my life who are so kind. Maybe I should be more thankful about that. The woman who works in campus ministry—what's her name anyway?—told me to think about being attracted to kindness as a kind of call. Like it's a kind of call from God—for me to be nicer. I guess I could be nicer to my mom and dad. Last time I talked to them I was short with them since I had that paper due. Sometimes I forget all that they try to do, and how happy they are that I'm even in college. Someone once told me that if I'm ever mad at my parents, I should think of all the things they did for me when I was a baby—things I don't even know about.

Lunch was a blur, basically. I can't even remember it. Wait a minute. Yeah, I grabbed a hot dog and a soda on the way to my next class at 1:30. Economics drives me crazy. I don't seem to be able to get the hang of it. And I guess I was in a bad mood when Rob asked if I could give him my notes from the last class. Maybe I should have just given them to him right away instead of making him practically beg for them. I can get mean when I'm in a bad mood. I guess I didn't respond to God's invitation to be generous. I'll have to think about that.

Class didn't turn out so bad anyway, and I think I'll be able to do okay on the test. I hope. How about a little help with that, God? Am I allowed to ask for that? Maybe I need to be more positive about things. I'm grateful that I had a chance to grab a nap after the gym and before dinner. I feel healthy. Sometimes I take my health for granted, but I'm nineteen and in decent shape, and I know a few people in my dorm who have health problems, like my roommate with asthma and that guy with food allergies. I'm grateful that I'm healthy, God. Thanks.

Dinner was awesome. It was fun to spend it with my girlfriend. I'm so lucky to have such a great girlfriend. She gets me to laugh at everything, even myself. And man, that vegetarian lasagna in the cafeteria is amazing. Can't believe I had two helpings. Maybe I should work out more tomorrow! I probably should have studied more after dinner too, instead of surfing the web. And looking at porn too. That always gets me down. Why do I do that? I have my girlfriend, what do I need all that for, like every day too? Also, I was glad to find a quiet study carrel in the library, and at least I got through what I needed to cover tonight. Anyway, it's 12:30 a.m. now and it's been a pretty good day. Thank you, God. Get me through tomorrow!

The review helps you to find God in your day. It makes up the bulk of the examen, as you prayerfully consider the places where you encountered God. In our example, the fictional college student sees God in many places—in the friend who playfully teases him as well as the professor who is kind to him. This leads him spontaneously to recall other people who are kind to him, such as his parents and grandmother. He also sees his health and his girlfriend as blessings.

But his life isn't perfect. He was testy with someone who wanted to borrow his notes. He recognizes that he's not treating his body as he should, and he sees that insight as an invitation. And he remembers a woman in campus ministry telling him that being attracted to the ways that others are kind may be a call, inviting him to be kinder to others. These digressions and insights happen often in an examen; something that happened today might remind you of an earlier event, and a link might be drawn, a pattern recognized.

In his review, our college student can see that recognizing his shortcomings is one way God can invite him to a new life. God raises things in the examen, so that we can grow in love, joy, and holiness during the day. Were our college student less reflective, he might never think about these things—either the positives or negatives—and thus might overlook God's considerable presence.

4. Sorrow

The next step is looking at anything you've done that was selfish or sinful during the day. Many people recoil at this step, seeing it as a stereotypical example of the way "religion" forces unnecessary guilt on them, causing them to feel bad about themselves. But all of us are human and therefore imperfect. It's healthy to recognize our failings and sinfulness.

This step helps us to grow, to increase in healthy humility, and to remind ourselves of our need for God. Besides, making mistakes is an inevitable part of our lives as human beings and finite creatures. Jim Manney, who describes this stage of the prayer as "fixing what's wrong," has a good description of why this part of the examen is necessary:

> Sin hobbles our relationship with God, not because it's a black mark in the book kept by the Divine Scorekeeper, but because the lies, illusions, and self-serving excuses that cloud our minds make us less able to give and receive love. Looking at our sins and faults allows us to take responsibility for them. We can possess them; they no longer possess us. We become more and more able to give our whole selves to God, and to become the people God created us to be.[9]

We need, however, to distinguish between guilt and shame. Guilt says, "I did a bad thing." Shame says, "I am a bad person." Too often guilt, which can be healthy, leads to shame, which can be unhealthy.

There are exceptions to this generalization. Guilt can be unhealthy if it simply weighs you down and prevents you from accepting God's mercy. And if you are truly acting badly or have done something reprehensible, some shame is not a bad thing. But in general, most people who pick up a book on prayer are not doing reprehensible things.

Guilt, often maligned in spiritual circles, can have some salutary effects. It can remind you of the need to change. It can humble you if you are vain. And it can remind you of your reliance on God—and that you're not God.

Guilt is also one way that our conscience works. If I have treated someone shabbily, been curt with them, or gossiped about them, I feel a pang of guilt. That's conscience speaking, so it's important to listen. It's God's voice echoing in your soul.

After you have reviewed the day, then, you will naturally notice some actions that you regret. Perhaps like our fictional college student, you realize that you are not as kind as you could be, that you lost your temper when you were stressed, or that you are, in a general way, not as grateful as you could be.

One helpful question was suggested by my professor of moral theology, James F. Keenan, SJ, who noted that in the Gospels Jesus usually does not castigate people who are trying hard, but rather those who aren't trying at all. The objects of Jesus's criticism are people who could love, show mercy, and be generous but don't—like the people who pass by the beaten man in the Parable of the Good Samaritan. The Gospels show Jesus critiquing those who could love, but just don't *bother*. As Father Keenan put it, for Jesus sin is often a "failure to bother to love." So one question I ask myself during the examen is "Where did I fail to bother to love today?"

What happens after you name your sins? You can ask God for forgiveness. You can resolve to ask for forgiveness from a person you've offended. If you're Catholic and it's a significant sin, you might seek out the sacrament of reconciliation, confess your sins to a priest, and receive absolution. A recognition of sinfulness may also lead you to say to yourself, *I don't want to live like that any longer.* Our college student might say, *There was no need for me to be a jerk to Rob.*

Some examinations of conscience focus on sin. In fact, St. Ignatius suggested the "particular examen," which invites you to look at a "particular sin or fault." His particular examen has three steps. First, in the morning you ask God for the grace not to engage in that pattern. Second, at the noon meal, you recall how many times you engaged in that fault or sin. For our college friend it might be remembering how he was ungenerous. Ignatius suggests that you write this out. (He includes a homey example in the *Spiritual Exercises* of writing a *g*, probably for *giorno*, or "day" in Italian, and placing dots next to the letter indicating the frequency.) Then you commit yourself to avoiding the behavior. Finally, at the close of the day, you again recall how many times you committed this fault or sin and write it out again. The goal is to focus on a specific behavior.

George Aschenbrenner wisely notes that during the examen we are usually not called to amend our entire life. "We are deficient in so many areas and so many defects must be done away with. But God does not want all of them to be handled at once. Usually there is one area of our hearts where God is especially calling for conversion, which is always the beginning of new life." As Father Aschenbrenner points out, it's usually the one aspect that we want to forget and perhaps "work on later," so we tend to avoid it. But God's bringing it up in the examen is his way of "interiorly nudging" us to attend to it.[10]

And we should not despair about changing, for it is God who is encouraging us to grow, to change, to be converted, to undergo what the Gospel writers called *metanoia*, a change of mind and heart. Aschenbrenner writes, "A great hope should be the atmosphere of our hearts at this point—hope not founded . . . on our own powers for the future—but rather founded much more fully in our God."[11]

In general, the sorrow portion of the examen calls us to recognize our own imperfections, flaws, sins, and especially our need for God's grace. That brings us to the final step.

But before the next step you might include an optional one. Many people find it helpful to return to a place in the examen that was especially meaningful. If there was a significant occasion for gratitude, say, a major event in your life, if you received a significant grace, or if you finally understood a sinful pattern, it's worthwhile to return to that grace and savor it even more.

5. Grace

The examen looks forward. Thus, the final step is to ask for God's help. You might ask for grace to help in a particular area that you know will be a challenge in the next twenty-four hours: "God, you know that I am having a hard time with my boss (parent/sibling/spouse), so give me the grace to be more patient and loving."

As you can see, the examen begins with a recognition that God gives us graces throughout the day and ends with a reminder of our need for God's grace. And by "grace" I mean God's help, encouragement, or presence. Karl Rahner called grace God's "self-communication," something we would hope for every moment of the day.[12]

Why Pray the Examen?

The foregoing sounds like a lot to remember for such a short prayer. But the examen is actually simple—just five steps: *presence, gratitude, review, sorrow,* and *grace.* Now that we understand what it is, let's discuss *why* we pray the examen.

As mentioned earlier, the examen works against our tendency to view our lives as a series of problems to solve, challenges to surmount, or obstacles to overcome. It also invites us to pause to appreciate God's presence in our lives, which works against the urge to put today behind us and plow ahead to tomorrow. Mainly it helps us to *notice*.

To begin with, it helps us to notice individual events that we might have appreciated at the time, but that we need to recall, savor, and cement in our memories. The examen solidifies grace by helping us remember it.

Imagine that you're commuting to work one morning, standing on a train or a subway platform, when you unexpectedly run into a friend you've not seen for some time. Upon seeing you, she delightedly throws her arms around you, hugs you tightly, and says, "I've missed you!" Her warm and spontaneous gesture fills you with joy. But she's rushing to catch her own train, and the conversation ends quickly. "Bye!" she shouts, smiling.

In the afterglow, you might feel a rush of gratitude for her friendship and even thank God. But then, rushing to catch your train, you hop on, pull out your phone, and start checking your emails. Suddenly you're consumed with work. By the time you've reached your office that warm moment is buried under so many tasks that it barely registers. You may end up having a terrible day and that joyful moment is submerged under a sea of troubles. You may even forget that incident entirely. As a result, your day may seem unrelentingly joyless, and if this kind of perspective is not challenged, you may see life as unrelentingly joyless.

The examen is an antidote. When you pray the examen at the end of your difficult day, you will be reminded of that moment of grace, remember to be thankful for your friend's embrace, perhaps remember other times you spent with your friend, and thank God. Consequently, you may experience several things. First, you will be grateful to God. Second, you will be grateful for your friend. Third, you may see your day as more joyful than you had initially thought.

Finally, you may feel relief when you realize all these things: *My life is not so bad after all*.

The examen also invites us to see God in what may seem like *small* moments, and small moments can carry great grace. Recently, I went to the zoo with my sister and my then eleven-year-old nephew Matthew. There, we came upon an ingenious exhibit. Designed to let people interact with birds, it was a spacious caged area filled with small trees on which were perched hundreds of colorful parakeets. At the entrance, Matthew purchased a popsicle stick dipped in honey and covered with small seeds.

When he held out his stick, a hungry parakeet flew over to him and started pecking away merrily. My nephew laughed for joy. His laugh delighted me and filled me with a burst of joy. All at once I was so happy for his being in the world and for my being with him during this moment. At one point a pure white parakeet alighted on his hand. He held out the little bird and said to me, jokingly, "Look, the Holy Spirit!"

Matthew was right. That little incident—being happy that he was happy—was indeed a sign of the Holy Spirit. The moment, lasting no more than a few seconds, was packed with grace. These are the kinds of things that we need to pause to appreciate. They are not earth-shaking, but they are carriers of grace. And the Holy Spirit.

The examen also helps us see *patterns*. Practicing the examen daily helps you to see where you are missing something on a daily basis. If during every examen you find yourself grateful for a particular friend, your gratitude will register, and you will naturally be grateful the next time you see your friend. The examen helps you to see God *in the moment*.

Likewise, you might find yourself continually prone to one nagging fault, selfish action, or sinful pattern. Perhaps you find yourself noticing, in one examen after another, that you are rude to someone in your family, you're not giving friends the time they need because you're too busy, or you're too lazy to reach out to someone at work who needs comfort. These things come up in your examen over and over.

The more you see the pattern recur, the more likely you will be to resist the temptation to be rude or selfish or lazy the next day. It's surprising how having something come up repeatedly in the examen serves to dissuade further bad actions. Never underestimate the persuasive power of saying to yourself night after night, "I can't believe I did *that* again."

Mainly the examen helps us notice God in the past twenty-four hours. And usually it's easier to look back and notice God in the past than it is to see God in the present. Many of us have passed through difficult times when God felt absent, only to look back months or years later and see God's activity clearly. You might have suffered through the death of a family member and realized only in retrospect how God was helping you.

When my father was dying from lung cancer twenty years ago, many friends were especially generous. One, Janice, a Catholic sister and one of my professors in graduate school, traveled all the way from Boston to Philadelphia, on her limited sister's budget, simply to visit him for a few hours before he died. Another, Regina, a healthcare professional who was also the sister of a Jesuit friend, helped to answer all my questions about my father's illness, spoke with my family about hospice care, and visited him many times.

In fact, it was Regina—not anyone in my family—who was with my father when he died. After weeks of painful physical decline, one day, after we had spent a long day sitting by my father's bedside, the doctors and nurses said that there was nothing anyone could do and that we should go home. Regina said that she would stay overnight. The next day, when the hospital called to tell us of his death, we also got a phone call from Regina, who described his last moments.

That day I was too overwhelmed by grief to fully appreciate what Regina had done for my father, my family, and me. I thanked her but was also consumed, along with the rest of my family, with planning the wake and the funeral. Looking back, I can see so clearly how God was present—through the presence of friends like Janice, and her kindness, and Regina, who was praying for my father at the hour of his death.

Peter-Hans Kolvenbach, the superior general of the Jesuits from 1983 to 2008, put it well. More than twenty years ago, I asked if he might contribute an essay for the book *How Can I Find God?* Some contributors talked about finding God through their children, others through nature, prayer, or reading Scripture. Father Kolvenbach, a scholar and a linguist, surprised me with a fictional tale about the abbot of a monastery who used to speak to his monks every day about encountering God. Kolvenbach said, "I see myself more or less in his story":

> [The abbot] carried on until the day on which a monk dared to ask if he himself had ever encountered God. After a bit of embarrassed silence, the abbot frankly admitted that he had never had a vision or a one-on-one meeting with God. Nothing surprising about that, since God Himself had said to Moses, "You cannot see my face" (Exodus 33:20). But this very same God taught Moses that he could see His back as he passed across his path. "You will see me pass." And thus, looking back over the length and breadth of his life, he could see for himself the passage of God.[13]

Noticing the "passage of God" is one way of describing what happens in the examen. God allows himself, concluded Kolvenbach, "to be recognized once he has really passed." Then he quotes what God says to Moses in Exodus 33:23: "You will see my back."

Seeing where God has passed makes it easier to see the places where God is now. If you are consistently reminded in the examen that you have found God in nature, for example, it is more likely that when you have a rich experience in nature you will say, in the present, "Here is God."

Often people ask me if they're doing the examen wrong. But unless they're skipping the basic steps—presence, gratitude, review, sorrow, and grace—the answer is usually no, because there are many ways of doing the examen.[14] You might even pray what you could call a "life examen," akin to what Andrea invited us to do during the Lab summer intensive when we placed a sheet of paper on the floor and started tracing out our lives. If you have a few days or an extended period, you can begin with gratitude for some of the blessings in your life, then gradually work your way through your life, year by year, looking for moments of God's presence, seeing patterns of generous and sinful behavior, and asking for God's grace for the rest of your life.

Often I've suggested this method to people recovering from addictions. Alcoholics Anonymous suggests a "fearless moral inventory," which is often more focused on behavior associated with addictions. (I like adding the graces one received as well.) Also, for those new to the spiritual life, a life examen can be a catching up, as they see where God has been present over the years. In her book *Inner Compass*, Margaret Silf compares the process to strolling alongside a river, against the current, all the way back to its source.[15]

Common Questions About the Examen

Since the day I entered the Jesuit novitiate, I've prayed the examen every night. And in the past twenty years as a spiritual director I've spoken to hundreds of people about their prayer; I always ask about their experience praying the examen. So it's not surprising that I've run across some common questions.

1. *What if I always fall asleep?* This is the most common question, since most people pray the examen at the end of the day. An easy suggestion is to shift the time of your examen to the morning (reviewing the previous day) or the afternoon or early evening (reviewing the past twenty-four hours). There's nothing sacrosanct about doing it at night.

Or you might need to look at the position you're praying in. A few years ago, a young Jesuit said that he was always falling asleep as he did his examen.

"How do you do it?" I asked.

"Well," he said, "I brush my teeth, turn out the lights, get under the covers, and then start. But somehow I find that I always fall asleep."

I laughed and suggested that perhaps he could at least try not getting under the covers! Overall, though, try switching up the time or your posture.

2. *What if it feels like I'm racing through a boring list of what I did today?* Sometimes the examen becomes, paradoxically, just another thing to do. We sit down, stressed or rushed, wondering how much time we can give to it, grit our teeth, and begin. We may say something like, "Okay God, I'm in your presence," then call to mind a few good things that happened, zip through the last twenty-four hours, remember a few sins, and ask God for some help the next day. Then we jump into bed. Soon we wonder why our spiritual lives seem dry.

If that sounds realistic, it is, because that's sometimes how I pray the examen. If you're a busy person, you might be tempted to rush through it. Even if you're not busy, you might resist spending time with God because you think it's a waste of time, are worried about what might come up, or are just lazy.

In these cases, it helps to recall that you're in a conversation with God. One of the perils of the examen is that it can feel like a monologue. Jim Manney recounts something that a friend asked about the examen, which touches on the danger of a solipsistic approach: "What's to keep it from becoming a play starring myself as the hero of a one-person show?" Good question. Or "What's to keep the examen from becoming a *review* of that one-person show?"[16]

If it's turning into a one-person show, work harder to bring other people into your examen—be intentional about focusing on your relationships with other people and giving thanks for other people.

If it's becoming a monologue, there are few ways to remind yourself that it's a conversation with God. First, as I described before, look at the physical place of your prayer. Look long and hard at the chair, cushion, or pew that you're on and imagine God looking at you. Second, pepper your prayer with the word "God," just to emphasize the conversational nature of the prayer: "God, I remember my friend's warm embrace at the train station." Finally, close with a prayer that expresses your relationship with God. "Thank you, God, for this day and this prayer."

Jen Willhoite, an artist, wrote me just as I was writing this chapter. She said, "The examen helped me know God in my heart, rather than just know *of* him." The examen is not so much about you as about God *with* you.

3. *What if I don't feel anything when I pray it?* For many believers, emotions are the litmus test of whether a prayer is "successful." St. Ignatius and his followers may be partially responsible for this. St. Ignatius often spoke of the "gift of tears." He never implied this, but some people infer that if you don't have tears or at least strong emotions—joy, sadness, anger, frustration—then somehow the prayer is not working.

On a recent retreat, I didn't shed a tear once during the entire eight days. Even though I should know better, I felt cheated. My spiritual director laughed and said, "That's not the only way to experience God." Ironically, as I was packing up to leave, I felt deeply moved by something and started to weep. It was as if God was saying, "You know, I've been here all along, but you don't need to cry!"

In some spiritual circles there is the tendency to privilege feelings over thought, but our minds are surely as important as our hearts. Sometimes we do feel something during the examen. We might not only remember a moment and feel grateful, but we may also feel a sense of peace or calm or joy. And we may even receive the "gift of tears."

But in general people don't feel much during the examen. More often, they're *remembering a moment when they felt something*. The woman who ran into her friend at the train station would remember the warm feeling that she experienced at the time. Perhaps there would be just a flicker of that warmth as she recalled it. But if there were no warm feelings during the examen, that would not be surprising. Simply having the insight that her friend loves her is important.

In other words, insights are as important as feelings, in the examen and in other prayers. If your examen feels "cold" from time to time, don't worry. Sometimes you'll feel God's presence or a sense of joy or comfort. As in any relationship, not every encounter will be emotional. This is the case with the examen, which is primarily a prayer of insight, not feeling.

4. *What if my life isn't going well and I get sad just thinking about my day?* Life can be hard. "To thee do we send up our sighs," goes a line from the Salve Regina, the Catholic prayer asking for Mary's help, "mourning and weeping in this valley of tears." Maybe every day isn't a "valley of tears," but some days are. Is it cruel to ask someone to review their day when they are suffering from cancer, they have lost their job, or a family member has died?

In fact, it's quite the opposite. Often when a person is engulfed in sadness, I will recommend focusing on gratitude. This is not to dismiss or cover up the sadness. Rather, when we are sad, we tend to assume that there is no good at all in life. Focusing on gratitude helps to restore our whole vision.

God is always with you, and the examen helps you see that, even when things are going terribly for you, or you are sad, or you have suffered a loss, God is present. It might be a kind word from a physician, the healing touch of a friend, or an unexpected phone call or email that shows you that God is on your side.

It even might be something that you enjoyed *despite* your sadness. I remember one moment from the day of my father's funeral that made me laugh.

That day I felt submerged under an ocean of grief. One day after my father's death, my forty-five-year-old cousin, in perfect health, died suddenly. So our family was consumed with still more grief. Presiding at my father's funeral (the first funeral I had ever presided over) was healing for me, as it gave me a chance to enter the Gospels and the Mass and be reminded of my belief in the Resurrection. It was also consoling to have so many of my family, friends, and Jesuit brothers with me. But another moment ended up being a significant part of my examen that night.

During his wake (or "viewing," as they say in Philadelphia) the night before and the morning of the funeral, we had asked the funeral home to play some Irish music. (My father, of Irish descent, had a lifelong fondness for Irish music.) My father was a private person, and we weren't sure if there would be a big crowd, so I thought that any silences could be awkward. Happily, during the evening wake, a sizable crowd came to pay their respects. Beneath the conversation you could hear mournful Irish tunes.

The next morning, however, there were only a handful of people at the funeral home. Toward the end, as we were leaving, present along with me were just my mother, my sister, my sister's husband,

and two of my friends—a longtime friend from high school named John and a Jesuit named Chris. Mournful Irish music continued as we stared at my father's body in the casket. All of us had run out of things to say, so we prayed silently.

Then we heard a click on the tape machine and suddenly a sprightly tune came booming over the loudspeaker. I couldn't immediately identify it until I heard the first line. "It's a *great* day for the Irish!" sang the Irish Rovers. It was one of my father's favorite songs. My friend Chris suppressed a laugh—barely.

John said, "Well, it's not a great day for *one* of the Irish!" Everyone laughed.

"No, no," I said. "It *is* a great day for him! He's in heaven."

When I prayed my examen that night, I remembered that little spark of joy. It dawned on me that, in addition to professing my faith in God during the Mass, I had professed it before my friends at the wake. I really *did* believe that he was in heaven, that he was with God, and that, yes, it really *was* a great day for him.

Even if your day is not especially sad, but simply feels dull, you might be tempted to skip the examen. But as Jim Manney says, "You might have the impression that your everyday life is the dreary same old, same old. It isn't. Daily life is rich and meaningful. Every encounter, every challenge, every disappointment, and every delight is a place where God can be found."[17]

5. *What if I'm not sure how it's supposed to change me?* Many times the examen invites us to change by focusing on an aspect of life that we may be overlooking or an area where we might need to improve. Sometimes it also helps us see the way that we are noticing, or not noticing, God.

Just as I was writing this chapter, a co-worker dropped by to tell me this story. Thanks to a session on the examen for the staff at America Media, Shawn decided to introduce it to his children. The night after our session, he was talking to his eight-year-old son.

Shawn at the time was a divorced father whose children stayed with him a few days a week.

"Let's go over our day today," Shawn said to his son. Then he remembered the morning with his son. "Remember how I got you and your sister out of bed, and then your sister lost her sock, and I had to rush you through your cereal? And then remember that I was in a rush and on the way to work I got so angry when that other car cut us off and almost hit us? And then remember how you ran into school after you kissed me goodbye?

"So," he said to his son, "I think God was there when I saw you and your sister waking up. That always makes me happy."

"Daddy," said his son, "that's not where God was."

"It wasn't?" said Shawn. "Then where was he?"

"When that car almost hit us! If we were there a few seconds earlier, we would have gotten into an accident!"

Shawn was, he told me, disappointed in himself for missing a possible moment of grace. "My son taught me not to get so 'caught up' in my own stuff, that I miss God." The examen enabled his son to see something that he missed. Ultimately, the examen helped to teach him something about noticing and changing. If we are attentive, we will be invited to change, often in very gentle ways.

6. *What if I don't have time?* When I hear this frequent complaint, I am reminded of what I was told as a boy about going to church: "God gives you twenty-four hours a day, seven days a week. Can't you give God an hour on Sunday?" That kind of moralizing doesn't go over well today. And making people feel guilty in order to goad them into prayer usually doesn't work for very long.

Yet it's important to think about our commitment to God. Many people, perhaps most people, reading this book would say that God is the most important thing in their life. But how important can that relationship be if you can't spend a measly fifteen minutes on it?

Here's another way to look at it. Think about the things you do for fifteen minutes ungrudgingly. How much time do you spend watching television? Surfing the web? Wasting time? Could you not spend some of that time in the examen?

A gentler way to encourage people is to remind them how much better they will feel if they do it and how it will help them. This is a more selfish motivation, but it's motivation nonetheless. On the rare days when I've missed the examen before I go to bed, say, if I'm very sick or so frazzled that I forget, I usually remember before I nod off and wake up to do a quick one. Even if it's only for a few minutes or even a few minutes of gratitude, it's worth looking back.

If you skip the examen, you will also get out of the habit of looking for God every day. That will lead to a diminished awareness of God. And that will lead to greater stress, anxiety, and maybe even despair. Soon you'll find yourself wondering why things have gotten so rough.

Physical exercise is a good analogy. If you don't spend time exercising, your muscles will get weak. One day you'll find that you're not able to do what you used to do, or you pull a muscle or get winded. If you don't keep up your physical health, you will suffer. The same goes for your spiritual health.

Again, this may sound moralistic, but do you have ten or fifteen minutes anywhere in your day? Try to carve out an easy time to do it, and then stick with it. It may be the most important fifteen minutes of your day. And it will surely help you during the following day.

Overall, the goal of the examen is to teach us to notice God. We notice God so that we can respond to God. And we notice God in the examen, so that we can respond to God the next day as well. The more you do it, the more you will see God not only in the past, but also in the present, so that you can say, to paraphrase my friend Andrea, "I am here today, in this place, with you, God."

IO

What Happens When You Pray?

EMOTIONS, INSIGHTS, MEMORIES, DESIRES, IMAGES, WORDS, FEELINGS, AND MYSTICAL EXPERIENCES

The examen typically doesn't evoke intense feelings or strong emotions. Of course, that's not true for everyone or every time. Occasionally, I've prayed the examen and have felt deeply moved by a memory from the day, but the examen is more a prayer of insight than feeling.

This raises an essential question: What does it mean to "feel" something in prayer? More broadly, what happens in prayer? In other words, what happens after we close our eyes?

This is one of the most important questions in the spiritual life and one of the least addressed in spiritual writing. Sometimes books discuss prayer—practices, techniques, traditions—without saying what beginners want to know most: "What happens when a person prays?" "What is supposed to go on inside of me? Do I hear voices?

Do I see visions in my head?" "What is a good prayer experience? What do people mean when they talk about enjoying prayer?"

Those were my most pressing questions when I was a Jesuit novice, especially because I often heard my fellow novices talk about how "rich" or "satisfying" their prayer was. When I would sit down in the chapel, I used to close my eyes and wonder, *Now what?* And when things started to happen, I would wonder, *Is this right?*

With an eye both toward helping people who are new to prayer and encouraging people who have already prayed, let me answer this most basic question before we go any further. For me this question is at the very heart of prayer. So let's explore the most common "fruits" of prayer one by one.

Emotions

Although emotions don't often arise during the examen, they do in many other kinds of prayer. For many people an emotional response is the most noticeable and most frequent result of praying. To understand what that means, let's make a distinction between *unsurprising* and *surprising* emotions. The first are easier to recognize and understand.

Unsurprising Emotions

Sometimes the emotions that arise in prayer are not surprising. If you've returned from a funeral and pray about the life of the person who died or something that touched you during the service, it wouldn't surprise you to experience sadness. Likewise, if you've just received some good news, sit down to thank God, and feel a sense of joy, that emotion wouldn't shock you. In general, it's easy to see what's happening. The connection between your life and what you feel in prayer is clear—and unsurprising.

But there is a difference between experiencing these emotions in your daily life and experiencing them in prayer. Why? Because you are experiencing them with God in an intentional way. That is, God may be *raising up* these emotions within you.

If you're joyful over some bit of good news, your joy may intensify when you pray about it. Why? Perhaps you are being invited to see that God shares in your joy or that God is the source of that joy. Or maybe God simply wants you, out of God's boundless generosity, to enjoy the good news all over again, like a parent asking a child to retell the story of a success to help the child deepen his joy: "Tell me how it felt to hit that home run again!" Joy is magnified when brought into prayer.

What do you do in return? How do you respond to this joy? Enjoy it with God. Savor it with God. Sink into it with God. Bill Barry once told me, "The enjoyment can be prayer too." Then express your gratitude to God by telling God how happy you are or by deciding to do a good deed by way of thanksgiving.

However, if you have been going through a difficult period in your life, your emotions—sadness, anger, fear, frustration, anxiety— may not surface in prayer immediately. They may not be surprising when they emerge, but they may take *time* to emerge. If you haven't prayed for a while, frequently you may find that painful emotions arise when you recommence. It is as if God is providing you with a safe space in which to acknowledge difficult feelings.

You also may have emotions about your relationship with God. A friend of mine recently went on a retreat at a nearby monastery. During his time there, the monks spoke with him about prayer and various images of God. One day, after hearing about the God of mercy, he experienced a feeling of peace and started to cry. He realized that God was not what he had imagined. My friend had for years struggled with feeling judged by God, and no matter how many times he had been told that God is merciful, he felt stuck. When he revisited his images of God and made room for an image other than the one of a judgmental God, he experienced a feeling of "release" and an invitation to freedom.

Something similar may happen when we are busy. We may not be consciously avoiding certain emotions. Rather, we simply haven't given them time to surface. Remember my grade-school experiment of filling a glass with water from a stream and waiting for the silt in the glass to settle? Until we become quiet and attentive in prayer, it may be hard to settle. But only when we do can our true emotions become clear.

In most cases, once you identify the emotion that arises, you can relate it to an aspect of your life. The invitation may be mainly to acknowledge the emotions that arise in God's presence, speak in your own words to God, and to ask for God's help. Often, expressing these emotions brings relief, as you open yourself up to God. For me, it usually helps to get these emotions off my chest and "give them" to God. God already knows these things, but my sharing them helps me to know this in a deeper way.

Sometimes even a dimly felt awareness of the power of these emotions can block prayer. Someone once told me how frightened she was of prayer, because there was so much "in there." She was afraid to let these emotions surface, because she felt they might overwhelm her. They were too powerful. Others are afraid to share them with God, because they feel that they are inappropriate or because they feel guilty that they haven't shared them earlier. Encouraging someone in this situation often means encouraging them to see that God desires nothing more than to hear them, comfort them, and free them. Most of all, to be with them, as any good friend would.

Surprising Emotions

Occasionally, emotions arising in prayer catch you unawares. An emotion can be so unexpected that it can be frightening, even within the relatively quiet context of prayer.

Let's say you are reading—either in your daily prayer, during a retreat, or after hearing it in church—the story of Moses asking to know God's name, from the Book of Exodus:

> But Moses said to God, "If I come to the Israelites and say to them, 'The God of your ancestors has sent me to you,' and they ask me, 'What is his name?' what shall I say to them?" God said to Moses, "I AM WHO I AM." He said further, "Thus you shall say to the Israelites, 'I AM has sent me to you.'"[1]

As you ponder this, something surprising happens. You are drawn to the words "I am who I am."

In philosophy class in college you read that some scholars think that God is saying "I am being," in other words, "I am the source and ground of all being, of all existence, of all that is." But recently you read that many Old Testament scholars believe that this circumlocution most likely means, "None of your business." Names were important in the ancient Near East. To know someone's name was to have a kind of power over them. Here, God's name is God's own affair.

You start to think about Moses, who had been given a difficult task, but who doesn't get a satisfactory answer from God. You don't know the entire story of Moses other than what you remember vaguely from the movies and a few homilies, but you know that Moses ended up doing a lot for God. You wonder, *Why wouldn't God tell Moses his name?* It seems unfair. After all, it's a minor request from someone who wants to be in relationship with God.

Gradually you grow perplexed, and then disturbed, over the way that God seems to be treating Moses. Even though you've never thought about the story in this way, or much at all, you feel sympathy for someone who has been asked to do something difficult. Why wouldn't God just tell Moses a name? You find yourself *angry* with God for seemingly setting aside Moses's simple request.

It feels strange to feel this emotion when you are praying with this familiar story, and you feel a little guilty about it, but it's unmistakable: you're now *angry*.

You've just had one of the most common experiences in prayer—a surprising emotion. It is one of the prime ways God communicates with us. You wonder, *Where is that coming from? Why am I so angry about what happened to Moses, of all people? What does this mean?*

Anger is not the only emotion to arise unexpectedly in prayer. You might feel sadness when you read about Joseph being sold into slavery in the Book of Genesis, or joy when you read about Jesus healing someone in the Gospels, or disappointment when you compare your seemingly "boring" life to the exciting lives of the apostles.

Sadness, joy, disappointment. What other emotions can surprise us in prayer? The answer is any emotion that comes up in your daily life: joy, anger, fear, frustration, disappointment—anything.

You don't have to be meditating with a Bible passage to experience a surprising emotion in prayer. You could simply be praying quietly in your room, in a church, or walking down the street and be blindsided by a powerful emotion.

God is raising the emotion in prayer for a reason. Why? In the case of surprising emotions, it may take just a few questions to get to the heart of it.

First, *what is evoking this emotion?* Let's use the example of reading that passage from the Book of Exodus. God's response to Moses initially strikes you as unfair. So you are angry at the way God seemed to treat Moses. The answer to this first question is usually straightforward. It's easy to identify something in that Bible passage as the spark for your emotion.

Second, *is this emotion related to something going on in my life?* Now we begin to go deeper. Often emotions relate not only to the focus of prayer—in this case the story of Moses—but to something in your own life.

These experiences in prayer are similar to your emotional reactions to something you read in a book, watch on television, or see online. Let's say that a friend has died. A few months later, you watch a movie that has a scene of a funeral. Although the movie is not even that good, you start to weep. You don't have to be a psychiatrist to see what's happening: the funeral scene in the movie has called up your feelings about your friend.

Something similar may happen in prayer. When we read a passage that strikes us with its immediacy or raises strong emotions, this is often a cue that God is inviting us to notice something. "Hidden feelings," as Mark Thibodeaux calls them, are raised for us to name, examine, and understand—and just as often to have them healed. God is doing this *for a reason*. That's an important insight about prayer. Surprising emotions in prayer are one way that God invites us to look at our hidden feelings.[2]

Perhaps your strong response to the Book of Exodus stems from your anger about how you've been treated at your workplace. You worked on a project for many weeks, and suddenly, through someone else's carelessness, it's canceled. Or you've been planning a big vacation and your boss tells you that you can't go. Even worse, you have been fired or laid off.

You feel an anger out of all proportion to the Bible story you've just read. The story of Moses asking God for a name was the avenue through which God surfaced something about your own life. You even feel a bit like Moses (or more accurately, as you imagine Moses might have felt).

The emotion might be buried deep, something you've not allowed yourself to feel yet. Sometimes, if we are too busy or afraid of confronting these emotions, we don't allow ourselves to feel them. In prayer, God gently raises difficult emotions to invite us to look at them, share them with God, and to heal them. In the end, it's not only about Moses's experience; it's about yours, and about how God might want to reach you and heal you.

Third, *is this emotion telling me something about how I perceive God?* A more subtle reason may relate to how you feel about *God*. Here you see God's answer to Moses as unfair. You may ask yourself what feels unfair in your life. Perhaps you have been treated shabbily in your family and wonder why God isn't helping you. In fact, God seems absent from your life overall. God is mysterious, as you've heard, but you realize in a new way that you don't like that about God.

You are angry at God for what's going on in your life, and you are angry at God for being so mysterious. *Moses might have been angry too,* you think. *Or maybe not. Maybe Moses was more accepting.* You're not sure.

But you don't need to be a Bible scholar to pray with the Bible. You're aware that *you're* angry. Why isn't God more present to you? You think, *Where are you, God?* Your anger is less about how God is treating Moses and more about how God is treating you.

Fourth, *what might the fact that this emotion came up mean for me?* The key response to both surprising and unsurprising emotions is to pay attention. We pay attention not only because it's important to understand our own emotional lives, but because it came up during prayer, and so it is likely something God wants us to look at.

This emotion, then, may be something God is raising *for a reason*. I cannot stress this enough. Prayer is a conscious conversation with God. Thus, if God is raising something in prayer, in your one-on-one time with God, pay attention. Imagine if God walked through the door and said, "I invite you to think about this part of your life." You would naturally listen. Think of these emotions in the same way.

So now a surprising emotion has come up in prayer, you've pinpointed its immediate source, and found a possible connection to both events in your life and how you feel about God.

Now what do I do with it? Three steps follow.

First, *consider if your surprising emotion makes sense.* Emotions, by definition irrational, are often based on our perceptions. That's one of the insights of the branch of psychology called cognitive behavior therapy: perceptions influence emotions. Thus, it's important to test if your perceptions reflect reality.

In this case, why are you angry about work? Are you upset because someone said something that could have been meant as playful, but which you interpreted as offensive? Are you focusing only on the negative parts of your life and "universalizing" them?[3] That is, are you taking one problematic incident and saying, "Everything at work is terrible"? It's important to see if your emotions are based in reality.

Likewise, why are you angry about God? Is God really absent, or have you just not been looking? Sometimes people tell me how angry they are that God is absent, and I ask if they have been doing the examen or at least noticing God's presence. "No," they might say sheepishly. "I guess I haven't been noticing." To quote Richard Leonard again, "If you feel distant from God—guess who's moved?"[4]

Sometimes simply stopping to think about these emotions in a rational way can be clarifying. Are you reacting to reality? Seeing things clearly? Or overreacting?

But if you feel that your emotions are a reasonable response to your situation, then it is time for the second step. You may now *feel free to express these surprising emotions, pleasant or unpleasant, in prayer.*

Can you tell God how joyful you are when you think of your newborn child? Can you tell God how relieved you are that your time with your family over a recent Christmas break went off without any major arguments? Can you share how happy you are to have found a new friend?

Can you also ask God for help, and be open to the many ways that God might help—by relieving the situation, through the kind word of a friend, even by enhancing your sense of God's presence in prayer?

If you are angry, feel free to express that too. God has been handling anger for a long time. It's as old as the Psalms. "How long, O LORD?" prays the psalmist. "Will you forget me forever?"⁵ God can handle your anger.

Some people believe that strong emotions—especially anger, disappointment, and sadness—are inappropriate for prayer. It's unseemly to bring these before God, some say. Others say that feeling supposedly "negative" emotions shows you don't trust in God. "Why should you be upset about anything?" goes the argument. "Don't you trust that God will make it right in the end? Don't you have faith?"

I believe that God wants to know us in our beautiful, complex, messy humanity—and emotions are part of being human. To begin with, expressing your emotions to God is a way of unburdening yourself, and it's healthy to unburden yourself of painful emotions. It is unhealthy to keep everything bottled up, as psychologists know. That doesn't mean all emotions must be expressed at all times and in all places—only babies do that. But sharing strong emotions about important matters in your life is part of an emotionally healthy life. Sharing them with God is part of a spiritually healthy life.

Sharing emotions also helps *unblock* your relationship with God. Again, think of your relationship with God as you would a relationship with another person. If you refrained from expressing something that is meaningful to you or that is getting between you and the other person, the relationship may grow formal, distant, or cold.

I can't count the number of times people have told me that their relationship with God seems stale or cold. They'd like more intimacy, but are not sure how to get closer. When I probe and ask what is going on, I usually come across a great loss, a crushing disappointment, a dashed hope, a persistent worry, or a nagging fear that they haven't shared with God. Or I discover something about God is bothering them—perhaps God's seeming lack of care for them.

When I ask if they're sharing how they feel with God or talking honestly in prayer about what's bothering them, they usually shake their heads. They may feel that such emotions aren't appropriate to bring before God. Or they hadn't considered it. Or they've been told not to. Or they think God won't care.

Recently, a man who sees me for spiritual direction told me about a turbulent situation in his life, one that had caused him many sleepless nights. His dropped his head, furrowed his brow, and pursed his lips when he told me about it. It was obvious that he was in some emotional pain.

I asked him one of the most basic questions in the spiritual director's handbook: "Have you spoken with God about this?"

He smiled and then laughed. "No!"

"Why not?" I asked.

"Good question," he said.

An inability or unwillingness to be honest in prayer about your emotional life can lead to feelings of distance. If you refrain from saying what is on your mind and in your heart, a closer relationship with God may become blocked.

One way forward is to remember that God desires an intimate relationship with you and so desires your honesty. Knowing that helps you to confidently share your feelings with God. That, in turn, can help to unblock a relationship that feels cold—with God or with another person.

In the third step, *consider responding to what you determine is an invitation to action.* This is also the case with many of the other prayer experiences that we will consider in this chapter: insights, memories, desires, feelings, and so on. Perhaps God is raising an issue so that you may respond.

Let's say that you are praying with a psalm that talks about the "cry of the poor." You start to feel sadness about all the poor people in the world today. Yesterday you read an article about refugees who were dying while trying to cross the ocean, and you felt an intense sadness. Now in your prayer you are surprised to feel even more sadness.

It's important to name this and express it before God, but it's also important to ask yourself: "What does this mean? Is my sadness God's way of moving me to action?" Because I would suggest that what you're feeling is *God's sadness*. How else would God move you? Again, pay attention.

Emotions are one of the most powerful fruits of prayer. When you close your eyes and emotions come up—whether surprising or unsurprising—consider that it might be God who is raising them up.

Insights

Once on a retreat I was praying with the Gospel story of a paralyzed man who is carried to Jesus by his friends. The Gospel of Mark tells the story of a man who lives in Capernaum, Jesus's base of ministry by the Sea of Galilee. His friends, desperate for his healing, carry him on a mat to the house of Jesus, who is preaching in front of a crowd so large that it blocks access to the doorway. Hindered by the crowd, the men clamber onto the roof (many houses at the time had a staircase that led to the rooftop), where they tear off the thatched roof and lower the man into the house, depositing him in front of Jesus. The original Greek in Mark says, wonderfully, that they "unroofed the roof" (*apestegasan tēn stēgen*).

When Jesus sees "their faith," he says to the paralyzed man, "Your sins are forgiven." The scribes present grumble about Jesus's effrontery. Who is he to forgive sins? Sensing their complaints, Jesus asks, "Which is easier, to say to the paralytic, 'Your sins are forgiven,' or to say, 'Stand up and take your mat and walk'?" Then, to prove that he has the power to forgive sins, he says to the paralyzed man, "Stand up, take your mat and go to your home." And the man does just that. All are amazed.[6]

It's one of my favorite Gospel passages—a moving and dramatic tale told in sure, swift strokes by Mark. Still, it wasn't until years after first encountering it that I noticed that the Gospel says not, "When Jesus saw the man's faith," but "When Jesus saw *their* faith." Many New Testament scholars agree that Jesus was impressed by the faith of the man's *friends*, rather than the faith of the paralyzed man.

The story, then, is not simply about Jesus's power to heal, but about how our friends can bring us to God. In the man's case, it's literal: they carry him. In our case, it's more subtle. When we are struggling, our friends can help us maintain our faith by encouraging us, showing us God's love, praying for us, or laughing with us. Also, at the start of our faith journey, it is usually another person who introduces us to the spiritual life—by giving us a book, inviting us to go on retreat, or recommending a good church. In those ways our friends "carry" us to God.

One year on retreat, however, as I prayed with that passage, a new thought occurred to me. Usually when I imagine myself in a Gospel passage (more about that practice later), I picture the participants as generic first-century men and women. It's as if I'm in a film with unrecognizable extras. That year, however, as I thought about this passage, into my mind came the faces of four real-life friends who were carrying me to Jesus. Three were Jesuits and one a layperson.

In real life, some of them don't know one another. In my prayer, I imagined introducing them to each other: "Do you know Kevin? He's a great guy: kind, sensitive, earnest. Do you know John? He's a terrific Jesuit: kind, prayerful, and hardworking. Do you know my friend George? . . ." It was a conversation between me and my real-life friends, in my prayer.

Then something dawned on me. Not only do I have good friends, but I also have friends who are good. In other words, my "good friends," in the sense of close friends, are also "good friends," in the sense of good and holy people. Had you asked before my retreat if my friends were good people, I would have said, "Certainly!" My friends are a signal blessing in my life. But perhaps because it was revealed to me in a new way, during an unusual experience in prayer, it sank in as never before: my friends are good and holy people.

Then, as I was thinking about them, many other friends, women and men, started to fill the scene. They were part of the larger crowd who were listening to Jesus. All the faces of my friends turned to me, and I saw that they were good too. So many friends who are good. Grateful for my friends, I realized how blessed I was.

Why am I recounting this? Because although I was grateful for a new awareness that was tremendously meaningful, I felt little emotionally. A lump didn't rise in my throat, nor did tears fill my eyes. Nor did I feel any excitement. My heart didn't skip a beat. Although I was aware of being thankful and aware that this was a new realization, it was primarily an intellectual experience: I came to know something. It was an *insight*, another important way that God speaks to us in prayer.

Let me share something about that same retreat: I was discouraged that I didn't cry. For those new to the spiritual life, being disappointed about a lack of tears may not seem odd, but in most previous retreats I had at some point been so deeply moved that I wept. It's a beautiful gift to be so touched by something in prayer that one has the "gift of tears." In the spiritual life, people tend to privilege emotions over all other responses. If you don't feel something emotionally, the thinking goes, then it isn't a real spiritual experience.

Yet that no-tears retreat was satisfying nonetheless, because it was filled with insights. Insights in prayer can be as important and transformative as emotions. And for people whose personalities are less emotive, this may be the primary way that God is revealed to them.

Recently, a friend told me that she was prayerfully reading a passage in a spirituality book that talked about helping the poor. The book mentioned that there were many types of poverty beyond material poverty: the poverty of loneliness, the poverty of anxiety, the poverty of fear. She said that it unlocked a side of Christian charity that she had never thought of before. When she recounted this story, her eyes widened, an unconscious sign of this insight.

That insight could help my friend live her Christian life in a new way. Thus, we need not denigrate it because it is unemotional. Insights are one of the primary ways that people learn. It may take time and effort to incorporate them into our lives, but they are essential.

After all, not all of Jesus's teachings would have evoked shouts of joy or buckets of tears among the people of first-century Galilee or Judea. When he was sharing a parable with the disciples, their first response might have been deep thought, which perhaps led to insights rather than emotion. One of the most famous definitions of a parable, in fact, comes from New Testament scholar C. H. Dodd. A parable is a story or tale from nature or everyday life that so arrests listeners with its strangeness or vividness that it "teases" the mind into "active thought."[7] Though the two are not mutually exclusive, for Dodd a parable is more about thinking than feeling.

Another insight that occurs in prayer is an answer to a thorny question. We come before God confused or disturbed about something. We can't see a way forward. Now, there is a Jesuit tradition of prayerful decision-making known as "discernment," but there are also times when something just clicks.[8]

One morning, several years ago, I was frustrated by something going on in my Jesuit community and was mulling it over in prayer. The Jesuit superior, the person in charge of the house, was planning to do something I strongly disagreed with, and I wasn't sure what to do. For days I had been stewing about it. Suddenly something obvious came to me: *If I just tell him what I'm thinking, I will have gotten it off my chest and can accept what he decides and move on.* It wasn't a life-changing insight, but it helped me see a path that I couldn't see before. And I trusted it particularly because it happened in prayer.

You may also be graced with an insight about God. One of my earliest experiences in prayer was thinking about Jesus. When I was on my first retreat, at age twenty-seven at a Jesuit house outside Boston, the retreat director asked me this question: "Who is Jesus for you?" Having had no experience with this type of free-form prayer, I sat down on the broad green lawn and came up with some answers. Let's see, Jesus is the Son of God, Savior, Messiah, and so on. Suddenly I thought, *Friend.* I had never thought of Jesus as a friend before. It pleased me to think about this, but again there weren't any strong emotions. It was an insight, and one that changed the way I relate to God. I didn't break down in tears. I simply enjoyed the insight.

Memories

On a retreat a few years ago, I was wondering what was up with God. Plowing through the Bible passages assigned to me by my director, I was moved at times but also wondering about God's love for me. I had been experiencing grace in my prayer and in my daily life as well, but I still questioned God's love. That may sound ridiculous—after all, doesn't the experience of grace show that God loves you?

It does, but during my retreat prayer seemed, for want of a better word, impersonal. It was as if a friend sent a birthday gift with no note. Yes, that shows love, but it seems vague. At the time, my desire was to experience God's love for me, to hear God say, in a way, "I love you." Perhaps that sounds greedy, and perhaps it was. But at base was a sincere desire to enter into a deeper relationship with God.

After speaking to my retreat director, I decided to ask for something clearer. St. Ignatius often encourages us to ask for what we desire in prayer, while being willing to accept whatever we receive. In my next prayer period, then, I asked for the grace to see God's love for me. Out of the blue I had an odd memory.

I was in my childhood home on Christmas Eve, which was surprising because it was the middle of the summer and I hadn't been thinking about Christmas. When I was a boy, my family owned a tall candle in a glass that was brought out every year for Christmas. The ten-inch candle was nothing special; it probably cost a few dollars. On the outside of the glass, which was covered in sparkly dust that rubbed off a little each year, was the image of a red ornament hanging from the branch of a Christmas tree.

The candle was unpacked with the rest of our holiday paraphernalia in mid-December. Every night after dinner around that time of the year, the Christmas tree, electric candles in the windows, colored lights on the evergreen bushes outside our house, and the candle would all be lit. The candle sat atop our old Magnavox stereo system in the living room. Sometimes we would turn off all the lights in the house and "watch the tree." The only light in the living room came from the colored lights on the tree and the warm glow of the flickering candle.

Here's what I wrote in my journal, unedited:

> I remember such a feeling of warmth and of being loved by God. Very gentle . . . and a feeling of security and of being happy. It was very lovely and I saw this as one way that God loves.

Then, after that prayer period, grateful for the seeming response from God, I went on a bike ride on a perfect summer day. Later I wrote:

> I was coasting down the hill and felt the wind rush past my ears, and I was transported back to riding my bike to school

down the hill. And I could see and feel myself so clearly, in
my blue jeans and blue corduroy jacket and baseball cap, and
I felt an intense burst of love—for me, and God's love for me
as a boy. I was moved to tears. So strong and vivid a memory.
A real experience of God's love *for that boy, who I am.*

I share those experiences not because they are unusual. Memories
arise for many people in prayer, and my memories are no more important or interesting than anyone else's. Nor am I sharing them to
make myself out to be some sort of mystic, which I am not. I don't
have these experiences that frequently, certainly not with that level
of intensity. Rather, I'm sharing them to let you see how God can use
memories in prayer, in this case to remind me of God's love for me as
a boy, and God's love for me now.

Memories are among the most powerful spiritual experiences.
They can arise at any time, unbidden, as they did with me. I didn't
say, "God, please give me a happy memory," nor did I consciously
begin to think about my past.

Memories can also be bidden, as when you intentionally cast your
mind over a certain time in your life or try to remember a person, an
event, a place, or an experience in prayer. (Yes, you can even have a
memory of an earlier prayer.)

Often memories arise when meditating on a Scripture passage. If
you are thinking about Jesus feeding the crowds in the story of the
Multiplication of the Loaves and Fishes, you may remember a memorable meal in your life—on a birthday, an anniversary, a holiday—
when there was an unexpected bonanza of leftovers.

That may prompt you to think about how much fish and bread
was left over in the Gospel story—twelve baskets. You recall how
food from *your* memorable meal fed you for days and how you passed
it out to friends and family, neighbors and co-workers.

Then you start to think about the loaves and the fishes not simply as the physical food with which Jesus nourished the crowds, but as symbolic of his words as well. Jesus's nourishing, life-giving words would have been spread around too. And that starts you thinking about how you yourself spread Jesus's words around. "What am I doing," you ask yourself, "to give away Jesus's words?"

What has happened? The memory enabled you to see the passage anew. More accurately, God has raised up that memory to help you see more clearly what you are being called to do.

Memories may also be raised up in prayer to help you heal. Take the example of a memory of a great wrong that has been done to you, something that still causes you pain. Gerard Hughes reminds us, "We need to pray over these memories in order to be released from the stifling effect they are having on our lives, whether they have suddenly come into consciousness or have always been there." He suggests praying with various Gospel passages where Jesus heals someone.[9] (More about entering into Gospel scenes later on.)

Memories can also console you. One of the most common prayer experiences is a memory that encourages you during a tough time. If you are asking God how you can make it through a dark time, you might remember another difficult time that you survived. It comes back to you with new clarity: you recall the initial fear, who calmed you, and how you moved through the crisis.

What is God saying? It may be an encouragement that, as Blessed Julian of Norwich said, "All shall be well." It may be a reminder that the God who was with you in the past is still with you. "You got through that, didn't you?" you feel God saying. "Wasn't I with you? Why wouldn't I be with you now?"

Let's take another example. Say you are praying about being lonely. Suddenly you recall that last week a good friend emailed you out of the blue, just to say hello. You were so surprised. Yet you had forgotten about it until this prayer period. What might God be saying? Perhaps God is inviting you to notice less obvious signs of love or to appreciate signs of affection that you might otherwise overlook. Such memories are God's way of comforting you.

Childhood memories are frequent visitors in many people's prayer—and my own. Often on retreat I have a memory of a childhood experience in the natural world—mowing a lawn, walking across a meadow, exploring the woods near my house—that pops up in prayer. Sometimes it's clear what's going on, and the memory relates to what I'm praying about.

A helpful question to ask is "What occurs to me when I think about this?" This is one way to ponder what God might be telling you. You don't have to be a trained spiritual director (or psychologist) to get to the bottom of this. The connection between your memory and what you're praying about or what's going on in your life may be obvious.

Sometimes, though, it takes more reflection. It may be curious that God would bring something up that doesn't seem to relate easily to your prayer or your current situation, but sometimes the meaning will be revealed as you reflect on it over time, like a dream that makes sense only days later.

Or perhaps nothing occurs to you. In that case, it may simply be a gift. Why, on so many of my retreats, do I continually find myself on a particular patch of ground near my old elementary school? Often I imagine myself sitting in a clearing just a few feet from the school playground surrounded by tall dry grasses, watching the grasshoppers and crickets jumping from blade to blade. I have no idea where this memory comes from or what I was doing sitting in the weeds that day, when I was probably five or six.

I've come to realize that this may simply be a gift. Why should we always seek meaning or message in these memories, or indeed in the graces of prayer itself? Everything that happens in prayer doesn't have to "mean" something, "be about" something, or answer some question. It may simply be a gift. Why can't God simply give us a lovely memory?

It's like the old story I've heard many times about a composer, variously identified as Beethoven, Mozart, or Shubert. The composer sits down at his piano and plays a beautiful new song for a friend. When he has finished, his friend says, "But what does it mean?" In response, the composer plays the entire song again and says, "That's what it means."

Let me share a meditation that uses memories. It changed the way I look at transitions and may help you use memories to navigate a transition.

After my father died, my mother remained for another ten years in our family home. Eventually, she sold the home and moved to a retirement community, as I mentioned. As anyone knows, selling the home in which you had been raised is an emotional experience. Frankly, selling any house and moving in any way can be emotional. Recently I moved out of the Jesuit community in which I had lived for eighteen years, and that too was emotional. I shed tears as I closed the front door for the final time, knowing that even the sound of that door closing had become a familiar part of my life.

Saying goodbye to our family house was much sadder. It felt like part of my anatomy was being torn away. It was hard to believe that I would never again see the sights that I had known all my life: the view of the backyard from my bedroom window, the way the sunlight slanted into the dining room, the feel of the living room couch when I sank into it after a long day at school.

A few months after my mother moved into her new apartment, I made my annual retreat at St. Joseph's Abbey, a Trappist monastery outside Boston, during wintertime. My director was a former Jesuit turned Trappist, a good friend named Jim.

Around that time I had been reading a great deal about Jesus's house. In the Gospel of Mark, one passage speaking about Jesus in Capernaum remarks that he was, in the Greek, *en oiko*—"at home." It's not clear if that means in his home or in the home of another person, say, Peter. But it's possible that it was Jesus's home. (That same house is the one that the friends of the paralyzed man visit.) So I was captivated with the idea of Jesus's home. What would it have been like? Did people visit him there? Was it hard for him to leave? Did he bring anything from Nazareth to his home in Capernaum? The idea fascinated me.

But I was also thinking a great deal about my mother's home. So I was confused about what to pray on: Jesus's home or my mom's home. I asked Jim.

He stared out the window at the snowy landscape. Finally he said, "Why don't you invite Jesus into *your* home? Why not go through every room of your house together and recall what happened there? Happy occasions, the sad ones, events both big and small that you remember about that room. Start with your bedroom. And in each room, speak to Jesus."

Then something happened that sometimes happens in spiritual conversations: as soon as Jim suggested that prayer, I felt an urgent longing to pray it. That desire happens often on retreat, but also in regular conversation. Someone suggests a way to pray, mentions a Bible passage to pray over, or gives you a prayer that is already written, and you feel an urge to pray it *right now*. It's another sign of God's call. (More about desire in the next section.)

Jim's prayer was both easy and profound. It was no problem calling to mind what had happened in my bedroom—so much! In elementary school, sitting at my desk and doing homework, writing long reports, painting poster boards for class projects, and struggling over algebra homework, while I gazed dreamily out the window at the sparrows hopping around in the snow looking for food. In junior high school, gathering with friends and taping on a cassette player silly "plays" that we had written, some of which I discovered when I was cleaning out my mom's house. In high school, writing my college applications and wondering what the future would hold.

I remembered being sick. My mother bringing me chicken soup and crackers, my father bringing me little gifts when he came home from work, and being happy I could watch TV, but then being weirdly excited when my school friends brought me my homework to do. (Yes, I was that kind of kid.) In the wintertime, I would lie in bed listening to the world get quiet as the snow fell and wondering if school would be canceled the next day. And in the summertime I'd try to fall asleep early (my parents were sticklers for that) while it was still light outside and the older kids were still playing. All those memories—and that was just my bedroom!

In the meditation was Jesus, beside me in every room I "visited." I said, "Thank you," not only for the experiences themselves, but for his being with me. I saw difficult moments as well and felt Jesus's sorrow and concern. There were many tears.

As the meditation drew to a close (I was running out of rooms), I grew sad. I anticipated that at the end of the meditation Jesus and I would walk into the living room, then leave through the front door, and close the door. For good.

Then something surprising happened. As Jesus and I left the house, I noticed that the door was still open, and I had a wonderful insight: I could return to my house any time, in memory and prayer. It was so consoling. And unexpected. I don't think I could have ever said "goodbye" to my house in as fruitful a way as Jim had suggested in prayer.

Memory is one of God's greatest gifts, because it allows us to return to a past filled with grace.

Desires

"Pray for what you desire" is a frequent refrain among spiritual directors, especially those trained by Jesuits. Throughout the *Spiritual Exercises*, the classic text of St. Ignatius Loyola in which people are invited to imagine themselves in scenes from the life of Christ, re-treatants are invited to ask for the "grace" they desire in prayer.

In the first part of the Exercises, we ask for the grace to know ourselves as a sinner who is nonetheless loved by God. In the second part, we ask for an "interior knowledge" of Jesus, an intimate know-ing of him, as we follow him imaginatively through his birth, early life, young adulthood, and the whole of his public ministry. In the third part, when we imagine Jesus's crucifixion and death, we ask for sorrow for our sins. The fourth part of the Exercises focuses on the Resurrection.

In that final part, St. Ignatius suggests asking for something spe-cific in what he calls his "prelude" to prayer. It is a good example of the importance of desire in his spiritual worldview:

> It is to ask for what I desire. Here it will be to ask for the grace to be glad and to rejoice intensely because of the great glory and joy of Christ our Lord.[10]

At every stage of the Spiritual Exercises, then, we are invited to pray for what we desire. This practice flows in part from Ignatius's recog-nition that all prayer is a gift from God and that our desires can be holy.

Yet desire is somewhat disreputable in some religious circles. We are supposed to be freed from desires, aren't we? Aren't desires selfish?

Not necessarily. It's both natural and human to pray for what we want. How could anyone stand before God and *not* feel a longing to ask for the help they need?

So one kind of holy desire leads us to ask God for help, as St. Ig-natius has us do in the Exercises. Jesus himself emphasized this kind of desire during his public ministry. In the Gospel of Mark, Jesus meets a blind man named Bartimaeus, who is sitting by the roadside in the town of Jericho, waiting for Jesus to pass by. "Son of David," says Bartimaeus, "have mercy on me!" Jesus stops and asks the man, "What do you want me to do for you?"[11]

Notice that Jesus doesn't heal the man without asking him first what he wants—and obviously Jesus could see that the man needs help. Jesus asks him what he wants, it seems to me, for several reasons.

First, Jesus wants to know Bartimaeus. Rather than healing the man without engaging him, Jesus wants to make this into a genuine encounter. Their meeting is not simply an exchange: you ask me for something, and I give it to you. No, he wants to come to know the person, as in many other Gospel stories—for example, the one in which Jesus has an extended conversation with the Samaritan woman.[12]

Second, Jesus wants to afford the man dignity. Jesus does not impose himself on the man. He first asks the man what he desires.

Finally, Jesus asks the man what he wants because desires are important. Bartimaeus knew immediately what he wanted: he wanted to see. But for many of us, coming to know our deep desires is a lengthy process. Yet in naming our deepest desires we name the deepest part of ourselves, for our deepest desires are God's desires within us.[13]

There is another kind of desire, one that arises in prayer. This is not the desire that prompts us to pray or the desire that leads us to ask for things in prayer, but rather a desire that comes *during* prayer. Let's look at several kinds of desire that may arise in prayer.

A Desire to Be Closer to God

Perhaps the most common is a desire to live a more God-centered life. You may be reflecting on a Bible passage you've read, a homily you've heard, or a movie you've seen and feel a burst of desire for closeness with God. You wish that you were closer to God; you wish God were more a part of your life; you wish that you could feel God's presence more than you do. You feel an almost tangible longing for this kind of union.

What's going on? You're experiencing your deepest desire, which is to be in union with God. "You have made us for yourself, O Lord," St. Augustine wrote, "and our hearts are restless until they rest in you."[14] It's the most human of desires, manifesting itself in a longing, a feeling of incompletion, or a desire to be part of creation. Even though it may feel confusing, it's something to celebrate. But something else is going on: God is calling you.

What better way would God have of calling you than *placing within you the desire for God*? In my experience as a spiritual director, I have seen this as one of the most common ways that God calls people into a relationship. Once people are made aware of this phenomenon, it can be freeing, exciting, and sometimes overwhelming. The desire for God is God's desire for you. As the plaque on that retreat house wall said, "That which you seek is causing you to seek."

A Desire to Follow Jesus

The desire to follow Jesus Christ is more specific. It often arises while people are meditating on the New Testament. A few years ago, during a spiritual direction session, a young woman told me that when she thought about the scene in which Jesus called the first disciples and imagined Jesus saying, "Come and I will make you fishers of people," she imagined herself at a considerable distance from the four fishermen on the shore and felt a powerful longing to be in the group of soon-to-be disciples.

"It wasn't that I felt left out," she told me. "I just wanted to follow Jesus so much. I wanted to be a part of the group." I invited her to see this desire as the means through which Jesus was calling her.

The desire to follow Jesus takes many forms. First, you can be attracted to Jesus, find him appealing in all sorts of ways, and admire his compassion, freedom, and boldness. You want to be with him, even though you may not understand why. Don't worry: it was probably hard for the first disciples to understand why they were so attracted to the man.

Indeed, one of the constant themes of the Gospels is the personal magnetism of Jesus. Crowds follow him everywhere. When he preaches at his house in Capernaum, the crowds are so great that they block the entrance of his house. When he feeds five thousand people and sails to the other side of the Sea of Galilee, they follow him there.

And when he calls the first disciples, they follow him immediately. Why? They might have heard of him, heard of his miracles, or even witnessed some of his miracles. They might have found his preaching irresistible. They might have already encountered him in the company of John the Baptist (as the Gospel of John indicates). They might have been ready to turn their lives over to a religious leader. Or they might even have been young men who were bored with their lives as fishermen and might have seen this as an opportunity for an exciting new adventure. Remember, nothing in the Gospels suggests that the first disciples were old or even middle-aged men. Peter was (either then or at one point) married, but he could have married (and have been widowed) at an early age. But all the rest could have been young—teenagers even.

But I think something more was at work: it was *him*. Holiness is appealing. It is one way that God has of drawing us closer to the divine.

That may sound like an abstract statement until you recall times that you've been with people whom you considered holy. Think about what it was like to be in their presence, how you wanted to do nothing but spend time with them, listen to what they had to say, ask them for advice, look at how they lived their lives, and figure out how they could live so freely, so openly, so lovingly. Now think of Jesus and how much more people must have experienced this in his company. Jesus's own holiness must have been irresistible. This, in addition to the preaching and miracles, helps explain the crowds that followed him everywhere. Holiness attracts.

A Desire to Be a Better Person

When I have done something foolish, childish, stupid, or selfish, I reproach myself and wonder why I'm not further along on the spiritual path. If we're not careful, this feeling, itself healthy, can degenerate into crippling shame. Remember, guilt says, "I did a bad thing"; shame says, "I'm a bad person."

But the desire to become a "better" person, for want of a better word, is a desire that God plants in us to encourage our spiritual progress. It's a desire to be your "true self," as Thomas Merton and other spiritual writers have called it, the person God created, or what you might call your "best self," the person God intends for you to become. It's a delicate balance: recognizing your inherent goodness as you are, the person God created, and hearing the call to become the person you're meant to become. Sometimes you feel as if that other person—a freer, more loving, more joyful one—is within arm's reach. That's a call from God, an invitation to grow.

The desire to become a better person gets its motivation from both negative and positive sources. When we are made aware of our shortcomings and failures, whether by recognizing them or having someone point them out, we realize that we are not the person we think we are—or hope to be—and we know that we have to move in that direction. Or we can simply make a conscious effort to take steps to lead a more loving and generous life, confident that we can move closer to the life we want to lead.

But the original desire comes from God. Being the person you were created to be is God's desire for you. Why? Because God knows that being your true or best self is the state in which you will be most fulfilled as a person.

So when in prayer you feel a desire to progress spiritually, pay attention. Then take steps to become the person you want to be. First, act *as if* you were that person. The branch of moral theology known as "virtue ethics" and, earlier, the writings of Aristotle suggest that the most effective way to acquire a virtue is to start acting as if you already had that virtue. For example, if you're not naturally patient and need to grow in that virtue, start acting that way, and gradually you will become patient. The desire that becomes a practice will become a habit that will become a virtue.

A Desire to Emulate a Holy Person

While convalescing from the injury that ended his soldiering career, St. Ignatius (still Iñigo de Loyola) ended up in the family castle. Desperate for something to read, he opened a book on the lives of the saints. Not an especially religious man, Iñigo took up the stories about the saints mainly because there were no books containing the tales of chivalry that he preferred. As he leafed idly through the stories, he caught himself thinking, "What if I should do this which St. Francis did, which St. Dominic did?"[15]

Iñigo found himself attracted to the lives of two holy men, both founders, one of the Franciscans, the other of the Dominicans. There is some irony, of course. Here is someone with little religious background assuming that he could emulate two of the greatest of saints in Christian history. There is no little pride involved there—but God can use that too. Underneath the pride was something deeper—a desire to be like a holy person, which is another way that God calls us.

This call happens in many ways. You may be offered the opportunity to focus on certain aspects of holy persons. For example, you may meet someone who leads a holy life, prompting you to feel an appeal that may be hard to put into words. One of my Jesuit friends is a great guy: open, prayerful, free, loving, kind. One thing I admire about him is that I've almost never heard him speak ill of another person. Last year when I spent time with him and prayed about it, I felt a desire to be more like him in that regard. That's a holy desire.

You may also feel something more wide-ranging, a desire to pattern your whole life on that of a holy person. When I was twenty-seven and miserable working in the business world, I stumbled upon a TV documentary about Thomas Merton. Until then, I'd never heard of Merton and hadn't a clue what a Trappist was. The documentary, called *Merton: A Film Biography*, was so compelling that I found and read his autobiography, *The Seven Storey Mountain*. In that book, Merton tells the story of his own conversion, which caused him to leave a rather dissolute existence in favor of life as a cloistered monk.

His story hit me like a freight train. And my primary response was not that I wanted to join a monastery—even at the time it seemed a stretch for me—but that I wanted to be like Thomas Merton. He seemed to have lived such a purposeful life—fulfilling, satisfying, and happy. At least more fulfilling, satisfying, and happy than mine. Basically, I wanted to be more like him—in my whole life, not just a part of it. That led, eventually, to my entering the Jesuits.

Such desires arise in many ways in prayer, for example, when thinking about friends you know, people you've read about, or figures in the Bible. For Christians, it may center, naturally, in Jesus. In that last case you may not feel so much the desire to follow Jesus as to be like him. (The two are similar, but also different.) Overall, if your desires lead you to want to be a holier person, listen to them.

A Desire to Do Something

I should help those refugees! you think when you're praying. You can't get the story of a refugee child you saw online out of your head. You might ask yourself: "Why am I still thinking about it? I feel like I want to do something. But what can I do?"

When Jesus sees someone who is poor or struggling, the New Testament tells us that he "has compassion" or is "moved with pity." It's one of the most common expressions in the Gospels. The Greek word is *splagchnizomai*, which means, literally, that he was moved in his bowels. Jesus felt things in his guts.

After experiencing that feeling Jesus always *does* something. The Gospel of Matthew describes Jesus disembarking from a boat on the Sea of Galilee: "When he went ashore, he saw a great crowd; and he had compassion for them and cured their sick." Shortly afterward he feeds the multitudes with an abundance of loaves and fishes. His feeling of compassion and his desire to help translated into healing and feeding.[16]

None of us can do what Jesus did in that Gospel story, but we can pay attention to the desire to do something. This goes beyond emotions of sorrow over a person's plight and moves into the realm of action. So, if you are praying about the refugee child you saw on TV, and you feel a sense of urgency to donate money, to volunteer at a detention center, or to advocate, then *do it*.

How else would God's plans for the world be fulfilled other than by moving our hearts with desire?

Images

Not long ago, I moved into a new Jesuit community. The new community was a renovated former convent filled with recently purchased furniture. Our efficient Jesuit superior had arranged it so that, on the day we moved in, almost everything was in place. Despite those blessings, I found myself focused on a few small problems, which were simply part of getting used to a new place. But I couldn't get them out of my mind. For some reason, I was focused on the negative, unable to appreciate the new house.

The next day I prayed for the first time in our house chapel, a narrow, stark, elegant space with wide wooden benches lining both sides, high windows that let in the light from the street outside, and a polished concrete floor. The reading from the Daily Gospel was the one mentioned earlier: Jesus feeding the multitudes with the loaves and fishes. I was drawn to meditate on the reading, but also felt that I should bring to prayer my frustrations over the one or two small problems.

Then a strange image came to my mind. In my imagination I saw a cloth spread out on the ground covered with an assortment of foods, a kind of muslin cloth with plates and dishes full of food, a veritable feast set out in front of me. It came to me that I was being given in this new house a smorgasbord of wonderful things: a new clean space, a friendly community, a comfortable room, a good location, and, more to the point, something that many people in the world don't have: a house. It seemed a reminder not to focus simply on the parts of the smorgasbord that I didn't like, but rather to see the banquet that God was offering me.

Images can come to us in prayer unbidden. Like memories, they are ways that God consoles us. The image of a mentor, teacher, friend, child or grandchild, nephew or niece can delight us. A remembered glimpse of a physical place—the ocean last summer, a field we like, a favorite running path—brings us peace. The face of Jesus, a saint, or a holy person we knew may pop into our mind, or images that surprise us with their freshness.

A friend suffering from terminal cancer recently visited the French shrine of Lourdes. There Catholics believe that the Virgin Mary appeared to a young girl named Bernadette Soubirous in a series of apparitions beginning in 1858. You may be skeptical about "private revelations," but the church has approved pilgrimages there and has also authenticated dozens of miracles that have occurred there—using the careful records of physicians. In any event, even if you don't believe in the apparitions (I do, and have visited Lourdes many times), you can still appreciate it as a holy place where the faithful come to pray.

Carlos, who has since died, was there for an eight-day pilgrimage, sponsored by a Catholic charitable organization called the Order of Malta, which brings sick and suffering men, women, and children there to pray for healing, physical and otherwise.[17] A few days after he returned, Carlos told me of a surprising image he had there, which he described as one of the peak spiritual experiences of his life. Over lunch, he struggled to find the words.

"I had a strange image. I felt so close to heaven. You know the thin plastic wrap you use to cover food? You can hold it up and poke your finger into it and it will just stretch and stretch and get really thin around your finger. You feel like you're almost through, on the other side. You're not quite through, but you're almost there? That's how I felt in Lourdes."

I asked him what that image made him feel interiorly.

"New. Connected. Refreshed," he said.

Some images seem to come from nowhere and may seem like interruptions in prayer, but often they are ways God helps us get to the heart of the matter. As with memories, a question to ask might be, "What occurs to me as I meditate on this image?" Not every image that pops up in prayer is from God, nor does every image deserve our attention. If an image of a hamburger arises when you're hungry, it may be less from God and more from your stomach. As with everything in prayer, perspective and discernment are key.

Words

Yes, words arise in prayer. Not every word or phrase that pops into your head while you're praying is coming from God, however. And by the way, I'm not talking about *hearing* words in a physical way but rather intuiting them, having them enter your consciousness. This has happened enough times in my life, the lives of friends, and the lives of those who see me for spiritual direction that I trust it as authentic. But it is rarer than experiencing emotions, insights, memories, desires, and images.

It may be rare, but perhaps not so surprising. If we are thinking about God's communicating with us in prayer, why wouldn't God use words? Perhaps it doesn't happen frequently because even during prayer most of us are too self-aware to allow something as concrete as words to freely enter our heads.

Also, if we open ourselves to words, we can end up talking to ourselves. If we're seeking an answer to a specific question, like "Should I move to a new job?" we might be tempted to manufacture an answer ("Did I hear a yes?"), which would be incorrect to attribute to God. Overall, we're usually not free enough to allow God to speak to us in that way. Our desire for an answer usually gets in the way.

But occasionally we are free enough that God enters our consciousness with words or phrases that startle in their immediacy. To be clear, it's not that God can only do this when we are open. God can do this whenever God wants, but we are not always open enough to hear God so directly.

Many years ago, my mother told me that she was looking out the window of her house and asked God, "Do you love me?" Into her mind came the words "More than you can know."

Likewise, once on a group pilgrimage to the Holy Land, I was struggling with a difficult problem. One morning, I rose early to watch the sun rise over the Sea of Galilee. I decided to bring my cares to Jesus directly, as I gazed upon the ruins of Capernaum on the shoreline beneath me. Within just a few seconds of bringing Jesus to mind and thinking about this problem, these words came to me: "What is that to me?"

It was completely unexpected. Maybe because I was just starting my prayer, I was still free and unselfconscious. The words seemed blunt and direct, like many of Jesus's words in the Gospels.

Those words seemed to invite me to ask this question: "What is that problem when compared to your relationship with Jesus?" Likewise, what is that small problem compared to my vocation, which seemed spread before me, like the view of the Sea of Galilee, flushed in soft pink tones as the sun rose? What indeed was any problem compared to what Jesus offers?

The next day, on the bus another pilgrim told me that he had heard words in his prayer while our group was praying silently in the Garden of Gethsemane. Again, that "hearing" is not audible, but akin to recalling a line from a song or poem; the words just arrive and are felt or intuited.

After we returned to the States, when asked, my fellow pilgrim wrote me about that experience:

> In the Garden of Gethsemane, I was aware of Jesus's suffering and told him that I was often asking for things from him. What did he want from me? And I heard him succinctly answer, "Your prayers and attention." "Hearing" is problematic in such instances, as you know. I do recognize a voice other than my own, but it doesn't come through my ears.

To me, that sounded authentic. When speaking to my friend, I mentioned Vinita Hampton Wright's observation: God's voice has the "ring of truth."[18] It sounds like something God or Jesus would say.

How can we be sure that these words are coming from God and are not simply something we have manufactured? Well, we can never be 100 percent sure. But in my experience as a spiritual director these words or phrases often share certain characteristics:

1. *They are short.* The words are not usually a series of long sentences, but rather are aphoristic: "More than you know." "What is that to me?" "Your prayers and attention." My unprovable theory is that, since we are so hardwired to embellish and question, if these experiences were longer than a few words, we'd start to overthink them. Also, our openness to this kind of communication usually lasts only briefly. Once we become conscious of our thinking, our ego starts to get in the way.

2. *They are surprising.* They nearly always catch us unawares. When I was standing before the Sea of Galilee, I wasn't expecting anything. I didn't say in my prayer, "Jesus, talk to me." These moments surprise not only in timing, but in content.

Perhaps the most noticeable attribute is that these words do not seem to come from us. "There is no way," people often say, "that I could have come up with something like that." There is a sense that they come from outside of you; there is an otherness about them.

3. *They make sense.* The words fit your situation, the question that you've been asking God, or your needs at the moment. If someone else had heard the words I heard, "What is that to me?" they would have said, "Huh?" Granted, sometimes prayer is mysterious, but in the case of "felt" words, they usually make sense. And they are also true. My problems *are* nothing compared to my vocation. God *does* love my mother more than she knows. And God *does* want my friend's prayer and attention. They are both tailored to the situation and true. In short, they make sense.

4. *They get to the point.* A few years ago, I was praying with the passage in which Jesus is reading from the Scriptures in the synagogue at Nazareth. In essence, Jesus tells all who are assembled that he is the Messiah. In response, the infuriated townspeople boot him out of the synagogue, drive him to the brow of a nearby hill, and try to throw him off.[19]

In my prayer, I was wondering how Jesus could proclaim his

words so boldly to all the people in his hometown, when he could probably anticipate that they would find his words offensive. Were it me, I would be worried about what people might think. So how was Jesus able to be so free? Suddenly, I felt him say, clearly, "Must everyone like you?"

Generally, words that come in prayer go to the heart of the matter. In fact, in their directness, you could say that these words sound like Jesus. Now, the way Jesus "sounds" varies throughout the Gospels. In the Gospels of Mark, Matthew, and Luke, Jesus often speaks in punchy sayings or simple parables, while in John's Gospel he often talks in long-winded, oracular, and sometimes repetitive sentences. But often the directness of the words intuited in prayer puts one in mind of Jesus's short, pithy responses.

5. *They leave their mark.* If they are authentic, they strike your soul in such a way as to make an indelible impression. I've been thinking about the words "Must everyone like you?" for the last few years. It was probably the same with the disciples around Jesus, who never would have forgotten his words.

When hearing or feeling or intuiting words, these characteristics are helpful ways to discern if they are coming from God, or from you.

Feelings

Sometimes what arises in prayer is not a specific emotion, image, or insight, but a feeling—of calm, or peace, or a connection with God. Often this happens during a period of stress. You might be frustrated by something in your life, sit down and pray, and suddenly feel at peace. This is part physiological and part psychological. Taking a few deep breaths and sitting quietly helps anyone feel calmer. But it may be something more, a way that God is consoling and comforting you. After all, if you are stressed, what better way would there be? This makes sense. So pay attention to feelings of peace.

Other physical feelings are common in prayer as well. A friend told me that he was speaking to his young child and was amazed at feeling a physical "chill" that he attributed to God's presence. Here's how he described it to me:

> The "chill" is when you are feeling so much love for someone internally that it echoes through your body until it can be physically released, through hugs, a kiss, or words. It is truly the greatest feeling in the world, and I think it's God's way of sharing his own love with us. The other night, for example, after I tucked my eight-year-old son into bed, I was lying next to him, just talking. I forget the topic, but I began speaking about how much I loved him, how he is my friend, and how I will always be there to protect him. He was staring at me in the dark with a huge smile, exposing his cute front two half-teeth, and he reached his arms around me to give me as big of a hug as his arms would allow. That was when the "chill" surfaced. I think it happens just when I most need it.

Sometimes it's a feeling of "presence." Recently a woman told me that on the Christmas Eve after her mother died, she felt—"really felt," she said—her mother with her in the front row in church. A friend suffering from cancer told me that at one point during his treatment he experienced a great feeling of peace. He was sitting with a fellow cancer patient when he felt Jesus's presence, thought of the prayer of St. Teresa of Ávila that God has "no hands but your own," and felt a call to accompany his fellow patient.

At times, you may not even be able to describe what you are feeling. It may seem like a strange combination of feelings and emotions and memories and desires.

On a recent pilgrimage to the Holy Land I was praying at the Western Wall (sometimes called the Wailing Wall), the remnant of the wall built around Jerusalem by King Herod. As is their tradition, many Orthodox Jewish men were gathered to pray there, wearing their distinctive long black coats and hats. One of my fellow pilgrims was a Jewish scholar of interfaith relations, and so before our visit to the wall he explained to the group the wall's history and significance for the Jewish people.

A few minutes before, I had been telling my fellow pilgrims about one of my closest friends, Rob, who is Jewish. I had known Rob since college days and roomed with him in New York City after graduation; his parents and I were also very close.

During my theology studies in Cambridge, Rob invited me to a Passover seder at his family's home in the Boston suburbs. During the seder, his mother posed some informed questions about Jewish history mentioned in the Haggadah (the text that tells the Passover story): Why had Moses done this? What was the meaning of this phrase in the Hebrew Scriptures? What was Aaron's role? Miriam's?

At the time, I was in the middle of my Introduction to Old Testament course, so I was able to offer answers with alacrity. Those gathered around the table seemed surprised that I knew so much Jewish history. Rob's mom turned to him and said sardonically, "Why don't *you* know as much about Jewish history as your Catholic friend?"

After dinner, Rob laughed and said, "That's the last seder I invite *you* to!"

As I was telling my fellow pilgrims this funny story in front of the Western Wall, my cell phone buzzed. I quickly shut it off, for fear of giving offense to the people who had gathered at this holiest of

Jewish sites. Then, remembering that memorable seder, I went to the wall and prayed for my friend Rob and his family. I closed my eyes and touched the wall, and as I did, I had a strong feeling of the ancient nature of God. Old. Lasting. Enduring. Connected to the earth.

Afterward, I left our group and walked through the Old City alone. Wending my way over the slick limestones always puts me in mind of Jesus walking through the city with his disciples. Some of the most ancient stones, huge Roman paving stones, almost two feet wide, dated from the time of Jesus. Who knows whether he trod on them?

As I left the confines of the Old City and entered the more modern part of Jerusalem, I remembered that phone call. I checked my cell phone and listened to a message that had, despite the miles, gotten through. It was Rob telling me that his mother had just died. At the very moment that I was praying for Rob and his mother, he was calling with news of her death.

After I listened, I had a powerful feeling of God's presence, which I still find hard to describe. It was comforting, moving, frightening, confusing, mysterious, consoling, and hopeful, all at the same time. I called Rob, offered my love and sympathy, and then told him what had happened, which in the retelling seemed almost impossible.

The feeling I had wasn't emotional. It wasn't an insight. It wasn't a memory. It wasn't words. It wasn't a desire. It was a complicated and beautiful feeling that I'll never forget, but I can't describe it adequately.

Simply because you can't describe a feeling or experience in prayer doesn't mean that it's not real. St. Ignatius himself felt this. Fragments from his diary from 1544 indicate experiences in prayer that he found difficult to put into words. He wrote, "I cannot explain anything else of what happened,"[20] and "I felt or saw in a way that cannot be explained."[21] Often our experiences of God are so personal, so unique, as to be almost incommunicable to others.

Mystical Experiences

In prayer can come experiences of rare intensity in which we feel an almost overwhelming connection to God. These we call mystical experiences.

Experiences of this nature are often dismissed as privileges of the super holy, but they are not confined to the lives of the saints. Nor does each mystical experience have to replicate what the saints describe. In her book *Guidelines for Mystical Prayer*, Ruth Burrows says bluntly that mysticism is not the sole province of the saints: "For what is the mystical life but God coming to do what we cannot do; God touching the depths of being where man is reduced to his basic element?"[22] Karl Rahner's spirituality was often called "everyday mysticism."[23]

"Mystical" is hard to define with precision. One definition is the experience of feeling filled with God's presence in an intense and unmistakable way. Another is feeling "lifted up" from the normal way of seeing things. Yet another is feeling overwhelmed with the sense of God in a way that transcends your own understanding and even past experiences of prayer.

By their nature, these experiences are difficult to put into words. It's the same as trying to describe the first time you fell in love, held your newborn child in your arms, or saw the ocean.

During his time of meditation in the town of Manresa after his conversion, St. Ignatius described experiencing the Trinity (the Father, Son, and Holy Spirit) as three notes that play one musical chord, distinct but unified. Sometimes people find themselves close to tears, unable to contain the love or gratitude they feel. One young man described to me an experience of feeling as if he were a crystal vase so filled with God's love that it was about to overflow.

Although not commonplace, mystical experiences are not as rare as most would believe. Burrows writes that they are "not the privileged way of the few."[24] Such moments pop up with surprising frequency not only in the lives of everyday believers, but also in modern literature. In *Surprised by Joy*, C. S. Lewis describes an experience from his boyhood:

> As I stood beside a flowering currant bush on a summer day there suddenly arose in me without warning, and as if from a depth not of years but of centuries, the memory of that earlier morning at the Old House when my brother had brought his toy garden into the nursery. It is difficult to find words strong enough for the sensation which came over me; Milton's "enormous bliss" of Eden (giving the full, ancient meaning to "enormous") comes somewhere near it. It was a sensation, of course, of desire; but desire for what? . . . Before I knew what I desired, the desire itself was gone, the whole glimpse withdrawn, the world turned commonplace again, or only stirred by a longing for the longing that had just ceased.[25]

That's a good description of this desire for more. I don't know what a currant bush looks like, but I know what that desire feels like. It may be difficult to identify exactly what you want, but at heart you long for the fulfillment of all your desires, which is God.

This is closely aligned with the feeling of "awe," which the Jewish theologian Abraham Joshua Heschel identified as a key way to meet God:

> Awe . . . is more than an emotion; it is a way of understanding. Awe is itself an act of insight into a meaning greater

than ourselves. . . . Awe enables us to perceive in the world intimations of the divine, to sense in small things the beginning of infinite significance, to sense the ultimate in the common and the simple.[26]

In her book *Prayer*, Joyce Rupp describes an experience that happened "on a crisp early March morning" when she started out on her daily walk:

> I started up a hilly street. When I looked up, I gasped a huge "Oh!" There before me was the full moon, filling up the entire end of the street and sky before me. The round, shining moon looked like it was sitting on the ground. What I remember most is an instant sense of the "biggest love" I ever knew and a feeling that I could die immediately and be completely happy.[27]

Rupp said that this brief experience drew her closer to God throughout the day and, even today, as she recalls that time, it fills her with the feeling of the "great love." She has no trouble calling it a "mystical moment filled with an unexplainable intimacy," which draws us into "communion with divinity that is beyond our comprehension."[28]

Children and adolescents may be more open to mystical experiences than are adults. A few years ago a Jesuit told me that the eleven-year-old son of a friend had a rare experience during Mass. During the consecration of the Eucharist, an important moment in the Mass, he told his parents that he saw "light beams" coming down from the ceiling. "Doesn't everyone see that?" he asked his parents later.

Burrows wisely warns against making these rare experiences any sort of criterion of progress in the spiritual life. They should not "become the 'thing,' the sign of an authentic mystical life. The tendency will be for those not susceptible to be considered less spiritual, not contemplative."[29] If you have not had such an experience, it does not mean that you are an immature believer or a bad pray-er. Mystical experiences are not the *sine qua non* of the spiritual life.

In my own life I have had these experiences a few times. I've already described my experience in the meadow near my boyhood home. Let me describe another person's. Better yet, let me let her describe it herself.

The poet and memoirist Mary Karr recently shared with me a powerful experience she had on Christmas Eve at the Church of St. Ignatius Loyola in New York City. Mary agreed to write it down and did so in her inimitable honest, forthright, and earthy style. All you need to know is that Dev is her son; Sarah, his wife; and Father Joe and Father Feely, two Jesuit priests. Remember, unlike emotions, memories, insights, and the like, mystical experiences are rare, but they do happen. It's worth including a lengthy description of one, so that if you are ever gifted with one, it might not be so surprising, or even frightening.

I'll let Mary end this chapter on what can happen in prayer:

> The big thing to know is how tentative I felt heading over to Mass that Christmas Eve. I even almost didn't go. My longtime boyfriend and I had finally broken up a few weeks before, and it was Dev's dad's turn to have him that Christmas. So I was facing a solo holiday after a minor surgery. Dev and Sarah had slept over in case I needed help post-anesthesia. We'd had a ball, but as they pulled away from the curb Christmas Eve morning with their smoky-eyed little pit bull looking back at me through the rear window, I had to stop myself from lunging after the bumper.
>
> Usually, I'd have made plans with pals or booked volunteer work or gone to see my godkids in London or pals upstate,

but I'd expected to be down for the count. Instead, I was physically as strong as an ox but edging into that desolation I grew up in and that you know I so wrangle with. My closest pals were all away for weeks. I resolved to head to the family Mass at St. Ignatius, where I knew two friends, Jacqui and Antonio, were meant to show up with their sprawling brood.

It was an icy night. The wind swooped down those city canyons like a velociraptor, and I stumped across town turtled down in my biggest parka. I was glad when Antonio and Jacqui showed up early to help me save a whole pew for their family—boatloads of Italian/Jamaican cousins that year. The church was packed, and when the Mondas came in just as carols were starting, I got squeezed out of the pew and across the aisle.

Then a big family showed up, and the mother asked could I edge in so her husband could have the aisle. She wore a huge mink coat, had diamonds the size of Chiclets on her fingers, and stank of gin. As a sober person who once guzzled martinis, it was like sitting in a juniper forest or at a skid-row bar. I obliged but conceived a towering and irrational spite for this woman.

Just as the organ started "The First Noël," she started slurrily bitching at her husband. He always made them late. Their daughter was bringing her new beau, and they'd have to stand, and maybe they'd leave. He wasn't Catholic and blah blah blah. The husband was trying to smooth it over in whispers, but she ramped it up. I swear, it was like listening to my soused mother berate my long-lost daddy. My head started to spiral down that dark drain where I can only hear the bad news.

The church was all decked out, but it felt grotesquely lavish, those poinsettias piled up red as a stripper's lipstick.

All the gold ornaments on the altar seemed phony and monstrous compared to the humble Nativity. A few rows ahead, a young mother was gently trying to corral three red-headed kids under age four, and the foursome seemed to represent the animal urge to move and grasp and get. All of us are so futilely enslaved by ego and want, I kept thinking.

The drunk woman's daughter showed up to stand behind us (we were in the back row), and the parents rose to shake hands with the new beau. I briefly caught a glimpse of them. She was round-eyed and angelic looking, with long dark hair. But her fellow looked like a forty-year-old skinhead biker with crazy piercings and scary facial tattoos, including two tears coming out of one eye to mark prison stints. (Judge not, I now think . . .)

You see how insane I was going inside my dark skull. I actually started to cry, which embarrassed me, which made me cry harder. I picked up my purse, thinking I'd slip out. But I was hemmed in by that enormous fur lady, and the introductory rites were coming up.

So I started to pray. At first, I prayed to stop crying, but that made me cry harder. So I just decided to let it out, just feel it, soften around it. I let myself mourn for so many losses: my boyfriend and me, the schism with my sister, Father Joe, my poor drunk parents—even my marriage to Dev's dad.

Somewhere in that tidal surge of grief, I began to pray to Jesus. But not with words. This deep aching from the core of my rib cage just started to cry out to that sacred heart of his.

Around me, the chords of "O Come, All Ye Faithful" started, and the drunk woman's husband broke out in the most angelic-sounding tenor. It was one of those round-toned voices that just grab your solar plexus. People craned around at him—it wasn't just me who heard it.

And that's when the miracle happened. Nothing had externally changed, but it was like every molecule of my whole being altered. I wasn't in my own skull anymore. Inside went super still. Time itself stretched and slowed to this massive pause. I started looking as if for the first time. Something—somebody was holding me. And out of that embrace—the comfort and stillness of it—I started looking for the very first time.

Everything in the church went all sparkly, and the faces of people got super specific. I could see that every single one of us was made. Like, created, forged, formed by loving hands, planned, chosen, brought forth, nurtured, cherished. In a flash, everybody I looked at became a child. I didn't hallucinate a room of children, but every person my eyes settled on I could envision as a little kid—like, about age four or five—sentient but ignorant enough to be infinitely curious and awe-filled. I looked at that little red-haired family, and their restlessness wasn't ego-fueled despair but simple struggling life. It had much wonder in it. The mother seemed busy but brimful of love. Her toddler's sparse hair had been gelled into this adorable little spiked red faux hawk! But I could see her as a child too. This, I thought, is why God can forgive us everything, no matter what.

It went on for I do not know how long. But there were a lot of data points to it. A lot of stuff that kept popping up inside me. Like, the idea of incarnation filled me. When I'd meditated on it that fall (remember I was redoing the Spiritual Exercises with Father Feely), it had been pretty arid. I could simultaneously see baby Jesus curled inside that girl's belly. Being inside one moment, then slithering out between her legs onto a rough cloak. The great and magnificent God had become simple human mud, a mewling, hungry, shitting infant, entering our helplessness. Looking back, I now think of your idea that when we hurt and reach out from that deep pain, we become vulnerable before God, and in those broken regions we are finally broken open. He can finally get *in*.

The experience was so powerful and pleasurable and joyful that I contacted the surgeon the next week to ask whether any of the anesthesia I had taken could affect me psychologically or physically so many days later. He told me it was the good stuff—but not *that* good. It was also twilight sleep and supershort-acting anesthesia.

What I've set down feels so thin compared to how unfathomably vast the phenomenon was. I could hardly talk after. And outside everything stayed sparkly. The whole walk home. My head was completely devoid of thought. I was just being alive in a simple way. Back home, I fell on my knees and savored it all in a long meditation. And the next few days alone, which I'd expected to suck, became perhaps the most exalted period of my life. Very quiet and simple, but full of love for Him and all of us. Days of quiet followed. I remember trying to tell Dev and Sarah over New Year's, and while they believed me and didn't think me insane, their heads cocked like the pit bull's does when I talk to her.

What happened? they wanted to know. And I felt mute. The silence is the answer, the mercy.

II

How Do I Know It's God?

DISCERNING GOD'S VOICE

We've just looked at what can happen in prayer: emotions, insights, memories, desires, images, words, feelings, and mystical experiences. I hope that you can now better understand how God can communicate with you in prayer.

God's communication, however, doesn't come only in prayer. "By no means!" as St. Paul would say. God communicates with us throughout the day, which is one reason the examen is so helpful. We are invited to be attentive to all the ways God speaks to us— through relationships, work, reading, nature, and so on—not simply during time spent in prayer.

In fact, restricting God's communication solely to prayer or looking for God only during moments of prayer can short-circuit our spiritual life. Not long ago a young man who was discerning a vocation to religious life had a dilemma. During the past few months he had been enthusiastic about joining a religious order. For him, it had been a choice between marriage (or at least the possibility of marriage, since he was not in any relationship) and entering a religious order.

This process had happened gradually, without any "aha" moment in prayer. As my friend learned more about different religious orders and talked it over with friends, he began to realize how much he wanted to join. During one of our spiritual direction sessions he said, "Now I'm sure about this!" He saw this as a great grace, and it was.

But he was frustrated that he couldn't discern which religious order to join. Franciscans or Jesuits? He was even more frustrated that he didn't seem to be getting any clear answer during his prayer, no matter how "hard" he prayed. In response, I reminded him that the ability to make his first decision—whether to join a religious order at all—had not come through some special moment in prayer, but simply by reflecting on his everyday life and gradually coming to understand his desires.

This is often the case with those of us who pray. We get so focused on the fruits of prayer, as described in the previous chapter, that we forget to look at our "walking-around life." Often our decisions are revealed not all at once in prayer, but gradually as we go about ordinary life.

Still, since this book is on prayer specifically, let's look at an important question: "How do I know what's coming from God and what's coming from me?"

In the previous chapter I offered a few ways of discerning if the words intuited in prayer might be coming from God. Yet that discussion related mainly to the specific and rather rare experience of words or phrases. What about the other experiences in prayer? Emotions, insights, memories, desires, images, feelings, and so on? How do I know if their source is God, or me?

A few years ago, as I mentioned, I was invited to help Martin Scorsese and his creative team on the film *Silence*, based on the novel by Shūsaku Endō, about seventeenth-century Portuguese Jesuit missionaries in Japan. The film starred Andrew Garfield and Adam Driver as Fathers Rodrigues and Garupe, Jesuits tasked with searching for their mentor, Father Ferreira, played by Liam Neeson. (In my discussions with Mr. Scorsese and his co-screenwriter Jay Cocks, we decided that, even though it wasn't in the book, Neeson's character had been at one time their spiritual director.) But Father Ferreira has publicly renounced the Catholic faith, a move that sets in motion the entire film.

For much of the film, Rodrigues and Garupe hide from the Japanese authorities, but are eventually captured and tortured. (Christianity was illegal at the time in Japan.) Throughout this ordeal, Rodrigues suffers from a great spiritual dryness; he does not feel God in his personal prayer, though he sometimes sees signs of God's presence in his ministry among the Japanese people. (This is one of the multiple meanings behind the title of the novel and the film.)

At a critical point, after an extended period of grueling questioning and physical torture, Rodrigues clearly hears the voice of Jesus asking him to do something shocking: to step on an image of him—that is, an image of Jesus. (Stepping on the image represents "apostasy," publicly renouncing his Christian faith.) In order to dramatize the scene, the voice is heard on-screen.

In response to the voice, Rodrigues assents to what the voice asks and tramples on the image, thus denying his faith. Earlier he had been presented with a terrible choice: either he renounced his faith or Japanese Christians would be tortured and killed.[1] This was Rodrigues's dilemma throughout the film and another reason why

God's seeming silence tormented him. Stepping on the image meant symbolically rejecting the most important person in his life, Jesus.

After the film's release, I was on a panel discussion where a questioner asked something that many moviegoers were asking: How did Rodrigues know that it was the voice of Jesus?

My answer was twofold: one cinematic and the other spiritual. (Martin Scorsese might disagree with that dichotomy!) First, cinematically, as I saw it, the film intended the audience to understand it as the voice of God. In other words, it's presented in a straightforward manner. Rodrigues looks at the image and then he hears Jesus's voice asking him to do something that seems completely contrary to his faith, to trample on it.

From a more spiritual and perhaps subtle point of view, I responded that Jesuits are trained to recognize what is coming from God and what is not, a practice known as "discernment." Does this mean that every Jesuit can always tell what is coming from God in prayer and what is not? No. Clearly there will be mistakes, because we are human. But does this mean that over the course of a lifetime people can grow in their ability to recognize the voice of God? Yes.

So my response was that over the years Father Rodrigues had learned how to recognize God's voice in his own life. So if he had no reservations, we can take the command, at least in the film, to be what Jesus had asked of him, strange, confusing, and offensive as it may have seemed to the character—and to viewers.

But let's bring that question from the world of film to our own spiritual lives: How do we know, as I once asked my first spiritual director, that it's not all in our head?

First, a theological consideration: God's communication with us is always mediated, at least on this side of heaven. In other words, we are never speaking to God face-to-face. Why? For one thing, we would no doubt be incapable of bearing it. As God says to Moses, "You cannot see my face; for no one shall see me and live."[2]

Rather, God's voice comes through various media—through prayer, though the sacramental life, and through the events of our daily lives. On a more fundamental level, God's voice comes to us through the processes of our minds. Thus, to ask if it's God's voice or my voice begs the question: How else would God speak to us other than through our own consciousness?

Leaving behind such fine theological matters, when I ask, "Is it God's voice or my voice?" most people know what I mean. There is a difference between daydreaming and intuiting God's voice, between a random coincidence and God's activity, between God's voice and our voice. Yes, sometimes these things overlap, and it's hard to distinguish between them. But God's communication is always mediated through our consciousness. This means that if we don't grasp some essential differences, we run the risk of thinking that everything that pops into our heads is God's voice, when that is assuredly *not* the case.

Sometimes God's voice is obvious. In fact, sometimes God hits you over the head with a baseball bat. Maybe I should use a gentler metaphor, but at times God's voice seems unmistakable.

God's Baseball Bat

A few years ago on a retreat at the beautiful Linwood Spiritual Center in Rhinebeck, New York, I was praying with the Gospel passage in which Jesus asks the disciples, "Who do people say that I am?"[3] With this mysterious question Jesus seems to be trying to ascertain whether the disciples understood his identity, or his mission, or both.

The disciples answer as follows: "Some say John the Baptist, but others Elijah, and still others Jeremiah." That's probably a fair summary of what people in first-century Judea and Galilee were saying about Jesus. Finally, Jesus says, "But who do you say that I am?" Peter responds, "You are the Messiah." Jesus declares Peter "blessed" for understanding this.

It's a familiar passage for anyone who has ever gone on a retreat. Spiritual directors will often say, "Imagine Jesus asking *you* that question: Who do you say that I am?" And when people meditate on that question, they discover new ways to think about Jesus. But on this retreat my director said something unusual. After having me pray with that question and hearing my response, she told me to ask *Jesus*, "Who do you say that *I* am?"

That was new. During my next prayer period, I imagined myself with Jesus and asked him that question. Then . . . nothing.

Sometimes that happens in prayer. Nothing. Or at least nothing *seems* to happen. Your mind wanders, you can't concentrate, you're distracted. And even in those moments when your mind is focused, you can concentrate, and you're not distracted . . . silence. I listened to the clock ticking in the retreat house chapel for a long time.

At times the silence is easy to accept. You can say, "That's okay, it doesn't bother me too much. I'll just rest in the silence, knowing that God is with me."

But sometimes—when you feel the need for God's presence, when you are desperate about a situation, or, as here, when you ask for an answer to a specific question—accepting the seeming silence is more difficult. This was the reason for Father Rodrigues's torment in the film: he wanted an answer. Sent on an arduous mission to find his mentor and after his own capture and torture, Rodrigues pleaded for some response from God.

For several prayer periods I asked my own question and waited. I'm not comparing my situation with that fictional Jesuit's awful torment, only saying that I was praying for an answer. After two days of prayer, I gave up. Maybe Jesus didn't want to tell me "who I was" to him. Maybe it was presumptuous. Despite my belief that God wants to be our friend, I sometimes still feel guilty asking Jesus for answers.

That evening the retreat house was going to hold a reconciliation service in the chapel. It was not going to be the traditional kind in which a priest offers the sacrament of reconciliation (or confession); that was offered earlier in the week. Rather, it would be one in which the retreat leader read passages from the New Testament, another spiritual director offered a reflection, and a quiet time followed during which the retreatants—there were about fifty of us—could meditate on our need for forgiveness. An informal ritual in which we prayed for one another silently would close the service.

In the center of the main aisle was a single chair. At the end of the service, we were each to sit in the chair and wait for someone to come up to us, place their hands on our shoulders, and pray over us. It seemed hokey, but after a few minutes of watching retreatants take tentative steps toward the chair and sit, and other retreatants stand and place their hands on their shoulders, I found it moving. It wasn't choreographed; people rose when they felt moved to sit in the chair or "lay on hands" and pray. It was all done in silence.

As I thought about my need for reconciliation, I wondered again why Jesus hadn't responded to my prayer. At some point, I saw an elderly woman with a kind face get up and sit in the chair. As prescribed, I went up to her, placed my hands on her shoulders, and prayed that God might help her. Then she and I switched places. I sat down in the chair, and she stood up and positioned herself behind me.

After placing her hands on my shoulders, she surprised me by bending down. She leaned in close, almost touching my left ear, and started to whisper. *What is she doing? We aren't supposed to say anything*, I thought.

She whispered, "Know that you are God's beloved son."

It nearly knocked me out of the chair. No one else, as far as I could tell, had said anything to the person in the chair. She stood up, and I returned to my seat, slightly stunned.

I knew that I was God's beloved son. We're all God's beloved sons and daughters. But this was a different way to hear it: clear, direct, vivid, surprising. I felt God's love not only in the content of the message, but in the way it was delivered.

Like the words that we intuit in prayer, this was to the point, unexpected, and true. When I asked the question, I think I expected God's response to be, "You're a Jesuit," or "You're a priest," or "You're a Christian." But this was even simpler: "You are God's beloved son." Resonances with Jesus's baptism also came to mind: "You are my Son, the Beloved; with you I am well pleased."[4] Although I'm obviously not the Father's beloved son in the same way Jesus is, it still made me feel close to Jesus. When I told my spiritual director, she smiled and nodded. "That's wonderful! And it's true too!"[5]

Sometimes God is clear. You would have to work hard to deny that this was God's voice. It was true, was clear, made sense, came as answer to a prayer, and was not something I had manufactured. But sometimes God is not so clear, especially in personal prayer. So how can we tell?

Discerning the Spirits

A good place to start is, as ever, with Father Barry. In his article "How Do I Know It's God?" Barry turns to the insights of St. Ignatius Loyola, who himself had to discern what was coming from God and what was not.[6] In St. Ignatius's worldview, the question was not so much what is coming from God and what is coming from me, but something more serious: What is coming from God and what is coming from the "evil spirit"?

Coming across the term "evil spirit" may be a surprise. It can be either frightening (you think about being "possessed"), off-putting (you roll your eyes), or confusing (you have no idea what I'm talking about). Nonetheless, it's an important part of the way to discern God's voice in our lives. So let's briefly discuss what St. Ignatius means.

Opposing forces are always at work within us. Some forces come from God, and some do not. Most of us know this from experience. Basically, we feel pulled between good and evil, between hope and despair, between selfless and selfish impulses. All of us have felt this, sometimes in subtle ways, sometimes in overt ways. St. Ignatius understood that with practice we could learn to distinguish between the two "voices," one coming from God and one not, and in this distinguishing, which he called "discernment," we could begin to learn God's desires for us.

But what is the other "voice"? St. Ignatius calls it the "evil one," the power that moves us away from God. Is this to be identified with Satan? In my estimation, yes. Ignatius also calls this the "enemy of human nature." Today Jesuits generally call it the "evil spirit."

That may sound antiquated and alarming, conjuring up images from films like *The Exorcist*, but it's essential to the Christian worldview. And all of us have felt from within the pull toward selfish motives, uncharity, and evil. Moreover, we can see what happens when we give in to those impulses.

These impulses have certain identifiable qualities, which we can learn to recognize. St. Ignatius says that the evil spirit often acts in three ways in our interior lives. First, it acts like a *spoiled child*. The petulant, childish, selfish voice that says, "I have to have this *now*!" or "Why isn't everything going *my way*?" is not coming from God. Nor is the voice of the *false lover*, which encourages us to keep our sinful attitudes secret. No, says Ignatius, inclinations that would lead to sin need to be brought into the light. As the Alcoholics Anonymous saying goes, "We're only as sick as our secrets." Finally, the evil spirit acts like a *military commander*, trying to find your weak spot and catch you "off guard." Think of yourself as a castle under attack from an enemy commander who is trying to locate the weakest part of your defenses.

It's important to put the discernment process in perspective. Not every impulse is a temptation from the evil spirit and not every decision or act of discernment means that if you choose the "wrong thing," you're going to hell. Better to say that there are different forces working on us (and in us) that pull us different ways.

Full disclosure: I believe in the existence of Satan. I've had enough experiences in my own life and have seen the way the evil spirit works in other people's lives to confirm St. Ignatius's three "ways." They're easy to recognize once you start paying attention. And they're like the wind: you can see the effects. As C. S. Lewis said when asked about believing the devil, "I'm not particular about the hoofs and horns, but yes, I do believe."[7] And I believe that this force without hoofs and horns moves us to do things contrary to God's desires for us, contrary to our well-being and that of humanity. Follow the wrong voice, and you may end up causing harm to yourself or to others, or even to humanity.

If you don't agree with me or if your conception of the evil spirit is vaguer, you'll probably still agree that there is a definite force that pulls you away from God. Or a "voice," if you want to look at it that way. Ignatius's insight is that we can learn to recognize that voice and see it in contrast to God's voice, the voice that we want to follow.

Those voices move us in different ways, depending on whether we are trying to lead a moral life. They will sound different to a person leading a good life than to one leading a not-so-good life. Father Barry writes, "The first rule of thumb is that one should look at one's ordinary orientation with regard to God and to one's life as a Christian. Do I try to lead a good Christian life?"[8] That will influence how God's voice sounds.

At first this may sound confusing, but upon reflection you can see that it makes sense. If you are leading a good life, then God's voice will act quietly, gently encouraging you to continue along that good path. St. Ignatius has a beautiful image for it—it will act like a "drop of water on a sponge," gently and quietly. Encouragement takes this quiet and gentle form.

Discouragement, however, takes the opposite form. The evil spirit, who wants to lead you away from the good path, will try to disquiet you with "gnawing anxiety," "setting up obstacles" for you and generally acting like a "drop of water on a stone," which has a noisy and almost violent effect.[9]

George Aschenbrenner offers a good summary of what listening to the "good spirit" meant in the life of Ignatius:

> Whenever he found interior consonance within himself (which registers as peace, joy, contentment again) from the immediate interior movement and felt himself being his true congruent self, then he knew he had heard God's word to him at that instant.[10]

It's not only congruence with yourself, but congruence with God, because you are on the right path. It feels right because it is right. It's not as if God zaps you with a certain feeling. Rather, because you feel in sync with God's desires for you, you feel a sense of rightness.

That may sound abstract, so let's take an example. You are a good person trying to move closer to God. When you pray, you feel a sense of comfort and peace. You love praying, and it seems that God is encouraging you to lead an even more prayerful life. When you think about devoting yourself to praying more, spending more time in spiritual reading, perhaps seeing a spiritual director or going on a retreat, you feel a sense of calm, of peace, of rightness. It's pretty clear that this is God's voice, gently encouraging you to continue.

Now let's assume that you are moving toward a life of working with the poor. Suddenly in prayer you seem to hear a disturbing voice saying, "Are you *kidding*? You think you're so great? Who are you, Mother Teresa?" It's like someone's trying to push you off balance. This is probably the voice of the evil spirit.

By contrast, let's take a person who is cutting corners morally and going in the opposite direction, from bad to worse. In this case the evil spirit, paradoxically, chooses encouragement, gently urging the person to continue the bad behavior. Barry gives the example of a landlord gouging his tenants. The evil voice says, "These tenants are a lazy lot anyway; at least you're giving them a roof over their heads." Here the evil spirit is the drop of water on a sponge, gently encouraging this man, "It's not so bad. Go on."

St. Ignatius offers a marvelous image of why he thinks this is so:

> The reason for this is the fact that the disposition of the soul is either similar to or different from the respective spirits who are entering. When the soul is different, they enter with perceptible noise and are quickly noticed. When the soul is similar, they enter silently, like those who go into their own house by an open door.[11]

Gradually, the good spirit will move in and work through this man's conscience. It will alarm him, perhaps wake him up at night, and make him think, "What am I doing?" So now it's the *good* spirit that acts like the drop of water on a stone. "Wake up!" It's up to the man to listen. Sometimes people in those situations are so dead to the voice of their conscience that they are unwilling, or unable, to listen. Father Barry sums it up succinctly: "If I am not in tune with God in my life, I can expect that God will try to get me to change my life; I will feel pangs of conscience or concern."[12]

For most of us, those wanting to lead good lives, the voice of God will most often be a voice of comfort and consolation. The evil spirit will be the one that worries us, causes us anxiety, and moves us to despair.

Overall, it's important to see that God wants us to live happy and healthy lives, which is one reason God is speaking to us. God is trying to move us closer to happiness. Barry writes:

> God wants us to be happy and fulfilled. But the only way we can be happy and fulfilled is to be in tune with God's desire for the world and for us. For those who are trying to lead a life in tune with God's intention, consolation is the order of the day for the most part. This does not mean that life will be without pain and suffering; it means that God wants to be a consoling presence to us even in the inevitable pains and sufferings life has in store.[13]

God's Voice and My Voice

We now have some good rules of thumb for helping us see what is coming from the "evil spirit" and from the "good spirit." But what if it's a voice that's coming from neither? What if it is our *own* voice? How do we tell what is coming from God and what might be simple wish fulfillment, daydreaming, or a manufactured idea of God's will? Our own voice may not be anything evil, but it may be extraneous.

Not long ago a woman came to me for spiritual direction. As most spiritual directors do, I started by setting out some guidelines: how often to meet, what times, what direction will entail. Then I asked her what she hoped for in spiritual direction. The first thing she said was "I want help in understanding what's coming from God and what's coming"—she pointed to her head—"just from *here*."

These are difficult questions, sometimes not covered in books on spirituality. But they are essential because, as this woman realized, not everything that pops into your head comes directly from God.

Let's say you're praying about the Multiplication of the Loaves and Fishes, the Gospel story in which Jesus feeds an immense crowd with only a few loaves and fishes.[14] You reach the phrase "loaves and fishes," and the word "fish" hits you. You remember a bad meal you had last week at a seafood restaurant. You're still not sure if it was food poisoning, but it definitely came from that salmon mousse. Your mind wanders, and you promise yourself never to return to the restaurant. After a while you think, *What is God telling me? Am I not supposed to follow Jesus? Is following Jesus going to make me sick?* You're not agitated, but you start to wonder about the meaning of this.

In response I would say that it's probably something that just popped into your mind and there may not be any deep message here. It's most likely a distraction.

Now imagine that you're praying with that same passage, and something different comes up. You have a desire to sit down and eat with Jesus. Not simply out of physical hunger, but out of a desire to be with him. You imagine how good it would be to spend time with him, as a companion. You've never thought about what it would mean to eat a meal with Jesus, and then you have a memory of eating with your beloved grandfather when you were younger. He was always so kind and listened so attentively to you, as if you were the only person in the world, even though you were just a child. He made you feel special and loved. You see him as a real wisdom figure. Strangely, you start to think of Jesus in the same way that you do your grandfather—someone you would want to spend time with, someone who loves you.

That second memory sounds different from the first, doesn't it? What distinguishes the two? How can I discern what's coming from God and what's coming from me? What's a distraction and what's not? Or maybe a better way to put it is: What should I pay attention to?

Let me be clear: there is no one way to discern these things, and what I offer here are only a few questions to ask in these situations, which I've found helpful in my own life and in helping others in their discernment.

1. *Is the evil spirit involved?* Let's return to your getting sidetracked by a thought about that bad fish. If that causes you anxiety, disquiets your spirit, or moves you away from your prayer, it may indeed be not simply a distraction, but the evil spirit trying to move you away from God, or more precisely the evil spirit using the distraction to do so. The last thing that the evil spirit wants is for you to get closer to God. Even using a piece of fish will do, for its purposes.

Likewise, you could be thinking of following Jesus and then start to think, *If I follow him, I'll probably have to work with the poor, and then I'll get sick! Just like when I ate that fish.* That's clearly not coming from God either. Generally speaking, as we know, the evil spirit tries to move someone toward either evil purposes or, initially, a feeling of despair and hopelessness.

According to Ignatius, in a good person the evil spirit seeks to

> ... cause gnawing anxiety, to sadden and to set up obstacles. In this way he unsettles them by false reasons aimed at preventing their progress.[15]

A simple way to understand it is that if you are feeling despair, hopelessness, or uselessness, this is not coming from God, because, as Ignatius understood, these feelings lead to the "prevention of progress" in life.

Also beware of the "universal" language usually characteristic of despair, especially when coupled with negative statements about yourself. Anytime you find yourself saying things like "*Nothing* will ever get better," "*Everyone* hates me," "*No one* loves me," "I'm *always* failing," or "I'll *never* be able to change," it's usually a sign of the presence of the evil spirit. Catch yourself when you use those universal terms and try not to listen to those impulses.

By contrast, says Ignatius, the good spirit, the spirit that leads to God, is one that acts as follows:

> It is characteristic of the good spirit to stir up courage and
> strength, consolations, tears, inspirations, and tranquility.
> He makes things easier and eliminates all obstacles, so that
> the person may move forward in doing good.[16]

The evil spirit can be recognized when you feel despair, the good spirit when you feel hope. When you are trying to discern what is and what is not coming from God, this is a good place to start. Let me give you an example from my own life.

For some time as a young man I struggled with a mild case of hypochondria. It was not debilitating, but it made me overemphasize physical problems and be overly fearful of getting sick; in the process it led me to focus on my own well-being in a selfish way.

Twenty years ago I was slated to have some surgery, which brought up a welter of emotions and triggered some hypochondria—and some "universal thinking": "This is the worst thing *ever*." "I'm *always* getting sick." "I'm *never* going to be able to get through this." But I also felt a pull in the other direction: toward greater freedom, toward a letting go of the overweening ego that always made me focus on myself, toward hope. In the midst of this I saw my spiritual director. So I laid it out in the form of a question.

"It's a new experience," I told him, "of feeling freedom and hope when it comes to illness. And yet I feel pulled back to the despairing feeling. And that feels like the evil spirit. But the more thoughtful, positive, hopeful feeling, even though it's new, seems as though it might be coming from God. That's a new place for me to live, but I'm wondering: Is that the good spirit?"

He practically leapt out of his chair and shouted, "Yes!"

When you feel despair, don't listen to it; when you feel hope, follow it.

2. *Does it make sense?* If I am praying during a difficult time in my life, and I spontaneously remember another time when God was with me during my struggles, perhaps I can see in that God's desire for me to trust. Or perhaps I have a memory of a place that brings me a great deal of calm, and I relax. This is one way that God has of calming us.

By contrast, if I am praying during a difficult time and remember an email that I forgot to answer, the thought may not be coming from God. In the context of what I'm praying about, it doesn't fit.

Remember, you want to know if it makes sense. Does it make sense that God would reach out to me and invite me to trust? Yes, that seems to make sense, or at least squares with what is going on in my life at the moment. Does it make sense that during a period of prayer about something serious God would remind me to answer my emails? Probably not.

3. *Does it lead to an increase in love and charity?* This standard comes from the Gospel of Matthew, in which Jesus says, "You will know them by their fruits."[17] God's voice can be known by its effects. If following this impulse leads to an increase in charity and love, then it's most likely coming from God.

Let's say you're praying about someone you dislike. Perhaps you're asking God for help in dealing with this person. Suddenly you get enraged by something that he has done to you. *Oh I would love to just punch him in the face!* you think.

My friend Vinita Hampton Wright offers a way of understanding these feelings. You would probably realize that even though you had that feeling during your prayer, God is not moving you to punch this fellow in the face. So you move from that initial desire to thinking about how you might confront him about some fault of his that drives you crazy. You might even pray about what you would like to tell him about his fault—to get things off your chest. That seems to make sense, so you might be tempted to think that God was behind it. "Yet upon further reflection," as Vinita told me, "you realize that the confrontation might be quite satisfying to you, but would probably not increase your love for this person, nor would it help move this person to change for the better—so, no increase in love or charity."

If an action doesn't lead to an increase in love and charity— somewhere—its impetus is probably not coming from God.

4. *Does it fit with what I know about God?* Does it fit with the God you know from Scripture, tradition, and your own experience? If you are a Christian, does it fit with what you know about Jesus?

God is not going to make you hate yourself or believe that nothing can ever go right again, because that's not the God of the Old or New Testament, that's not the God of church tradition, that's not the God revealed in Jesus, and that's not the God you know. God gives hope, not despair.

For many people God is manifested in a feeling of calm. As this happens for you, you can start to recognize what God "feels" like in prayer. St. Ignatius started to see that this was the way God worked in him. In a sense, you come to know God's voice, so that when you hear it again you can recognize it.

5. *Is it a distraction?* Sometimes it's obvious that a stray thought that comes into your head may not be from God. If you're praying, your stomach growls, and you think about having a nice hamburger with all the trimmings, that notion is probably not coming from God.

The more you pray, the more you'll be able to sift through distractions. Think of it as a conversation with a friend. If you are talking with someone about an important issue and you suddenly notice a spot on your shirt, get sidetracked, and start complaining that the dry cleaner ruined your clothes, you would realize that you're distracted.

It's the same in prayer. You can usually tell what's part of the conversation and what's not. Likewise, with practice you can tell when a distraction is an invitation to another, new conversation. (More about how to deal with distractions later).

6. *Is it wish fulfillment?* This is perhaps the most difficult question, and one not often addressed. How can you tell if it is what you *wish* God would say to you? This is where it's especially important to test things out. Sometimes what we want to hear is indeed what God tells us. If you're lonely, pray to God for consolation, and feel calmer, that is probably God. There is nothing wrong with getting what you want in prayer. This is not necessarily wish fulfillment; it is God giving you what you need.

By contrast, you need to be careful not to simply conjure up the response in prayer that you desire. The best antidote for this is patience, waiting for the time when God speaks clearly.

I was directing a young Jesuit who was thinking about leaving the order. This is an exceedingly difficult situation for some, especially when they have felt so clearly the initial call to religious life. (It's also a mystery why God seems to call people into the priesthood or religious life and then out of it.) The temptation for many in this situation is to leave immediately without any careful discernment—especially if they are leaving because they've fallen in love.

But in this case the person spent months patiently waiting for experiences in prayer that would confirm his departure, a process that began in earnest in October. I'll let him describe what happened several months later:

> The biggest moment came when I was on a retreat in January. I remember walking outside, just admiring the trees, and a moment came where I heard Jesus telling me that I am meant to spend my life with someone. The second moment came as I sat with Jesus along the river (probably in February), and I heard Jesus tell me that I will be a wonderful spouse and

father. All this came about after reading Anthony de Mello's book *Awareness* and freeing myself from the trivial things of the world. Only in doing so was I able to tune out the noise and really listen to the quiet voice of God.

In May, he left the Jesuits, confident that he had made a careful discernment.

Notice that it took him *months* to discern and to feel confident that this was God's path for him. Compare that to someone who simply closes their eyes and says, "Should I leave my religious order?" and then imagines God saying, "Yes!"

Often in these situations it takes time, and the way God responds is not the way that we would initially imagine God responding. Thomas Green writes, "If the prayer is authentic, God comes when I don't expect it, and sometimes when I would prefer God not come, so that I find myself not controlling the situation."[18]

7. *Is it important?* In my experience, God enters our prayer in these direct ways most often when there is an important matter at hand. This is not to say that God cannot enter into our consciousness whenever God wants or about any matter whatsoever. But *usually* (again, in my own life and in my experience as a spiritual director) if this entrance comes during a time of urgency, it can be taken as a sign of God's presence. In the example of the Jesuit discerning his departure, the two messages from Jesus were clear and, of course, very important.

Clear, Warm, and Assuring

Here's a story that my friend Wyatt, a former colleague at America Media and a recent graduate of Marquette University, shared with me. When I was writing this chapter, he happened to tell me this story about something he experienced when he was working with an aid agency in Haiti. He agreed to let me share it with you:

Standing in line at the Haitian bank is the purest test of patience I know. The security guard with a shotgun strapped across his chest says no cell phones. I jam my hands into my pockets. Some rules just aren't worth bending.

More than four months passed since I landed in Haiti, eager to work as a journalist. For years, I said my dream job was to be a human rights journalist. And now, I am.

Reality wasted little time burning up my ignorant optimism. My sister got engaged. Friends trained and completed marathons. There were first days of school, first days on the job, and first days of life. I was not there for those days. I am in a different country.

My journeys around the world—Italy, France, El Salvador, and India—taught me the importance of traveling to the margins, reporting the truth, and being a microphone for those whose voices are often suppressed to a whisper. I never doubt the importance of this work. What keeps me up at night is the toll it takes on those I love. My prayers fill with questions of whether I am doing more harm than good.

My thoughts swayed back to that question while I stood in the bank, hands in pockets. My fingers brushed the plastic cover of my passport. As a distraction, I flipped from the pages filled with stamps to the registration page. My eyes rested on the numbers beside my baby-faced, teenage portrait—the passport's expiration date.

A sense of warmth covered my body. A voice—clear,

warm, and assuring—cut through my clouded thoughts in a whisper: "You don't get to do this forever." That was it, but the voice brought a sense of comfort. My body relaxed. Clarity replaced my anxious thoughts.

I knew immediately that "this" was being able to travel, report from foreign places, and tell stories like those from Haiti. I knew immediately the voice came from God. He was saying I will not be able to travel and live like this forever, but this is where I am meant to be for now.

Wyatt is not a saint (yet), which means that he doesn't have complete access to God's voice. For that matter, neither did the saints. But if we work through the questions I offered earlier, I think we can see that it was authentic.

1. *Is the evil spirit involved?* There is no indication that anything in this prayer could come from anywhere other than God.

2. *Does it make sense?* It makes sense that God would encourage Wyatt to stay where he was initially drawn and where he can do good for the poor.

3. *Does it lead to an increase in love and charity?* Wyatt's presence will surely lead to more charity and love, and he himself, freed of the burden of wondering if he is in the right place, will be able to move ahead confidently.

4. *Does it fit with what I know about God?* God is consoling and encouraging and invites us to work with the poor.

5. *Is it a distraction?* Quite the opposite. It's an important insight about Wyatt's life.

6. *Is it wish fulfillment?* It could be, but given that it happened so spontaneously, it's unlikely.

7. *Is it important?* Yes, it affects the course of Wyatt's life.

Discerning between what is coming from God and what is not is more an art than a science. For the most part, what happens in prayer can be trusted as coming from God, because prayer is a time when we are attuned and attentive to God's voice.

These are not hard and fast rules, but guidelines to help you begin to understand that God can enter your consciousness at any time and in any way God desires. The key is using whatever form of discernment you find helpful.

What Comes from God

In her book *Close to the Heart: A Practical Approach to Personal Prayer*, Margaret Silf offers a slightly different approach to distinguishing between a prayer and a daydream. She offers three helpful insights:

> *What comes from God will last and will bring about real change within us.* It will change our perspective on things and become a part of our life. That's a sign of how deeply it hits us, and also how much we can say yes to that experience.
>
> *What comes from God has a peculiar characteristic of weaving itself, seamlessly, into our own personal experiences and our memories.* This is another way of saying that "God meets you where you are." There is the sense not only of God using your own history but also of using and drawing upon what is already there. As Silf writes, "There is a consistency between our own experience and God's self-revelation."
>
> *What comes from God will draw us closer to him and closer to one another.* Without a doubt, God's voice will lead us more and more toward love.[19]

In time, you'll learn to recognize the feel, sound, and quality of God's voice. And God will help you with this process. God wants you to hear that voice and will help you recognize it.

Kuja Hapa!

One of my goals in life is to be attentive to even the smallest hint of God's voice, and when I think of "recognizing" that voice, I remember my time in Nairobi.

When I worked in Kenya as a young Jesuit, I helped refugees who had settled in Nairobi to start small businesses and support their families. Many of the refugees made handicrafts—woodcarvings, paintings, batiks, dresses, and so on. Eventually we opened a small shop in a slum in Nairobi, where we sold these handicrafts and also met with the refugees and discussed their businesses. The neighborhood, called Kangemi, was semirural, near many small farms.

One morning, the Kenyan woman who worked with us came into my office and said, "Brother Jim, *kuna kondoo!*" I was still learning Swahili, so I wasn't sure what she meant. So she said it in English, "There are sheep!" I followed her out the front door onto the porch of our shop, where refugees were gathered and chatting away. On a small lawn in front of our house was a modest flock of sheep grazing placidly, while a Maasai shepherd, perhaps in his teens, wearing the traditional red and black plaid cloth, watched them. I figured that there was nothing wrong with their grazing there, so I let them graze and went back into my office.

An hour or so later, after meeting a number of refugees, I returned to check on the progress of the sheep. The Maasai shepherd smiled and waved to me, apparently grateful that his flock could graze there. Then he said to the sheep, *"Kuja hapa!"* (Come!)

The sheep instantly raised their heads from the grass, looked at the boy, and started toward him. Now, there were many other voices at the time—the refugees on our porch chatting, people passing by on the dirt path, stray voices carried on the wind—but the sheep recognized *his* voice alone.

Naturally I thought of these lines from the Gospels:

The gatekeeper opens the gate . . . and the sheep hear his
voice. He calls his own sheep by name and leads them out.
When he has brought out all his own, he goes ahead of them,
and the sheep follow him because they know his voice. They
will not follow a stranger, but they will run from him because
they do not know the voice of strangers.[20]

As the boy led the sheep away, I saw again that the goal of the
spiritual life is not only to recognize God's voice as easily as the
sheep knew their shepherd's, but also to follow God with as much
alacrity as the sheep were showing.

12

The Gift of Imagination

IGNATIAN CONTEMPLATION

The tradition of prayer most associated with the Jesuits goes by many names: *Ignatian contemplation*, *composition of place*, *imaginative prayer*, and *imaginative contemplation*, among others. If you spend time with Jesuits or those trained by Jesuits, chances are that you have been introduced to this kind of prayer. And if you've ever been on a Jesuit retreat, you may have prayed this kind of prayer without even knowing it. And you probably enjoyed it. But when I first encountered it, I was disappointed.

A few weeks after I entered the Jesuit novitiate, the assistant novice director, David Donovan, said that he wanted to introduce me to "the way we pray." Excited, I imagined that he would share some arcane practice that would usher me into instant contact with God. Instead, he patiently described how St. Ignatius suggested in the *Spiritual Exercises* that people pray with their imaginations. He called it "composition of place."

"What do you mean?" I asked.

David described using your imagination to "place yourself" in a scene from the Bible and then paying attention to what came up in prayer.

I remember saying something like "That's it? That's the 'Jesuit way to pray'? Making things up in your head?" For a moment I thought that I had been duped into joining a crazy religious order (which would not be the first or last time someone thought that about the Society of Jesus).

David smiled and took a sip of coffee. "Let me ask you something. Do you think God can work through the feelings of love that come from the relationships you have?"

"Yes," I said.

"How about through your appreciation of things like the beauty of nature?"

Again, "Yes."

"How about through the inspiration or feelings you have during Mass?"

"Sure."

"Then why couldn't God work through your imagination?"

I took this in for a few seconds. "Your imagination," said David, "is another gift from God, just like all those other gifts. So it can be used to experience God." That made sense.

For those with similar doubts, William Barry offers a response in *God and You*: he advises trust in tradition. Remember, he says, that God used the imagination of saints like Ignatius Loyola, Francis Xavier, and Margaret Mary Alacoque to "draw them into a very deep intimate friendship with him." We should not distrust the natural gifts that God gives us, including our imagination. If the use of our imagination leads us to God, "then we can have confidence that the Lord is using our imaginations for his purposes and our good."[1] In fact, we are actually being invited to trust in something far more fundamental: "Trust the Holy Spirit of God who dwells in our hearts to guide our imaginations, to reveal the truth of God to us."[2]

But I was still unsure of how to do it. Fortunately, David, with whom I met for direction regularly, was used to dealing with, well, novices to the spiritual life. That day in his office, he laid out the process in several easy steps, but it took me a few months to get the hang of it.

Composing the Place

St. Ignatius did not invent this type of Christian prayer. It probably dates from the first person who heard the story of one of Jesus's miracles and imagined what it would have been like to have been there. "Jesus healed a man with a withered hand?" It would have been nearly impossible for that original hearer *not* to imagine the scene—seeing the fingers on the man's hand unfurl, hearing the reaction from the astonished crowd, and feeling the man's joy. Later on, when the Gospels were written down and edited, it would have been natural for readers and hearers to ask themselves, "What must it have been like?"

More than a thousand years later, St. Francis of Assisi encouraged people to place themselves in the scene when he created the tradition of the Christmas crèche, in which the story of the Nativity is recreated with figures of the Infant Jesus, Mary, Joseph, the shepherds, and the Wise Men. St. Francis had made a pilgrimage to the Holy Land and visited Bethlehem. Back in Italy, in the town of Greccio, in 1223 he created a Nativity scene with living actors in a cave. In *The Life of St. Francis*, St. Bonaventure, an early Franciscan, describes Francis's approach:

Now three years before his death it befell that he was minded, at the town of Greccio, to celebrate the memory of the Birth of the Child Jesus, with all the added solemnity that he might, for the kindling of devotion. That this might not seem an innovation, he sought and obtained license from the Supreme Pontiff, and then made ready a manger, and bade hay, together with an ox and an ass, be brought unto the spot.[3]

But it was Ignatius who popularized imaginative prayer in his sixteenth-century manual *Spiritual Exercises*, where it is the basis of much of the prayer in that book. As a result, it is Ignatius who is probably most closely associated with this practice. Remember that the Exercises map out a four-week retreat that leads a person through the life of Christ. From almost the beginning of the Exercises, Ignatius asks us to place ourselves in scenes from Jesus's life.

This was one of Ignatius's favorite ways to help people enter into a relationship with God, and it flowed from his own experience. As David Fleming, SJ, writes, although Ignatius was an excellent analytical thinker (even if he would never have thought of himself as an intellectual), the "mental quality of thought that drove his spiritual life was his remarkable imagination."[4]

It begins during the first week of the Exercises:

The First Prelude is a composition made by imagining the place. Here we should take notice of the following. When a contemplation or meditation is about something that can be gazed on, for example, a contemplation of Christ our Lord, who is visible, the composition consists of seeing in imagination the physical place where that which I want to contemplate is taking place. By physical place I mean, for instance, a temple or a mountain where Jesus Christ or Our

Lady happens to be, in accordance with the topic I desire to contemplate.[5]

In other words, when we're imagining something "visible" from the life of Christ, we can try to use our imagination to "contemplate" the physical place.

Ignatius gives specific instructions early in the *Spiritual Exercises* (that is, early in Jesus's life) on how to "compose the place" of the Nativity:

> Here it will be to see in imagination the road from Nazareth to Bethlehem. Consider its length and breadth, whether it is level or winds through valleys and hills. Similarly, look at the place or cave of the nativity: How big is it, or small? How low or high? And how is it furnished?[6]

As you can see, Ignatius asks us to imagine with as much specificity as possible. In Ignatian contemplation we use all five of our "imaginative senses." And, in my experience, the most helpful way of approaching this is by "composing" the place one sense at a time, beginning with sight.

But first a common question: "How 'accurate' does my imagination have to be? In order to see it in my mind's eye, how important is it to know what a biblical location would have looked like? Do I need to be a scholar of the history of first-century Galilee and Judea just to imagine things?"

It's important to consider the historical backdrop of each Gospel. When reading about Jesus's life, some historical context is essential. Obviously people in Jesus's day lived differently than we do. Reading as much as you can about life in first-century Galilee and Judea can help you better understand Jesus.

There's a memorable passage from the wonderfully named book

Stone and Dung, Oil and Spit, by Jodi Magness, about daily life in first-century Galilee, which depicts towns like Nazareth as "filthy, malodorous, and unhealthy" by contemporary standards and describes in Jesus's day garbage and sewage being tossed into the alleyways that ran between the small stone houses.[7] This kind of knowledge may help to guard against overly sentimental images of life in Jesus's time. Some knowledge of the times is helpful for your meditation. Why not picture things as accurately as possible?

At the same time, historical research is not a prerequisite for Ignatian contemplation. You don't have to be a biblical scholar to pray with the Bible.

If you pray about the Nativity scene, it may help if you know a little about journeys in the New Testament era, but you don't need to drop your Bible and consult a book about life in first-century Roman colonies. Go with what you know at the time. Even if you're praying with a Bible passage about which you know little historically (say, an Old Testament passage), take it at face value and trust that God will help you with the meditation. Overall, you want to strike a balance between obsessively researching every Bible scene and ignoring the fact that Jesus didn't live in modern times.

With that in mind, let's take our earlier example of the Nativity scene as presented in the Gospel of Luke, one of the most familiar of the Gospel stories:

> In those days a decree went out from Emperor Augustus
> that all the world should be registered. This was the first
> registration and was taken while Quirinius was governor of
> Syria. All went to their own towns to be registered. Joseph
> also went from the town of Nazareth in Galilee to Judea,
> to the city of David called Bethlehem, because he was
> descended from the house and family of David. He went to
> be registered with Mary, to whom he was engaged and who

was expecting a child. While they were there, the time
came for her to deliver her child. And she gave birth to her
firstborn son and wrapped him in bands of cloth, and laid
him in a manger, because there was no place for them in
the inn.[8]

With this reading, you could focus on either a part or the whole.
You might imagine the journey from Nazareth to Bethlehem, or you
might think about Mary and Joseph inquiring of the innkeeper, preparing the manger, having the child, or resting after the birth.

How do you determine which part to focus on and allow God
to lead you to the place God wants to lead you to? See which parts
of the story appeal to you. Likewise, notice parts of the story that
repel you. Both might be places where God is inviting you to spend
time. In the case of the appealing parts, it's easy to see how God is
drawing you. In the case of the repelling parts, remember that God
might be inviting you to look at a passage that is initially difficult
or uncomfortable in order to reveal something to you or teach you
something.

As with any prayer, first ask God to be with you and help you.
St. Ignatius often suggests asking for a specific intention, for example, to be closer to God, to understand Jesus more, to experience
healing.

He also asks us to be generous in our prayer, not only with our
time, but with how much of ourselves we give. By "giving ourselves,"
I mean being as present, aware, and attentive as possible; remaining open to wherever God might lead us; and being willing to spend
whatever time we allotted for our prayer, even if it seems dry. The
opposite would be letting our mind wander, not paying attention to
something God seems to be raising up, or cutting our time short because we get bored after a few minutes. Charles Healey writes, "Ig-

natius wants this spirit of generosity to be present at every stage of the prayer, particularly when the prayer seems unproductive."[9]

Then ask the same types of questions that Ignatius posed, focusing on the senses. I always start with sight. (The following are just suggestions for prayer, not a strict template.)

What Do I See?

Close your eyes and try to visualize the scene with as much detail as possible. Now, there are some scholarly debates over precisely how the birth of Jesus took place. The story of Jesus's birth in the Gospel of Matthew describes Mary and Joseph as living in Bethlehem, fleeing to Egypt, and then moving for the first time to Nazareth, while Luke has the two living originally in Nazareth, traveling to Bethlehem in time for the birth, and then returning home again.[10] Some scholars say that if it did happen in Bethlehem, it was likely in a cave, not a stable. Other scholars say that portions of the Nativity story were edited in such a way to emphasize Jesus's connections to King David to legitimize his claim to be the Messiah. And so on.

It's important to look at the Bible in a historical context or, as scholars say, "critically." To treat it "critically" here doesn't mean that we needlessly find fault with it, that our primary goal is to critique it, or that we don't believe it. Rather, a critical reading means we use all the tools available to try to understand how the Gospels were written and edited: what type of literature they are, which Gospels rely on other Gospels, when each was written, what the intent of the authors was, what the communities to whom they were writing were like, and so on. This is part of being an intelligent reader of the Bible. For example, we know that the Nativity stories are not 100 percent accurate for the simple reason that Matthew and Luke don't even agree on the sequence of the events. So it's important to bring critical (read: intelligent) eyes to the Bible.

Consequently, it is helpful to bring whatever you know about the Bible to your prayer. This doesn't mean, however, that you have to be a historian to pray, that you have to research a passage before you pray with it, or that you must picture the scene precisely as it was written. If it seems reasonable to you that Jesus was born in a cave, feel free to picture that. Although it may help you to know, for example, that many people in Bethlehem lived in caves at the time (some of which can still be seen on the hillsides surrounding the town), you don't need a degree in archaeology to picture Bethlehem.

For the most part, when we pray over a certain Bible passage, we set aside any desire to either construct a 100 percent historically accurate image or pick apart the accuracy in favor of the desire to experience the story. Prayer is not the time for flipping through history books or scrolling through even the most reliable sites online. Optimally, that's done as part of our ongoing education as believers. Prayer is a time for praying, not researching.

Moreover, you don't have to have seen a real-life stable to use the image in prayer. Nor do you have to have seen a single sheep in person, though it helps. (I remember my surprise when I first came upon an actual flock of sheep in East Africa: they were loud!) *Your* stable could be one you saw in a movie or on a Christmas card. Overall, enter the prayer trusting that God will help you see what God intends for you to see. You're not manufacturing a scene as much as allowing God to invite you into it.

So how do you compose the scene visually? Here are a few questions to keep in mind.

What do the surroundings look like? What does the stable look like? How is it constructed? Is it attached to the back of the inn? Does it look like the ones in Christmas cards you've seen with the wooden roof and the straw and the animals? What does the manger look like? What kind of animals are in the stable? Compose the place with as much detail as possible.

What do the people look like? Now that you've constructed the stable, cast your imaginative gaze to the individuals in the passage. What does Joseph look like? In popular portrayals Joseph is often pictured as considerably older than Mary. But nowhere do the Gospels say that Joseph is elderly. Many scholars believe that the tradition of Joseph as an elderly man was inserted later to downplay any implication of sexual attraction between Mary and Joseph.

Likewise, what does Mary look like? We don't know her precise age at the time of her son's birth. The Gospels say she was a *parthenos*, Greek for "young woman" or "virgin," but leaves her age unspecified. So perhaps Mary was fifteen and Joseph was twenty.

What are they wearing? Recently I read a fascinating book called *What Did Jesus Look Like?* by Joan Taylor, professor of Christian origins and Second Temple Judaism at King's College, London. Of course the question that everyone wants to know—what Jesus looked like in person—is not answered, nor can it be. Professor Taylor's book is basically a commentary on the ways that Jesus has been portrayed through the years, with brief forays into the general appearance of people in first-century Galilee and Judea.

Taylor notes, however, that the traditional portrayal of Jesus in flowing robes with long sleeves may be inaccurate. More likely, men of the time dressed in what we would consider a Greek or Hellenistic style, in a short tunic and cloak. Still, especially for a poor carpenter from Nazareth, this would have been homespun and probably uncomfortable in the heat. Perhaps readings like this will influence how Jesus looks in your prayer.[11]

What are the expressions on their faces? And what might those expressions tell you? Do they look concerned, worried, pained, excited, joyful? As you enter the meditation, you might find that these small things—their expressions—speak to you in a deep way. What might God be asking you to notice about their lives—and yours?

You might be surprised at what your imagination evokes. If Mary and Joseph turn out to be two people from your own life—say, your parents—allow that to be a part of your meditation.

Look around and see who else is there. Although the reading includes only Mary, Joseph, and Jesus, most Christmas cards feature the shepherds and a few onlookers. In your own prayer you may notice other people there too—again, even people from your own life.

Your meditation may go beyond what the reading indicates. In one of his meditations on the Nativity, St. Ignatius asks us to imagine a "servant" helping Mary with the birth. There is no servant mentioned in the Gospels, but Ignatius included one to help us enter the scene. (Or perhaps, as Bill Barry pointed out to me, as a nobleman Ignatius could not imagine her not having a servant!) In his meditation for the Resurrection, although there is no Gospel account of Jesus appearing to his mother, Ignatius says that this may be "piously believed" and includes it.

Ironically, sometimes these "nonbiblical" scenes have the most power. A few years ago, a man making his way through the Spiritual Exercises spent a great deal of time as the servant, handing Mary a towel, helping her through the birth, and noticing Joseph. For him it was a profound experience of humility, and after his retreat it was this image that he returned to again and again.

How do I fit into the scene? Begin with *Where am I?* Where are you located? Are you looking at the scene from a distance? Many prefer this method. The benefit is being able to look upon the scene as a bystander and not worrying about being a participant. The distance itself may also be part of your prayer. Recall that the woman who prayed with the scene of Jesus calling the first disciples saw it at a distance and felt a desire to join them.

But Joseph Tetlow, SJ, an expert on Ignatian spirituality, cautions against being *too* distant: "You do not merely imagine the events as though you were watching it on film. You enter into the scene, letting it unfold as though you were a part of it, standing warm in the temple or ankle-deep in the water of the Jordan."[12]

As Father Tetlow implies, the other way of entering the scene is as a participant. At some point you need to answer the question: *Who am I?* My friend found himself drawn to being the servant at the Nativity. From time to time I've also imagined myself as one of the characters in the story: someone to whom Jesus speaks—a leper, a scribe, a tax collector.

You might be a central character, the person who is healed, for example, or even a named character. You might imagine yourself as Peter or Andrew when Jesus calls them by the Sea of Galilee, or Mary Magdalene at the tomb on Easter Sunday. Sometimes people even imagine themselves as Jesus, say, on the cross and feeling abandoned. Many people, myself included, find it hard to cast themselves as Jesus, but it helps others enter more deeply into his life, death, and resurrection.

Let's return to the Nativity. Now that you've composed the scene visually you can ask yourself the next question.

What Do I Hear?

Composition of place includes aural composition. Think about the sounds in the scene. Are there animals making noise? Have you ever heard a cow moo up close? It's loud! Are there horses nearby? Goats chewing on their food? Chickens pecking about? Mice scurrying? What do they sound like?

If you're imagining the scene before the birth, you might hear some commotion as Joseph or perhaps the servant is readying the stable for Mary. After the birth, you might hear a child crying. "But little Lord Jesus no crying he makes," says the Christmas carol "Away in a Manger." But *your* little Lord Jesus may cry at the top of his lungs. Why not? It's not a sin!

Sound can be a powerful invitation to prayer. During one Holy

Land pilgrimage, I was with a group of pilgrims on a boat on the Sea of Galilee. Initially, as one of the organizers of the pilgrimage, I balked at the idea of a boat ride, which sounded cheesy.

Once on the sea, I realized how wrong I was. As we sailed along the coast, we could see the towns where Jesus preached and healed: Magdala, Capernaum, Bethsaida. And I could easily imagine Peter and Andrew, James and John fishing on these waters, with Jesus in the boat. Soon after we sailed, I realized that Jesus must have seen this exact view from this vantage point. It was an amazing moment of connection.

In the middle of the sea, we asked the captain to shut off the motor, so that we could have silence. A fellow Jesuit read the Gospel passage in which Jesus stills the storm, to the shock of the apostles. "Who then is this, that even the wind and the sea obey him?"[13] It's one of the most dramatic moments in the Gospels.

After the reading I invited the pilgrims to "compose the place," which was easy since we were at the very place where it happened! The Holy Land may be the one place where you can compose the place without closing your eyes. Nonetheless, I closed my eyes and imagined the scene.

The fierce wind made the colorful pennants that hung from wires attached to poles on either side of the boat whip around loudly. The wind whistled past my ears and the pennants snapped sharply. Immediately I thought of how terrifying it would be if someone stood up and was able, with a word, to stop the wind. Of how frightening it would be if that noise—the pennants snapping in the wind—simply ceased.

Then I experienced a new feeling: pity for the disciples. I imagined what it would have been like to see someone change the weather with a word. The Gospel of Mark says that the disciples were "filled with great awe," and various versions of the passage in Luke say, "afraid," "frightened," or "terrified." But I don't think I began to understand that until I was on the boat. All that came from just one imaginative sense: sound.

What Do I Smell?

The imaginative sense of smell may not figure in your prayer with some Bible passages—for example, a Psalm that asks for God's help. On the other hand, in some narratives in both the Old and the New Testaments smell can be important. In the Nativity, the smell of the stable and the animals can help place us in the scene with great vividness. If you are at the Last Supper, the smell of the food may help you with your prayer.

What Do I Feel?

Feeling is sometimes overlooked in discussions of Ignatian contemplation, which often give precedence to sight and sound, but feeling can be helpful in multiple ways.

First, *overall, how do I feel physically?* Are you tired? If Jesus is preaching to you at the end of a long day, are you weary? If you're traveling from one city to another with the disciples, are you hungry? Or have you just had your fill of the loaves and fishes that Jesus multiplied? How does the weather or, more broadly, the environment make you feel? Is it cold outside? Hot? Rainy?

One of the most surprising things about traveling through Galilee on my first visit was how hot it could get—at least in August. One day a friend and I were journeying to a tiny monastery between Jerusalem and Jericho and had to pass through the traditional Valley of the Shadow of Death. It was 110 degrees. As the sun beat down on us, I knew that I would never read about Jesus and his disciples traveling from one city to another without thinking about how hot it could have been (or without thinking about how often they might have traveled mornings or evenings to avoid the heat of the day).

Second, *what physical reactions do I have to the details in the passage?* What effect would you feel from the particulars of the scene? If you are sitting in a boat with Jesus, you might feel the roughhewn seats. If you are walking to Jericho, you might feel the dust kicked up by your sandals. If you are in the Temple in Jerusalem, you might feel the cool stone walls of the building. How do the specifics of the passage make you feel?

One of the most vivid experiences I've had with this part of imaginative prayer is seeing myself in the Gospel story of the storm at sea and realizing that the disciples would have been soaked to the skin; the clothes on their backs in the midst of the raging storm would probably have been wet and heavy. It deepened my appreciation of their initial anger when Jesus did not immediately come to their aid. On top of the fear of drowning, they were already physically uncomfortable. Such small details about what you might be feeling helps to place you deeper in the scene.

What Do I Taste?

In some Bible stories, the imaginative sense of taste may contribute little, if anything. If Jesus is preaching the Sermon on the Mount, there might be nothing that prompts you to think about food or drink. But if you are with Jesus at the wedding feast in Cana, you'll certainly be wondering what the "good wine" tastes like. Or if you're at the Multiplication of the Loaves and Fishes, the bread and fish might be especially satisfying after being hungry for so long.

Entering the Scene

Now that you've composed the scene, enter the narrative. By the way, the preceding section, on each of the senses, does not mean that you have to laboriously work your way through every single one before you dare to start praying. This is not a strict regimen, but simply suggestions for what might work.

Sometimes it helps to reread the passage, especially if it's a long one, to enable you to remember the details. But, essentially, just let the story unfold in your imagination. If you forget where the passage is going, return to the text to remind yourself, but for the most part once you've started praying, there is little need to read the text.

As an aside, several events occur in more than one Gospel, with variations from Gospel to Gospel. There are several recountings of the storm at sea, for example; the event occurs in each of the Synoptic Gospels, Matthew, Mark, and Luke, with minor variations. This brings up another common question: "Does it matter which version I use? And how do I know which version to use?" (You might smile at so many questions, but all are frequently asked, so they need to be answered.)

Sometimes it helps to read several versions of the same story and see where your heart inclines. There may be one that appeals to you more than the others. Trust that God can lead you to that particular one. There's also nothing wrong with combining the "variants," as scholars say.

One of the most common places where variants happen is at the Crucifixion. Each Gospel offers a different treatment of the Passion and death of Jesus. Why? Well, the four evangelists drew on different traditions of the same story to tell it to four different communities. Not surprisingly, there are variations. Imagine four different friends telling your life to four different groups of people. They would include or stress different things. Thus, when reading the Passion narratives, people are often surprised to find that parts that they cherish (for example, Jesus's quote "My God, my God, why have you forsaken me?") do not appear in all four Gospels.

There's also nothing wrong with sticking to the passage that you've started with. Sometimes I'm curious to see what another Gospel says, but mostly I find it's fine to stay with the passage at hand.

As in any prayer, allow God to lead you. In the Nativity, if you are drawn to spend time quietly contemplating the scene and feeling a spirit of peace, that's fine. If you are moved to something more specific, that's fine too. Trust that God is leading you and will raise up what you are meant to look at.

Around Christmas a few years ago, I was a guest on a radio program called "A Conversation with Cardinal Dolan," hosted by Timothy Cardinal Dolan, the archbishop of New York. On the show, Cardinal Dolan recounted his experience with Ignatian prayer and related something I have heard from many people. When the cardinal was contemplating the Nativity, his retreat director suggested that he simply hold the Infant Jesus. It was a profound experience for Cardinal Dolan, who said that afterward the Nativity story took on new meaning, and no matter when he read or heard it, he thought of that moment in prayer.

Many people have had similar experiences when practicing Ignatian contemplation. Stories from the Bible take on new meaning, because it's a meaning that has become *personal*. It's one thing to read the Nativity or hear it preached about at Mass; it's another to experience it in prayer and have a personal insight about it. Certainly Cardinal Dolan had read countless times about the wonder with which the shepherds looked upon the child, but it was another thing for him to experience it for himself.

Also, in these passages God speaks personally to each person. Something in the narrative that may not strike another person as important moves you deeply. You may find yourself in the scene in a way that you would never have expected. My Jesuit friend Chris, whose late brother was physically disabled, told me that a retreat director suggested he bring his brother into the story of the Multiplication of the Loaves and Fishes to encounter Jesus. "It's one thing to imagine yourself just sitting with Jesus. It's another to push a wheelchair across the ground," he told me. "It opened up that scene in a new way to me."

As Chris's experience suggests, a good spiritual director who knows what is happening in your life may suggest a twist on the story to help you enter it, for example, bringing someone you know into the story, imagining yourself talking to a specific person in the scene (Peter, Mary, Joseph), or going off by yourself into a facet of the story.

After you have let the scene unfold in your mind, take a few minutes to return to parts of the prayer that seemed meaningful to you. This is a way to savor the prayer. Recently a young man doing the Spiritual Exercises said that he was overwhelmed when he imagined Mary handing him her newborn son. He said that he experienced a deep feeling of calm and warmth.

"Where should I go from there?" he asked.

"Back," I said.

In general, compose the scene, let the passage unfold, and then later write down what has happened. Resist the temptation to write things down as they happen, because that action can break up the prayer. It can also tempt you to be thinking more about the results rather than simply resting in the prayer.

It's worth noting that sometimes you don't even have to pick up your Bible to enter into the scene. If the story is familiar, you could use a painting or a poem to enter it imaginatively. For example, one of my favorite poets, Irene Zimmerman, OSF, writes poems that plunge us into the middle of various Gospel scenes. At times her poetry is as helpful as the original text in inviting me into the scene.[14]

Let the story unfold with as little judging on your part as possible. And resist the temptation to analyze it while it's happening. Let yourself be drawn to whatever seems attractive or interesting. For example, if you notice the disciples more than Jesus, try not to judge that as inappropriate or wrong. While you're in the meditation, just allow God to lead you through your imagination.

Paying Attention

God desires to communicate with you all the time, but when you *intentionally* open yourself up, you can often hear God more clearly. To use the metaphor of friendship, it is similar to saying to a friend, "Now you have my undivided attention." Ignatian contemplation—indeed all prayer—enables us to hear things more easily, or differently, and it becomes easier to recognize something that might have gone overlooked. Insights, for example, are common in Ignatian contemplation. And whenever insights come up in prayer, remember what David, my first spiritual director, counseled me: "Pay attention."

Let's return to the Gospel passage about the storm at sea, where Jesus stills a storm in front of the terrified disciples aboard a boat on the Sea of Galilee. While you are praying about this passage, you might notice how terrified the disciples are—not only by the storm, but by Jesus's display of power. His miracles could have been frightening to this band of Galileans. Though you may have heard this story dozens of times, you realize in a new way that watching the sea stilled by your friend would have been astonishing—and frightening.

You've just received an insight into the life of the disciples: sometimes it was frightening to be around Jesus. Maybe you've heard about "fear of God." It is a natural reaction. "Who then is this, that even the wind and the sea obey him?" they say afterward. For the first time, you see not only the excitement behind that statement, but also the fear. Then you wonder if they ever talked about this reaction with Jesus. What would Jesus have said in reply?

That might be as far as that insight goes—which is fine. If it goes further, all the better; but insight into Scripture alone will help deepen your faith.

Often an insight can lead as well to thoughts about your own life. It might prompt you to ask yourself, "Where am *I* afraid of God?" Are there places where you've seen signs of God's presence, but have been afraid to admit it—because you're afraid of God's power? Sometimes it's frightening to think about God taking an interest in your life. Is that fear preventing you from a deeper relationship with God?

One additional important aspect of paying attention comes after your prayer—writing it down. Take note of what happened while you were involved in the story: insights, emotions, desires, memories, feelings, and so on. This record will prove invaluable as you reflect on your prayer experience. (More on this later when we talk about journaling.)

What If It Doesn't "Work"?

Here are the most common issues that arise in Ignatian contemplation. (These issues arise with other kinds of prayer as well.)

I wasn't able to compose the scene. It was too complicated! Sometimes composing a Bible passage can seem a chore. If you are thinking about a complicated passage during the Passion narratives where Jesus's trials and inquests take him back and forth between Pontius Pilate and the religious authorities, the story may be too complex to keep straight. So composing the scene and remembering precisely what happened in the passage become not life-giving, but bothersome. In that case, focus on one part of the passage—whatever you feel most drawn to.

Likewise, in composing a scene you may find yourself too caught up with the details. For example, if you are with Moses and the Hebrew people journeying to the Promised Land in the Book of Exodus, you might be confused by trying to picture what all the people looked like, not to mention their animals, wagons, belongings, and so on. In these situations, simplify. You're not trying to be a film director, striving to make every detail authentic. Do your best to imagine in general what the scene *might have* looked like. It's more important to be open to encountering God in the Bible, and you can do that even if you've never seen an ancient wagon, a camel, or an Egyptian chariot.

I was able to compose the scene, but not a whole lot happened. A common complaint I very often hear is "I composed the scene easily enough, but I didn't notice much of anything happening," or "I went through the scene but didn't feel anything." Not every prayer yields dramatic results. Any time spent in God's presence is fruitful, but sometimes it's hard to see the fruit right away.

Why? For several possible reasons. First, there is something happening deep within you, but you may not notice it. Any time spent with God is transformative, but you may not be aware of a softening of your soul, a deepening of your appreciation for the passage, an increase in your love for God, or even something harder to explain.

Besides, God is always helping us express ourselves in prayer, even if we're not aware of it. As St. Paul wrote in his Letter to the Romans, "The Spirit helps us in our weakness; for we do not know how to pray as we ought, but that very Spirit intercedes with sighs too deep for words. And God, who searches the heart, knows what is the mind of the Spirit."[15]

Perhaps for some reason God is not offering you the grace of tangible results now. Instead, God may be preparing your soul for something in the future. God is like a gardener, who has to plow up the soil before planting new seeds. The gardener spends hours turning over the soil, pulling out weeds and old roots, fertilizing it, and then reworking it. The casual observer, passing the garden a few hours later, may see nothing happening, yet some deep work has been done.

Second, you might not have given yourself enough time to settle into the story. Often, Ignatian contemplation takes time before you are able to relax and let the story work on you, or in you. Sometimes you just need to slow down.

Finally, it may take a few tries before you notice anything. Don't be discouraged. This passage may not be offering tangible results right now, but that doesn't mean that you shouldn't be open to returning to it days, weeks, or even months later. Often I've returned to a passage that years ago seemed flat and have watched the passage open up. God may be waiting for the right time to invite you into the passage.

Keep in mind that this is a spiritual practice, and it takes repeated effort to become comfortable in it and free enough (free of any initial anxiety) to allow the process to work. Above all, be patient. Don't get discouraged.

I lost my place. I forgot what everyone says and does in the passage. Bible stories can be complicated, which means that people often lose their place. Sometimes I suggest rereading the passage to remind yourself of the sequence of events.

Or if you are reading the story of Abraham and Sarah greeting the angelic visitors and forget what the angels say to Abraham or when they greet Sarah, then perhaps you need to either reread the story or simply focus on another part of the story. What point in the story draws you? Which part of the story, as Ignatius says, holds the most "fruit" for you? For example, you might be wondering why Sarah laughs in that passage.

Another option is to have the story *in general* play out in your mind. You may not remember all the details, but you can remember the gist of the story. Feel free to enter the story as you can remember it.

I forgot to record what happened in my prayer. The other day a man who sees me for spiritual direction said that he had had a memorable experience in prayer, but he couldn't now say what had happened, because he had forgotten to record it. "Write it down," I practically shouted.

Do not, however, write *during* your prayer. Pray when you're praying. Delay anything else—writing, recording, analyzing—until after the prayer has ended. Even if you have had a great insight, try not to leap up from your prayer to write it down. Trust that you'll remember what happened afterward. The danger is that any deep prayer will be frustrated by constant interruptions. (This is distinguished from writing *as* prayer, which we'll discuss later.) But afterward, *do* write it down.

Why do you write things down? Mainly to remember what God has communicated to you. Sometimes I say to directees: "If Jesus Christ himself came into the room and told you something, what would you do?" Invariably they say, "I'd pay attention," or "I'd listen carefully." The same thing holds true in prayer. If God is speaking to us—through insights, feelings, memories, desires, or emotions—we are called to pay attention, and part of that attentiveness is recording how God has communicated with us.

Guard against two enemies in the spiritual life: forgetfulness and doubt. Think of them from the perspective of the evil spirit. What's the first thing the evil spirit would want when it comes to an experience in prayer? For you to forget it or doubt it.

Forgetting is easy enough. Things naturally fade from our memories with time. Writing it down can guard against that loss. So do record the fruits of your prayer immediately afterward. Don't be tempted to laziness, saying, "I'll write it down later."

Doubting is just as common. Often at the end of a retreat I will tell people, "You will inevitably doubt even those things that you have come to see as authentic." Our tendency afterward is to say, "I was just being emotional," or "I was just imagining things"—even "I was just trying to please my director." Writing down your experiences guards against this tendency, so you can return to your journal, read your original experiences in prayer, and remind yourself, "Yes, this really did happen."

I've tried Ignatian contemplation many times and have never been able to do it. Although most people are able to enter Ignatian contemplation, a few simply don't take to it. It's "content-rich" prayer, and some people seem better suited to more "free-form" prayer. Often their difficulty can be overcome with a few prompts: don't make it so complicated, don't have such great expectations, be grateful for whatever happens.

Some people lament that they "have no imagination," but that is highly unlikely. As Gerard Hughes says, "If you are capable of recalling even one event of your past life and reliving it in memory, however blurred the details, then you have the ability to pray imaginatively."[16] Father Barry notes that if you wince when someone describes the impact of a hammer hitting a thumb or if you can enjoy a good story, you have an imagination. Everyone has an imagination, though our imaginations differ. "We need to let God use the one we have and not bemoan the one we do not have."[17]

Imaginative prayer may not feel fruitful to some people, because they are still learning to use their imagination in this way. Some people are not attracted to this kind of prayer and may not consider themselves "made for" Ignatian contemplation. If that describes you, that's fine. Don't worry. Free-form, or "content-light," prayer might be better for you, like centering prayer, which we'll speak about later. But be open to trying it later, perhaps in a few days, weeks, months, or even years.

The Colloquy

A simpler way of doing Ignatian contemplation is by imagining God or Jesus in front of you and conversing "as one friend to another." For Ignatius this was an essential part of the Spiritual Exercises: he wanted you to come to know God, and Jesus intimately. Conversation, or what he calls a "colloquy," was one way of doing this. For many people who travel along the way of St. Ignatius, this is *the* most enjoyable way to pray.

At the end of many exercises, Ignatius recommends imagining ourselves speaking with Mary, Jesus, or God the Father. At one point during the First Week, Ignatius asks us to speak with Jesus on the cross and ask ourselves, "What have I done for Christ? What am I doing for Christ? What ought I to do for Christ?"[18]

Sometimes this prayer has worked wonders for me. On a recent retreat, as I imagined myself before Jesus and asked, "What am I doing for Christ?" I started to grow angry. That anger was an obvious sign that something was happening deep down. "I'm doing way too much!" I said to Jesus in prayer and listed all the unnecessary projects that I should have declined. And I felt Jesus say to me, "I'm not asking you to do all *that!*"

Many of the colloquies in the Exercises are freer in form, not attached to specific questions like "What am I doing for Christ?" Often, when you are reflecting on the ministries and miracles of Jesus, a retreat director will ask you to imagine speaking to Jesus, or one of the disciples, to review what happened during the prayer.

As ever, what you hear in prayer needs to be compared to your religious beliefs, what fits with your understanding of God, and what you know about yourself. Does it make sense? In time, you will be able to better discern what seems to be authentically from God.

Keep Trying

As I mentioned, even if Ignatian contemplation doesn't seem to work at first, keep trying. A few years ago I met a woman on a retreat who told me, with some sadness, that she had no imagination—she was too rational and literal-minded. One of her former spiritual directors had even cautioned her against trying Ignatian contemplation because of her supposed lack of imagination. Over the course of the retreat, we tried a few exercises designed to unlock her imagination and, among other things, I reminded her that if she could follow along when someone told a story, she had an imagination. Finally, I suggested the simplest colloquy.

She enjoyed sitting on a certain bench at the retreat house, and so I said, "Why not just sit there with Jesus? You don't have to imagine yourself in any scene from the Bible. Just sit with Jesus and speak to him, 'as one friend speaks to another,' as Ignatius said."

The next day she came into the room, beaming. She could barely wait to start. "Jesus and I had a wonderful day together talking!" she said. "We made up for a lot of lost time!"

I was glad that she tried again. So was she. And I'll bet so was God.

13

Praying with Sacred Texts

LECTIO DIVINA

Not everyone likes Ignatian contemplation. For some it is too "content heavy." Depending on your personality, you may not enjoy composing the scene, using your imaginative senses, or entering a narrative. It may be "too much," as one retreatant said to me a few years ago. By that she meant that she didn't like having to deal with all the "content."

Even if you shy away from composing the place, however, you may still want to pray with the Bible and other sacred texts. Fortunately, there is another method, called *lectio divina*, that can provide you with entrée into these texts.

Let's be clear: *lectio divina* (which means "holy reading" or "sacred reading") is an ancient prayer with a venerable tradition, not simply "Ignatian contemplation lite." In fact, it predates St. Ignatius himself and therefore predates what we know as Ignatian spirituality.

Lectio flowered in the great monastic communities of the Middle Ages, when monks were encouraged to read the Bible and the "Church Fathers" (early church theologians such as St. Augustine) as well as other texts, not just as part of their studies but also as an essential part of their spiritual life. *The New Dictionary of Catholic Spirituality* offers a succinct definition of *lectio divina* by Monsignor Kevin Irwin, an expert in the liturgy:

> In much patristic and monastic literature, as exemplified in the Rule of St. Benedict . . . *lectio* includes reading, private prayer, and *meditatio*, with "meditation" meaning the memorization, repetition, and prayerful rumination ("chewing over") of texts as a stimulus to personal prayer.[1]

The main purpose of *lectio*, in addition to union and communication with God is, a "thorough assimilation of sacred truth and a life lived according to this truth," says Irwin.[2] The words you chew over and digest become a part of you. The main difference between Ignatian contemplation and *lectio*, though the two overlap, is the absence of "composition of place." In *lectio* there is no requirement to "compose" anything, but it still enables you to engage sacred texts in prayer.

As with most prayer practices, there are many ways of approaching *lectio divina*. My favorite comes from Daniel J. Harrington, SJ, my New Testament professor in graduate school and one of the holiest people I've ever met. Father Harrington was a professor of New Testament at the Weston Jesuit School of Theology[3] in Cambridge, Massachusetts, the editor of the scholarly journal *New Testament Abstracts*, the author of hundreds of articles and dozens of books, and a regular preacher at his local parish. Dan's whole life revolved around the Bible. It was, he said, what got him up in the morning.

"I find God largely in and through the Bible," he wrote. "Most of

my academic, spiritual, and pastoral life revolves around the Bible.
It is for me the most important way to come to know, love, and
serve God."[4]

Given his love of the Bible, it's not surprising that Dan had his
own approach to *lectio*: four simple steps, in the form of four questions, offered with his trademark clarity. As with any prayer, we
begin by asking God to be with us and reminding ourselves that
prayer is a dialogue, not a monologue. Then we can turn to Dan's
questions.

Four Steps of *Lectio*

1. Reading

What does the text say? The most basic question about any spiritual
reading is: "What is going on?"

In the case of a Bible passage, at first it might be difficult to understand what the text says. You might have a hard time parsing it
if you aren't familiar with the Old and New Testaments. In the Old
Testament, one of the writers might say something that confuses
you, refer to a religious practice you know nothing about, or mention an event you've never heard of. In the New Testament, Jesus
might use an essential word (like *korban*) you're unfamiliar with,
coin a phrase you're not sure is hyperbole ("Let the dead bury their
own dead"), or mention a place whose location you don't know (the
Mount of Olives).[5] In these cases, it's helpful to look at the notes or
introductory essays related to the particular book in the Bible. Likewise, you might want to consult a Bible commentary for answers to
your questions.[6]

To begin to pray with the reading, you have to know what is going
on. More or less.

Occasionally, you *don't* have to know precisely what's happening and can luxuriate in the words. Suppose you are reading a passage from Psalm 137:

> By the rivers of Babylon—
>> there we sat down and there we wept
>> when we remembered Zion.
> On the willows there
>> we hung up our harps.[7]

You may read these verses, as I did as a Jesuit novice, and find them so moving that you can pray without knowing exactly what is going on. The image of the harps being hung up in the willow trees seemed a powerful symbol of grief, even though I knew nothing about the historical background of the verses.

Still, as with Ignatian contemplation, although you don't have to be a biblical scholar, it helps to know something about the passage. Here the psalmist is writing during the Babylonian captivity, the period after the Jewish people were deported to Babylon after that kingdom's conquest of Jerusalem in the sixth century BC. The rivers are the Tigris and Euphrates. At the time of the psalm, the Jewish people were waiting for deliverance by God from the hands of their captors. Knowing the historical, geographic, and theological backdrop of Psalm 137 adds immeasurable depth of meaning to those verses.

To illustrate *lectio*, let's use another kind of reading—this time not from the Bible, but from a modern spiritual master. This selection is from *New Seeds of Contemplation*, a book of meditations by Thomas Merton. It is the kind of passage that lends itself to *lectio*.

> Every one of us is shadowed by an illusory person: a false self.
>> This is the man that I want myself to be but who cannot exist, because God does not know anything about him. . . .
>> My false and private self is the one who wants to exist

outside the reach of God's will and God's love—outside of reality and outside of life. And such a self cannot help but be an illusion. . . .

The secret of my identity is hidden in the love and mercy of God. . . .

Therefore, I cannot hope to find myself anywhere except in Him. . . .

Therefore, there is only one problem on which all my existence, my peace, and my happiness depend: to discover myself in discovering God. If I find Him, I will find myself, and if I find my true self, I will find Him.[8]

To begin our *lectio*, we read the passage and see how much we understand. In this case, we are dealing with one of Merton's favorite themes: the distinction and occasional battle between the "true self" and the "false self" and the lifelong quest to become oneself. Earlier in the book he writes, "For me to be a saint means to be myself."[9] Thus, not being oneself, being the false self, is a barrier not only to wholeness, but also to holiness, to a relationship with God.

Perhaps you don't know much about Merton when you first come upon this passage. Perhaps you've never heard of him. Reading it cold, then, you might start with the basics. You might not know what "illusory" means, so you may have to look it up, as I did when I first stumbled upon the word. You may think about the complicated relationship between the false and the private self, and you might wonder what it means to "find yourself" in God.

You might also balk at the pronouns he uses. Like all of us, Merton was a person of his times, and you might be offended by his use of "man" for "person" and "him" for God. You may have to think about that, make peace with it, or even retranslate it in your mind in order to move ahead.

All this is part of understanding what the text says. In this first stage of *lectio*, you are, as Father Harrington says, simply reading, mainly for comprehension.

2. Meditation

What does the text say to me? Now that you've read the passage, pay attention to your reaction in prayer. What parts of the text are you drawn to? What, in a word, fascinates you?

One important aspect of *lectio* is trusting that God will draw you where you are meant to go. Mainly this comes with an attraction to a particular word, phrase, sentence, or idea. The attraction can be either positive (something that consoles or comforts) or negative (something that repels or shocks).

Negative attraction can be surprising, but that part of the reading, the part that is most shocking, may be where we need to spend time. If you are reading a passage in which Jesus talks about welcoming strangers and you think, "That's absurd. Why should I welcome some migrant?" it may be an invitation to pray with that passage. As one of my spiritual directors used to say, "Go where the energy is, either positive or negative."

In the Merton passage, you may feel alarmed to read about the "false self" and feel embarrassed or reluctant to think about it. What might your false self be? Pay attention to these charged passages. These may be where God wants to meet you.

The more common experience is being drawn to something appealing. When I first read this passage at age twenty-five, I was drawn to the notion of "discovering myself." Frankly, I had never thought of that before. That may seem hard to believe, but no one had ever asked, "Who are you?" or "Who do you want to become?"

Yet after graduating with a business degree and working in corporate America for several years, this question took on great urgency. After six years at General Electric, I didn't know what I was doing there, and Merton's notion of the false self struck a chord. *What* was *I doing there?* I didn't seem to be made for my work, and yet I went into the office every day trying to be someone I was not. I thought about that question over and over, as I drove to work, as I daydreamed at my desk, even as I fell asleep at night. *What would it mean*, I wondered, *to discover myself, to be my true self?*

This is an example of how God draws you in. For someone else, the idea of "discovering yourself" might not be as interesting as "discovering yourself in God." This, as Dan Harrington might say, is what the text wants to say to you—or rather what God wants to say to you through the text.

3. Prayer

What do I want to say to God on the basis of this text? Now that you've read the text and pondered what it might mean to you, it's time to respond. What do you want to say about all this to God?

This is a prime example of having a conversation with God in prayer. *Lectio divina* is an opportunity for God to bring things up for you to notice and then for you to respond to God about those things. Again, trust that God has pointed out something in this passage to you *for a reason*. If you are drawn to it in prayer, then most likely God drew you there.

Perhaps you've prayed over what Thomas Merton wrote and find yourself thinking, sadly, *I'm not my true self. I'm not the person I want to be.* You may want to talk to God about that. First, you might want to share your sadness with God. It might not be the first time that you've thought you're not the person you want to be, or the person that you think God wants you to be. But *lectio* helps you to see this more clearly. And this clarity may help you be more honest with God.

That was my experience when I first stumbled upon the idea of the true self. At the time, I was stuck in a job that I didn't like, but couldn't see a way out. Going to work, I often felt like an impostor.

I felt I was in the wrong place, that I was made for something else. When I first read these lines, I realized that I was living more like my false self than my true self, at least on the job. And that made me sad. Ironically, reading those lines made me even sadder than I had been—because it gave a name to what I was experiencing.

In other words, it was bad enough that I wasn't happy at work. Now I realized that things were more serious—I was living as my false self. Even though I had just been introduced to that phrase, it sounded dire—something I wanted to avoid. More positively, I wanted to become my true self, whatever that was. Maybe you have similar feelings when you read those lines.

In prayer, can you ask God to help you become that person? Even if that true self seems far away, the desire to move in that direction is healthy. Certainly asking God for help makes sense. Can you express your desire for change?

Maybe you'd like to say something else to God. Maybe you're grateful for the way you've been able to move closer to your true self. Maybe you've taken steps in your life—talked to friends, seen a therapist, gone on a retreat, joined a faith-sharing group, become more active in your church, started to live up to those promises you've made to yourself—that have helped you feel that it's possible you can change for the better. Maybe you'd like to thank God for the grace to do this. Prayer shouldn't focus solely on problems. This part of the *lectio* can be praise as well.

4. Action

What difference can this text make in how I act? What possibilities does it open up? What challenges does it pose?

Prayer is meant not simply to draw you into closer relationship with God, as essential as that is for anyone's life. It is also meant to move you to action. Being in relationship with God will naturally move you to action, because the relationship will always lead to some form of conversion. But the prayer *itself* should be the goad to some sort of action.

Let's look at each of Father Harrington's final questions one by one:

What difference can this text make in how I act? Again, you might discover in yourself a desire to live a more authentic life. Don't forget that this is not simply your own insight coming up, but God inviting you to something, in this case living more authentically. What might that mean for you?

What does it mean for others as well? Prayer is not simply about your own personal relationship with God, but also about your relationship with others. What difference will your prayer mean in the way that you treat others? What will your true self do for others that your false self refused to do?

In my case, reading Thomas Merton made me less comfortable with my false self. I was made aware of it, understood that I wanted to change, and started the stumbling process that led to change, which would take me from the corporate world to the door of the Jesuit novitiate.

It's okay if you don't know what precise actions to take. You don't need a detailed road map. All you need to do is take the first step. Trust that God, who has raised something up in prayer, will help you, will give you the grace you need to make these changes.

What possibilities does it open up? Prayer enlarges your world. God always expands our horizons, and so prayer naturally helps you see things afresh. Why would God *not* want to open up life for us? The evil spirit says, "Things can never change." God says, "Why can't they?"

Passages like this from Thomas Merton and other spiritual masters made me think about doing something else with my life, though I had little idea what that something else would be. All I knew was that I was miserable in my job, and that I felt an invitation to be my true self. So I started to *try* to live a more authentic life. I stopped trying to fit my square self in the round hole of the job, and I started to think about the future with something other than dread.

What challenges does it pose? That may be the hardest part of this prayer. It's well and good to have insights, emotions, feelings, and memories emerge during *lectio*. It may help you to say, "This will make a difference in my life," and "new possibilities" sound great. But how will it challenge you? Prayer should sometimes make us uncomfortable about ourselves and upend the status quo. For me, this passage meant not trying to go along with what others expected of me. And that was a challenge—as it should have been.

Yet how do you get there? One way, again, is to think about your true self and act *as if* you were that person. If you want to be freer, more loving, or more compassionate, act as if you were freer, more loving, and more compassionate, and in time, with God's grace, you will be moving closer to becoming that person. At first it will feel unnatural. That's okay. Eventually it will feel natural, and you'll find that you are closer to your true self. In this way the challenge leads to a new reality.

Lectio divina is a popular form of prayer. Those four questions are a wonderful way to do it, but you can also do it your own way. Many people do *lectio* in a less structured way, not stopping to ask each of the four questions, but taking a word or a phrase to rest on or letting the overall reading move them, wash over them.

For me, Father Harrington's way works best, but as with all prayers, it's only one way. Pray *lectio* in whatever way helps you encounter God through the sacred Scriptures or other writings. And let God encounter you in any way God desires.

14

Finding God at the Center

CENTERING PRAYER

The older I get, the simpler my prayer seems to become. This is not to say that I don't enjoy Ignatian contemplation or *lectio divina*, both of which we can call "content-heavy" prayer. Both forms of prayer involve multiple steps and anticipate mental images and intellectual insights. They appeal to people with active imaginations and a knack for visualization.

But some find that style of prayer unappealing—too complicated, too many steps, too many things to remember, too many things to hold in one's head. Years ago, one retreatant, after a few tries at Ignatian contemplation, quoted the famous putdown by the sniffy courtier about Mozart's music in the movie *Amadeus*. The retreatant came in, sat down, and said, "Ignatian contemplation? Too many *notes*!"

For those who don't want "too many notes," there are other, "content-light" forms of prayer, where the mind is not as concerned with images or insights. Perhaps the most popular is called *centering prayer*. Before we talk about the "how to" of centering prayer, a little theology will help our discussion.

Like two rivers, two traditions of prayer flow through the history of Christian spirituality, the *apophatic* and the *kataphatic*. The apophatic (from the Greek *apophatikos*, which means "negative") is an approach to God that consciously moves away from images, words, concepts, and symbols. It is more content-light. The underlying theology is that God is beyond our comprehension, beyond any mental images we might have, unknowable, and so one seeks to find God by emptying oneself of preconceived notions of the divine.

Harvey Egan, SJ, a professor of theology at Boston College, notes in *The New Dictionary of Catholic Spirituality* that this tradition is firmly rooted in both the Old and New Testaments.[1] In the Book of Exodus, God dwells in "thick darkness" and appears to Moses as a "cloud."[2] Moses cannot see God's face when God passes, which is another way of expressing the divine otherness. The medieval philosopher and theologian St. Thomas Aquinas said that one can only know *that* God is, not *what* God is.[3] Perhaps the most well-known writer on this way of praying is the (still anonymous) author of the fourteenth-century work *The Cloud of Unknowing*, who speaks more of what God is *not* than what God is.[4]

The other stream, kataphatic prayer (from the Greek *kataphatikos*, meaning "positive"), seeks to experience God in creation and makes overt use of images, concepts, words, and symbols in prayer. Kataphatic prayer is more "content-heavy." The theology here is that we can begin to know God through all creation.

Like apophatic prayer, kataphatic prayer is firmly rooted in Scriptures—another reminder that there is no "right" way to pray. The Old Testament stresses that God can be understood through God's visible works—that is, the natural world. In Christian theology this is made even more explicit: God is known as a person. As Jesus says in the Gospel of John, "Whoever has seen me has seen the Father."[5] And Aquinas—now arguing for the opposing side—says that although God is ultimately unknowable, we can seek God through the things that are "known to us."[6]

St. Thomas might be accused of wanting to have it both ways. But he's right in both cases: God can be known through his works (kataphatic), but not known fully (apophatic). Both approaches are true. Both streams of prayer are authentic. Both have been used by believers over the millennia. Moreover, many find themselves using these two different approaches at different times in their lives.

You've probably guessed where I'm headed. Ignatian contemplation, with its emphasis on the imagination, fits squarely in the kataphatic tradition. So does *lectio divina*. Centering prayer, a practice that seeks to find God at the center of one's being without the intentional use of images, is closer to the negative way. In a conversation a few years ago for my book *The Jesuit Guide*, Father Egan said bluntly, "Centering prayer is apophatic." As a result, centering prayer is sometimes associated with Zen Buddhism, transcendental meditation, or yoga rather than Christian spirituality, but there are clear echoes of centering prayer in the classic Christian texts.

At one point in the *Spiritual Exercises*, St. Ignatius talks about the "Third Method of Praying," which he describes as done "according to rhythmic measures." You choose a single word (he suggests words from the Our Father) and concentrate on the word while you breathe in and out. "This is done in such a manner that one word of the prayer is said between one breath and another," he writes.[7] This Ignatian practice, at least in its technique, sounds similar to Zen meditation as well as centering prayer.

But before going any further with comparisons, let's talk about what centering prayer is rather than, apophatically, what it is not.

Grace at the Center

The three men most responsible for introducing centering prayer into contemporary Christian circles in the English-speaking world were John Main, in the United Kingdom; and M. Basil Pennington and Thomas Keating, in the United States. Main was a Benedictine monk; Pennington and Keating were Trappist monks, like Thomas Merton. Pennington wrote that the term "centering prayer" was inspired by Merton's use of similar terms.

Pennington and Keating wrote a brief book called *Finding Grace at the Center: The Beginning of Centering Prayer* along with Thomas E. Clarke, SJ. Before his death in 2005, Father Clarke, a quiet and gentle priest, resided at a small retreat house in a rural area north of New York City. He offered a concise introduction to the method: "Our theme is *the center*, that is, the place of meeting of the human spirit and the divine Spirit, and, in that meeting, the place where the Christian at prayer meets the whole of reality, divine and human, persons and things, time and space, nature and history, evil and good."[8]

Who can possibly do that? I thought when I first read that. But Father Clarke's point is simple. Centering prayer is a move toward your center, where you encounter God. But it's not simple navel-gazing. Nor is it about God and you alone, for any encounter with God will inevitably lead you outward, to the rest of creation.

This simple framework may strike people as suspicious. Initially, I was even more leery of centering prayer than I had been of imaginative prayer. If Ignatian contemplation sounded ridiculous, then meeting God within you sounded arrogant and a little crazy. Who was I to say that God dwelt within *me*?

Other Christians see centering prayer as suspect, because it's seen as dangerously close to Zen Buddhism and other Eastern practices. (The misguided idea that Christians couldn't learn anything from Eastern spiritualities used to be a great source of frustration for

Thomas Merton.) But the more I read about centering prayer, the more foolish my objections became—for the idea of God dwelling within us is a foundational Christian belief.

For one thing, most believers recognize conscience as the voice of God within us. For another, multiple images of the indwelling God appear in the New Testament and in the early church. St. Paul says that our body is a "temple of the Holy Spirit," one place where God resides, and that God's Spirit "dwells" in us.[9] St. Augustine wrote that God is *interior intimo meo*, "closer to me than I am to myself."[10] Finally, what else is prayer other than encountering God in the depths of one's being? Where else would you encounter God in private prayer?

Centering prayer moves us to our center, where God dwells, waiting to meet us. So let's look at how to do it, according to three experts. As you would expect with this form of prayer, it's simple and straightforward.

Three Steps

Father Pennington's essay in *Finding Grace at the Center* breaks down centering prayer into three easy steps. (His first step combines what we might think of as the first and last steps, how we begin and how we end the prayer.)

> One: At the beginning of the prayer we take a minute or two to quiet down and then move in faith and love to God dwelling in our depths; and at the end of the prayer we take several minutes to come out, mentally praying the Our Father.[11]

"Faith," Father Pennington points out, "is fundamental for this prayer, as for any prayer."[12] When you move to the center, you trust that you're moving toward the God who is nearer to you than you are to yourself.

> Two: After resting for a bit in the Presence in faith-full love, we take up a single, simple word that expresses our response and begin to let it repeat itself within.[13]

In other words, you use a prayer word like "love," "mercy," or "God" to help you focus. Don't concentrate on the meaning of the word. Rather, let the word anchor you in the presence of God. As the author of *The Cloud of Unknowing* says, "It is best when this word is wholly interior without a definite thought or actual sound."[14]

> Three: Whenever in the course of prayer we become aware of anything else, we simply gently return to the prayer word.[15]

Distractions in prayer are, as I've mentioned, unavoidable. Even Ignatius mentions them. ("I was disturbed by someone whistling," he once wrote, "but was not so greatly disquieted."[16]) The prayer word gently recalls you to the presence of God. Distractions, as Keating writes, should be treated "like the weather, which you just have to accept. The important thing is not to pay any attention to them."[17]

And that's it. Centering prayer is simple in theory. In practice, it can be difficult for beginners, especially if your life is packed with content. The notion that you could meet God without doing anything may seem bizarre. Centering prayer is not about producing or doing or achieving. It's about being. Or rather being with.

As Margaret Silf says, "In the eye of the storm is a center of perfect peace, where our deepest desire is embraced by God's own desire for us."[18] To use the analogy of friendship, centering prayer is like a long silent walk with a good friend. Although you're not speaking to one another, there may be a deeper communication going on.

Invitations to Centering Prayer

Sometimes I find, paradoxically, that something content-heavy can lead to the content-light type of centering prayer. Sometimes reading a passage from a book, hearing a quotation, listening to a hymn, or walking into a church or a forest or along the seashore can lead to a wordless silence in the presence of God. Poems are especially helpful in this regard. They can conjure up an image of God that invites one instantly into prayer.

A few years ago I was on retreat at the Linwood Spiritual Center in Rhinebeck, New York, where a favorite spiritual director, Maureen Steeley, SU, gave me a poem by Joyce Rupp, which prompted me to centering prayer. The image of God was so surprising and so welcoming that it made me want to pray instantly. Let me share it with you:

Beckoner
Song of Songs 2:8–12

You tap at the window of my heart.
You knock at the door of my busyness.
You call out in my night dreams.
You whisper in my haphazard prayer.
You beckon. You invite. You entice.
You woo. You holler. You insist:
"Come! Come into my waiting embrace.
Rest your turmoil in my easy silence.
Put aside your heavy bag of burdens.
Accept the simple peace I offer you."[19]

The gentle image of a God who taps, knocks, calls out, whispers, and beckons invited me into contemplation in the presence of the

"Beckoner." It led me directly into a quiet, wordless, imageless time with God. Perhaps you have your own favorite poems or images. Be open to the various ways that you can be drawn into silent conversation with God.

What Can Happen?

What can happen in centering prayer? Almost anything—as in any prayer. But one common result is not, as with content-heavy prayer, the occurrence of images or insights—though we can be open to those things—as much as it is a feeling of closeness with God. This can be compared to what can happen in any close relationship.

A relationship may involve a good deal of active communication—talking, discussing, listening, questioning, even arguing. This may happen over a meal, driving in a car, while doing housework, during a time set aside for catching up, or in any other part of daily life. Most times the conversation is direct, and the communication is clear. Afterward both can look back and say, "We were together and talked about this or that topic."

But at other times you might find yourself in silence with the other person and experience a more passive way of communicating. A parent and child might be working together in the garden, building a birdhouse, or shoveling snow, all in silence; they become aware of the fact that they are doing this together, and the parent is filled with gratitude for the child. A couple might be silently washing dishes together, become aware of the joy they have found in one another, and realize that this is what they had long hoped for. Or a boyfriend and girlfriend are driving to a date together and realize that they like this activity, driving in the car in silence, as much as the other things they do together. Centering prayer is like this: enjoying being in God's presence, silently.

Take something more purposeful: the *intentional* spending of quiet time together. A couple, two friends, or a group of friends decides to do something that they know will be mainly wordless: walking on the beach, watching a sunrise, hiking through a forest. As they do this together, there is a sense of companionship, friendship, and love.

Although there is no talking involved, there is nonetheless deep communication happening. It is less "speaking with" and more "being with." (In fact, in these situations, talking might seem out of place.) Afterward those who have been together may feel a sense of peace and comfort, sometimes finding it hard to put into words what that silent time meant.

This is what I mainly experience in centering prayer. (Others may have different experiences.) It can sometimes feel as if nothing is happening, as if you are just washing dishes with your spouse or just walking beside a friend silently. But often a deeper feeling accompanies the nothing.

At the same time, images and insights also arise in centering prayer, as well as memories, desires, emotions, and the other fruits of prayer we have looked at. But in this form of prayer, it's important not to engage them as much; simply notice them and perhaps bring them to prayer in another session. This form of prayer asks us to treat everything other than the prayer word as a distraction to be gently let go. "It is important not to reflect on what is happening while doing centering prayer," writes Thomas Keating. "You can do that later. While in this prayer, dedicate the time to interior silence."[20]

Think of it this way. If you and a friend had decided to walk along the beach in silence, and you were reminded of something that you wanted to say, you would probably check yourself and allow both of you to enjoy the silence. You might make a note to bring it up later. Communicating verbally is important, but so is the silence. And centering prayer is the time for silence.

Speaking Prose

Remember the example of Molière's Monsieur Jourdain, who finds to his delight that he has been speaking prose all his life? A similar experience often happens to people with centering prayer. When I describe the practice as "placing yourself in God's presence," people's eyes often light up, and they say, "Well, I do that already!"

Some time ago a friend told me that she found meditation easier than prayer. "Prayer is too difficult for me," she said.

She explained that in meditation, she emptied herself of all her thoughts, found a mantra that she liked, and stuck with that form of centering herself. "It's so much easier than prayer," she said. "Is that okay?"

Here was a believer practicing the techniques of centering prayer, but leaving God out of the picture. In response, I suggested a small change.

"Instead of varying your technique, why not continue with what you call meditation and consciously remind yourself that you are in God's presence? Where it was once simply you by yourself meditating, why not invite God into your prayer?"

Her eyes lit up. She told me she had been missing God so much.

"I can do that!" she said with delight.

So can you.

15

Discovering God in Creation

NATURE PRAYER

A passage from Pope Francis's encyclical, or pastoral letter to the worldwide church, on the environment, *Laudato Si'* ("Praise to You"), changed the way I looked at both prayer and creation. It's called "The Gaze of Jesus":

> [Jesus] was able to invite others to be attentive to the beauty that there is in the world because he himself was in constant touch with nature, lending it an attention full of fondness and wonder. As he made his way throughout the land, he often stopped to contemplate the beauty sown by his Father and invited his disciples to perceive a divine message in things.[1]

Why did this passage from the pope's encyclical change my way of looking at creation? Because I had never thought of Jesus as participating in creation in such a direct way. I knew that Jesus lived in creation—among "the birds and the bees and the flowers and the trees," as the old song goes. And I knew that Jesus often used elements of creation to illustrate his parables, which, to quote the definition from the biblical scholar C. H. Dodd, are metaphors or similes drawn from "nature or common life."[2]

But it never occurred to me that Jesus *enjoyed* creation. "As he made his way throughout the land, he often stopped to contemplate the beauty sown by his Father," writes Pope Francis. Thinking of Jesus enjoying nature opened for me a new window into his life. I imagined him sitting on a hillside overlooking the Sea of Galilee and taking in the rocky landscape, dotted with wildflowers, that led down to the water.

Pope Francis was sharing his imaginative reading of the Gospels. It's impossible to know for certain that Jesus contemplated creation in this way, since nothing like this is mentioned in the Gospels explicitly. That is, there is no Gospel passage that says, "Immediately Jesus withdrew from the crowds so that he could enjoy the flowers."

But can we doubt it? Jesus had a sensitive heart and an inquisitive mind, so how could he not have enjoyed the natural world? It strains credulity to think of Jesus grimly marching through the landscape of Judea and Galilee, head down, teeth clenched, willing himself not to look at the flowers, steeling himself against a refreshing breeze, and stopping his ears against the birdsongs. The profusion of images from nature that he uses shows that he paid attention to nature and loved it.

Traveling through Israel makes it even harder to imagine Jesus ignoring creation. The first time I visited the Holy Land, I was stunned by its natural beauty. My first glimpse of the Sea of Galilee, to take one example, was unforgettable. A Jesuit friend and I were driving north from Jerusalem to Galilee in a tiny rental car. Toward the end of our journey the sea burst into view between some slender palm trees: the palest blue water under a cerulean sky with pinkish-gray hills on the opposite shore.

My friend and I stayed at a retreat house perched on a hill above the Sea of Galilee, where I could barely take my eyes off the water. At the time, however, the land itself was not quite so beautiful. We were there in late August, when the sun parches the Galilean landscape to a crisp and the dry grasses are varying in shades of brown. When I returned home, a Jesuit familiar with Israel said, "You should return in the spring when everything is green." Frankly, it was hard to imagine.

A few years later, I returned with a group of pilgrims in March and was delighted. In the springtime, Galilee is carpeted by vivid green grass dotted by bright red poppies and, best of all, countless mustard plants that burst into yellow flower. The profusion of yellow flowers of the kind that Jesus saw and used in his parables filled me with a joy unique to the Holy Land.[3] It was beautiful not only in itself, but because I knew that Jesus had seen it too.

Why do I place so much emphasis on the physical surroundings of the Holy Land? To help us enter our discussion of what we might call "nature prayer."

How to Pray with Nature

For most people who lived in the world of the Old and New Testaments, the question "How do you pray with nature?" would be nonsensical. The entire universe was under God's command, and everything spoke of God's presence. "The heavens are telling the glory of God; and the firmament proclaims his handiwork," as the psalmist says.[4]

Beyond the creation narratives in the Old Testament, the most beautiful expression of this belief might be contained in the Psalms. Psalm 95, a psalm prayed often in the breviary, says:

For the LORD is a great God,
    and a great King above all gods.
In his hand are the depths of the earth;
    the heights of the mountains are his also.
The sea is his, for he made it,
    and the dry land, which his hands have formed.[5]

While in graduate theology studies in Cambridge, Massachusetts, I would often walk through Harvard Yard and pass Emerson Hall, which had these words incised in foot-high letters on the granite lintel above the main entrance:

WHAT IS MAN THAT THOU ART MINDFUL OF HIM?

Even when I was rushing to class, seeing those words never failed to move me and remind me of the full question posed by Psalm 8:

When I look at your heavens, the work of your fingers,
    the moon and the stars that you have established;
what are human beings that you are mindful of them,
    mortals that you care for them?[6]

The psalmist is admitting that when he looks at nature—the moon and the stars—he not only thinks of God, but is also moved to ponder God's care for humanity. That insight comes from contemplation of the natural world and "God's heavens."

For people living during biblical times, creation was suffused with God's presence. I still believe it is, and I am not alone, but in many places today others no longer share that collective belief. As an overarching worldview, the idea of the world as "charged with the grandeur of God," to quote the Jesuit poet Gerard Manley Hopkins, has fewer adherents.[7] Therefore, we may need to be more conscious of God's presence in the natural world.

Here, again, is the question: How do we pray in nature and with nature? Let me suggest several ways, some of which overlap.

Let Nature Calm or Delight You

A massive study by the University of East Anglia discovered what many of us have always suspected: spending time outdoors is good for your mental, emotional, and physical health. Drawing on 140 previous studies, which canvassed more than 290 million people, the study concluded the following, according to the lead author Caoimhe Twohig-Bennett:

> Spending time in, or living close to, natural green spaces is associated with diverse and significant health benefits. It reduces the risk of type II diabetes, cardiovascular disease, premature death, and preterm birth, and increases sleep duration.
>
> People living closer to nature also had reduced diastolic blood pressure, heart rate, and stress. . . . In fact, one of the really interesting things we found is that exposure to greenspace significantly reduces people's levels of salivary cortisol—a physiological marker of stress.[8]

Greenspaces were defined as "open, undeveloped land with natural vegetation" but also included urban parks and street greenery. The study also mentioned something called "forest bathing" in Japan, where people spent time in forests either sitting or lying down. (I would call that simply "sitting or lying down in a forest"!)

Few people would quarrel with that finding; it makes sense to anyone who moves between urban and pastoral settings. The calm of most natural settings stands in striking contrast to the stress that is palpable in urban environments. Once I leave New York City, even if it's just a few miles out of town, my body relaxes. Some of this may have to do with psychological effects—leaving behind the stresses of work—but some of it has to do with the calming effects of nature.

I have another theory about this, probably unprovable. Perhaps there is a primitive part of our brain that is hardwired to connect with nature. Since we were nature dwellers for tens of thousands of years, it stands to reason that we would have, in some ancient part of our brain, a physiological desire and affinity for nature. It may be part of who we were, and perhaps who we still are.

Overall, it's clear that most of us enjoy nature, even if merely because it calms us, as that study demonstrates. But just as important as the physiological effects of nature are the spiritual effects.

The summary of that study didn't touch upon what I would suggest is the fundamental reason that we enjoy spending time in nature: it connects us with God at a deep level. When we are in nature, among the trees, looking into a pond, gazing at the ocean tides, contemplating the clouds, or standing dumbfounded before a mountain, we are encountering something created *directly* by God, and so the distance between God and us is decreased. Works of art created by human beings—paintings, songs, buildings, poems, novels, operas, musicals, sculptures—can move us, and we can appreciate them as inspired by God, but in nature we encounter something created by God alone. We are experiencing the creativity of God in a less mediated way. This may be one reason why time in nature can be such a powerful spiritual experience.

In fact, the physiological effects—slower breathing, lower heart rate, overall calming—may be another way that God draws us to spend time in nature and meditate on creation. We enjoy nature not only because we are closer to God, but also because this is one way that God draws us closer. Again, this is speculative, but it's been at work in my own life.

Every year, for the last thirty years, like every Jesuit, I have spent eight days on a silent retreat, usually at a retreat house. And every year, on the first day of the retreat, as I walk outside and look at either the ocean or a river or a forest, I am filled with joy. I think, *Yes, this is the way things should be.* In a few moments I feel calm and disposed to praying.

This is the first step to praying in nature: letting it calm you and invite you into prayer.

Celtic spiritual traditions call places that do that easily—the ocean does it for me—"thin places," places where the border between God and humanity is "thin." In her poem "Praying," Mary Oliver reminds us that it needn't even be an especially beautiful or grand place: "It doesn't have to be / the blue iris, it could be / weeds in a vacant lot, or a few / small stones; just / pay attention."9

Enjoy Nature as God's Creation

A few years ago, my nephew and I were walking along a path that encircles a pond near his family's house. We've been doing this for several years, and we always enjoy looking at the fish in the pond and listening to the birdcalls. (My nephew is also a champion rock-skipper.) A few autumns ago, when Matthew was ten, we were walking under the trees, whose leaves had turned gold, and he said, "Uncle Jim, I know you really like this, because where you live, there's no nature!"

"Yes, that's true," I said. "I enjoy being in nature."

"What parts do you like best?" he asked.

Matthew's comment was like unbidden spiritual direction. That night in prayer I thought about his question. The answer differs for each person, but a partial list of the things I most enjoy about nature includes seeing the leaves change in autumn, watching thunderstorms approach and break over a landscape, and, especially, seeing the varying colors of the ocean in different parts of the world. When

I'm on retreat in Massachusetts, the ocean is a steely blue. When I'm on vacation at the Jersey shore, it's a greenish brown. When I was in Jamaica as a novice, it was a pale translucent blue. On the coast of Kenya, it was grass-green.

Several scientists have told me that the color of the sea surface depends on the type of earth under the water, the currents, the level of plankton, and the sea temperature, among other things. Scientific explanations aside, these varying colors are always a way for me to appreciate the great variety of God's creative hand, as if God were saying, "The ocean is beautiful as it is. But I can make it even more beautiful by changing its color."

At this point in our discussion, I should probably show you photographs, since it's hard to explain the beauty of creation in words—and I'm no poet. But I'm sure you have your own favorite parts of the natural world. All sorts of things might delight you: sunsets, storms, animals, clouds, trees, flowers, insects, rocks. Can you enjoy all these beautiful things? Can you allow yourself to enjoy them as unique, wonderful, and strange things that God has created?

As Father Barry says, "You can be praying just by consciously sensing what [God] has made."[10]

Consider Nature As an Image of God

A few years ago, I was on a summer vacation with some Jesuit friends at the seashore. The Jesuits own a house in Cape May, a town on the southernmost tip of New Jersey. (Because we Jesuits take a vow of poverty and can't afford personal vacations, the Jesuits own a few houses for communal vacations.) That year I was struggling with some problem—which I have now forgotten—and was walking along the beach.

In the early morning, the Cape May beach presents a ribbon of sand that stretches for miles and is usually devoid of crowds. It's my favorite place for a run and a swim. After my run, I felt overwhelmed by my problems and turned toward the ocean. In its almost unimaginable immensity, it suddenly seemed an image of God.

Perhaps because I've spent so many retreats at Eastern Point Retreat House by the Atlantic Ocean, for me the sea has become intimately connected with God. Printed on the front page of the brochure for the retreat house, for as long as I can remember, are the words "Deep calls to deep" from Psalm 42:

> Deep calls to deep
>   at the thunder of your cataracts;
> all your waves and your billows
>   have gone over me.[11]

As an aside, here's an example of being able to fruitfully pray with something without knowing what the passage means—or in this case completely misunderstanding it. Recently I asked Richard Clifford, SJ, an Old Testament scholar, what this passage, so dear to me, means.

Father Clifford wrote that this "psalm of longing" is a "surprisingly modern internal dialogue of a frightened and discouraged psalmist who is doing his best to 'hold on.'" The psalmist is in the north of Israel, far from his fellow Israelites, who are close to God in the Temple in Jerusalem. "To dramatize his lost and alienated situation, he sees himself in the midst of the chaotic waters that characterize a world without the Lord's powerful protective presence. Those chaotic and godless waters are washing over him."

But what does the psalmist mean when he says, "Deep calls to deep"? Father Clifford said that he couldn't be sure, but instinct told him it meant "the tumult of the chaotic sea is being compared to the conversation of evil forces."

What a surprise! When I first read that line as a young Jesuit, it meant something else to me entirely—that the deepest part of ourselves calls out to God. "Deep calls to deep" seemed a perfectly wrought image of the ideal goal of prayer: communing with God. I thought about that often when I was near the ocean.

That morning on the seashore, however, the ocean felt more like an image of God's *immensity*. It is a powerful image for me—vast, deep, unknowable, and in some places literally unfathomable. The mass, weight, and power of the sea put me in mind of God.

Even the surface of the sea defies description, as glimpses of God always do. In one of my favorite books on nature, *The Sea Around Us*, naturalist Rachel Carson captures some of this mystery when she writes, "Crossed by colors, lights, and moving shadows, sparkling in the sun, mysterious in the twilight, its aspects and its moods vary hour by hour."[12] One cannot catch the sea in any one mood, any more than one can catch God.

That morning the sea was the perfect image of God. So I took a deep breath and exhaled my problems onto the surface of the sea and into God's care. As the waves receded from the shore, I imagined God taking all my problems into God's loving care and into God's immensity. What were my problems in the face of the vastness of these waters? To use the Psalm quote in a slightly different way, "Who am I that God is mindful of me?"

On other days, I would use the sea as an image of God in a different way. I would plunge into the cold ocean after my run and then float there, imagining myself surrounded by God on all sides. Sometimes I would dunk my head underwater, so that I was surrounded by the ocean. It was comforting to feel surrounded by God's love.

I know that the Atlantic Ocean is not God, but it helps me *imagine* God. You might consider other images that help you imagine God. Perhaps the sky is an image of God's overarching care, the changing clouds an image of God's playfulness, the driving wind an image of God's creative Spirit, a soaring seagull an image of God's freedom.

Each image may speak to you in a different way about one of God's attributes or about a way that God is active in your life, which may in turn help you relate to God in a new or deeper way.

Learn About the Wonders of Nature

As a boy, I spent an inordinate amount of time looking at things in nature. I would turn over rocks in our backyard to examine the bugs underneath, poke at the ant mounds on the sidewalks in front of our house, admire the wild snapdragons and goldenrod in the meadows near my elementary school—but most of all I watched birds.

One of the books I treasured was Roger Tory Peterson's *How to Know the Birds*. Peterson was both an ornithologist and a gifted artist whose graceful drawings and paintings of the birds filled his field guide, which was regularly pulled from my bookshelf. The author also popularized the use of "field marks," sometimes called the Peterson Identification System, which enables one to recognize species by noticing distinctive features like colored bars on the wings or the way a bird flies ("undulating," "hovering," or "straight and fast").

I spent hours staring out the window looking at the birds and flipping through my dog-eared book trying to distinguish between a catbird and a blackbird. Later, I would try to paint them with as much detail as I could, in the style of Peterson's book—though my juvenile watercolors paled in comparison.

One winter, my parents let me hang a bird feeder from a branch of the tree nearest our dining-room window. I took an empty plastic milk container and, after cutting out an opening and filling it with birdseed, I hung it from the gnarled crabapple tree. Over the next few weeks I watched dozens of birds swarm around the feeder: cardinals and blue jays, sparrows and juncos, catbirds and mockingbirds.

I still love birds and find that one of the blessings of being a Jesuit who has been sent to live in various places in the world and, lately, been required to travel a good deal is seeing so many birds that I could have never dreamed of seeing as a boy.

When in Gloucester, I see (and hear, because they're noisy) more red-wing blackbirds in a day than I could have in a lifetime in suburban Philadelphia. The pond near the retreat house hosts all manner of waterfowl: mallards that flaunt the purple patches on their wings, black cormorants that nosedive into the sea, and barn swallows that make their nest under the eaves of the retreat house, swoop and spin, and consume 850 mosquitoes over the course of a day. During my time in Jamaica as a novice, I saw a hummingbird for the first time and practically jumped out of my skin. And when I was in East Africa, it was as if I had gone to heaven, birdwise at least, when I saw my first weaver bird just outside our house in Nairobi, weaving its distinctive nest hanging from a flowering purple jacaranda tree.

I'm still a bird enthusiast, though not a "birder," someone who rises before dawn to traipse through a dark landscape looking for birds through binoculars or someone organized enough to keep a catalog of the various species they've seen. But I feel elated when I see a new bird, especially one that I recognize from my days poring over Peterson's guide. Sometimes I even remember the field marks that help me to identify it.

And a few years ago on a pilgrimage in Israel, I woke up before dawn and wandered down to the Sea of Galilee. I watched dozens of unfamiliar birds fly around and thought, *Where is Roger Tory Peterson when you need him?* Then I realized that I was probably seeing some of the same types of birds that Jesus saw, and I remembered that passage from *Laudato Si'* that I quoted earlier. Sometimes on pilgrimage I will just close my eyes and hear the same birdsongs that Jesus heard.

This lifelong interest in birds in their glorious variety and gorgeous plumage has led me to a deeper appreciation of God's creation as expressed through the creatures Jesus called the "birds of the air." To me, they are signs of God's endless variety and the way God blesses each part of the world with special birds: robins in America, hummingbirds in the Caribbean, weaver birds in Africa. And the more I learn about birds, the more I can see God's hand in nature in a specific way. I'm not just enjoying nature in general; I'm enjoying a specific part of it in the same way that you might enjoy a specific part of a friend—her sense of humor, knowledge of movies, ability to make you laugh. The more I know about birds, the more I appreciate God.

What part of creation might do that for you?

Let Nature Teach You About God

Directing a retreat, I once asked a woman, "What was your prayer like yesterday?"

"I hugged a tree!" she said.

Younger readers may not recall this epithet, but a few decades ago "tree hugger" was a derogatory term for someone interested in environmentalism.

Was she serious? In spiritual direction the last thing you want to do is laugh at something that is supposed to be serious, so I suppressed my smile. "What do you mean?" I asked, hedging my bets.

"Do you see that beautiful tree outside?" she replied. "When I hugged the tree, I felt connected to the earth and to the beauty of God's creation. Stretching my hands around the trunk made me feel grounded, connected to the earth, in a way that I never had before. And here I was holding on to a living creature, which reminded me that God is continually creating."

Her openness to nature helped me see God's creation in a way that was different from using nature as an image of God or learning about nature. Her nature prayer helped me see that creation could be used to understand not only God, but also God's *activity*—to see creation not only as something static, but as something active; to see not only creation, but *ongoing* creation.

One of the most moving passages in St. Ignatius Loyola's *Spiritual Exercises* is his invitation to consider how God "dwells" in creation in various ways: "in the elements [rocks and minerals], giving them existence; in the plants, giving them life; in the animals, giving them sensation; in human beings, giving them intelligence."[13]

Later on, Ignatius invites us to consider how God, in a beautiful phrase, "labors and works for me in all the creatures on the face of the earth."[14] This is a God who is still creating. Especially if you watch something grow—a plant in your yard, a puppy or kitten you've just adopted, even your own child—you may have had this experience. You have witnessed God not only creating, but continuing to create, "laboring" to create. Ignatius writes that God

> . . . acts in the manner of one who is laboring. For example, he is working in the heavens, elements, plants, fruits, cattle, and all the rest—giving them their existence, conserving them, concurring with their vegetative and sensitive activities.[15]

As you enjoy nature, can you see God's hand in creation and in the continuous creation of the world around you? That awareness can lead you to a deeper, more contemplative appreciation of God's continuing activity in the world, and in your own life.

Look for Epiphanies in Nature

On a recent retreat at the Eastern Point Retreat House, God had a surprise in store. For many years I had wondered about the validity of seeing signs in nature as a way that God speaks to us. I knew that I could gain insights from God through nature, but direct communication seemed fanciful, almost superstitious. As a friend of mine likes to say, "Just because a leaf falls in front of you on the sidewalk doesn't mean that God is saying anything special to you—or any-thing at all!"

In any event, although I wasn't going through any doubts about my vow, I was praying about chastity. Chastity is something that members of religious orders pray about from time to time in the same way that people might pray about their married life and ask questions in prayer: "How good of a spouse am I? How can I be more loving? Where am I failing to notice God in my relationship? Where is God asking me to grow?"

I thought about the times in the past when I had started to fall in love with someone (not acting on it, just noticing those feelings) and times when I was too focused on one person's attention. What could I do to avoid this in the future? One day, I was speaking to my retreat director, Joe, about this and wondering which Bible passages might be helpful.

We discussed a few, and then Joe said, out of the blue, "Don't for-get to see what epiphanies you might have in nature."

It wasn't a completely surprising comment, because I had been telling Joe how much I enjoyed nature. Still, I wasn't used to hearing things put so straightforwardly. It was an unexpected invitation to see God speaking to me more directly in nature.

Afterward, I walked from Joe's office into the main part of the re-treat house, an old mansion built in 1926. Many of the smaller rooms used for spiritual direction are still called parlors. In the hallway one of the Jesuit retreat directors, John, was peering into one of the par-lors, looking confused.

"A bird got into the house," he said.

On the floor between two wingback chairs was a small gray cat-bird, looking more confused than John.

"See if you can shoo him into the foyer," said John. After much flapping of wings, the bird was coaxed into the foyer, which connects the mansion with the dining room. Both sides of this small space are glassed in. Thus, the catbird was now in a room that probably appeared to be the outdoors, with grass, trees, and sky visible. In response, it started flying at great speed toward the windows, each time bouncing off the window and falling to the floor.

"He's hurting himself," said John. "He thinks he's outside."

Stunned, the catbird hopped on the floor erratically. It was easy for me to gather him up in a woolen blanket that had been draped across the back of a nearby chair. Underneath the blanket, I could feel his warm, lively body and his wings trying to flap. John opened the door, and when I unwrapped the blanket, the bird flew to the top of a wall that stood behind a statue of the Virgin Mary. Then it flew away.

Into my head came the thought, *Flying at false freedom hurts you.* I felt it was a kind of message from God. For me, false freedom is the appeal of something that is not in keeping with my vows—like an infatuation. True freedom comes when I accept the love that comes from all those in my life—Jesuit brothers, friends, and family—freely and deeply. We hurt ourselves when we try to seek love in places that are not going to nourish us. It is the difference between false love and real love.

The next day I related this experience to Joe, who said that it was important to see God's hand in this.

"I'm not sure whether I should trust it or not," I said.

"I'd trust it," he said. "Because it really spoke to you about where you were."

Incidents like this are rare and have to be discerned carefully. Not every leaf that falls in front of you is a message from God. And we have to be careful not to become superstitious or solipsistic: creation does not revolve around us! At the same time, we shouldn't be blind to the variety of ways that God speaks to us, one of which is often directly through nature. Father Barry once remarked to me, "Remember that God is in everything all the time. So a coincidence can be a way for God to communicate."

Reverence and Care for Nature

One of the most important messages in *Laudato Si'* is that the environment is to be reverenced. Many other thinkers and theologians as well as saints—especially St. Francis of Assisi—have spoken about creation in this way. But Pope Francis's encyclical may be the most comprehensive approach to the call to reverence creation and care for it.

The encyclical defies easy description, much less a quick summary, for *Laudato Si'* is about more than simply the environment. It looks at how the environment is intimately connected with the flourishing of humanity and especially how the degradation of the environment disproportionately affects the poor. The year the encyclical was released, I hosted a panel discussion at a Catholic university. There Cardinal Peter Turkson, the president of the Pontifical Council for Justice and Peace (the Vatican department that helped write the encyclical), said, "This is not an environmental encyclical; it is a social encyclical." Certainly that is true. But the majority of readers will appreciate it as much for what it says about creation as about the economy.

One of the encyclical's most important insights is Pope Francis's notion that "everything is connected." The decisions we make about natural resources *and* the decisions we make about economic policies will influence not only the planet, but also the well-being of our brothers and sisters.

Francis also notes that we are invited to see that every living creature—not only every human being—is valuable and therefore worthy of our care. The following passage is one of my favorite parts of the encyclical, and when I read it I thought of all the birds I had seen as a boy, each of them with infinite value:

Our insistence that each human being is an image of God should not make us overlook the fact that each creature has its own purpose. None is superfluous. The entire material universe speaks of God's love, his boundless affection for us. Soil, water, mountains: everything is, as it were, a caress of God.[16]

Yet we do not always reverence creation. In many instances we have simply used and abused it. Francis turns to the story in Genesis in which humankind was asked to "till and keep" the earth, that is, to work the earth and use it, but also to preserve it. It's not ours, only entrusted to us: "The earth was here before us and it has been given to us."[17] Overall, we have tilled too much and kept too little. What is called for is greater reverence, and that reverence includes care. That care then can be a form of reverence, of prayer.

Recently I read a marvelous biography of Rachel Carson called *On a Farther Shore*.[18] Carson was the author of *Silent Spring*, which awakened American society to the dangers of pesticides in the early 1960s. In her earlier books *The Edge of the Sea* and *The Sea Around Us*, she wrote movingly about the ocean and the seashore. *Silent Spring* was the heroic harbinger of the contemporary environmental movement. Her entire life, from biologist to nature writer to environmental advocate, could be seen as one long reverencing of creation.

But one doesn't have to be an activist to care for creation. And have you ever considered care of the environment as a kind of prayer? Working in your garden, trying to recycle, creating less waste, and using fewer natural resources as well as taking in a stray dog or cat and working for global change (less pollution and better management of natural resources) can all be forms of reverencing creation.

Pope Francis also recognizes the intimate connections that many of us have to nature, and he encourages that bond. He recognizes that it is in those places, and those moments with nature, that God often speaks to us most profoundly:

> The history of our friendship with God is always linked to particular places which take on an intensely personal meaning; we all remember places, and revisiting those memories does us much good. Anyone who has grown up in the hills or used to sit by the spring to drink, or played outdoors in the neighborhood square; going back to these places is a chance to recover something of their true selves.[19]

When I first read that, I thought of the meadow from my childhood, a "thin place" for me. Such holy places, places that ask us to pay attention, need to be reverenced.

In the same way that we would reverence others by caring for them, we can reverence nature. In this way our care for nature, for God's creation, for what Francis calls "our common home," becomes itself a prayer.

16

Talking About Prayer

SPIRITUAL DIRECTION, RETREATS, FAITH SHARING, AND JOURNALING

As you become more experienced in prayer, you may start to hear about four common practices: spiritual direction, retreats, faith sharing, and journaling. All are helpful ways of deepening your prayer life. Unfortunately, all four practices are sometimes considered the reserve of the extremely religious, when they are gifts meant for all believers. Anyone who prays can greatly benefit from them.

Let's talk about these four key practices, which are related to one another.

Spiritual Direction

Spiritual direction is a practice in which one person seeks help from a more experienced person in noticing God's activity in prayer and daily life. The one providing guidance is the spiritual director, and the one seeking help is the spiritual directee.

In their now classic book *The Practice of Spiritual Direction*, William Barry and William Connolly offer a more comprehensive definition:

> We define Christian spiritual direction, then, as help given by one believer to another that enables the latter to pay attention to God's personal communication to him or her, to respond to this personally communicating God, to grow in intimacy with this God, and to live out the consequences of the relationship. The *focus* of this type of spiritual direction is on experience, not ideas, and specifically on the religious dimension of experience, i.e., that dimension of any experience that evokes the presence of the mysterious Other whom we call God. Moreover, this experience is viewed, not as an isolated event, but as an expression of the ongoing personal relationship God has established with each one of us.[1]

That definition reminds us of a few things. First, the director helps the directee notice and appreciate how God *is* communicating with the directee, whatever form that takes—not what the director believes about how God *should* be communicating. A good spiritual director will not impose ideas, expectations, or presuppositions.

For example, if a person is going through a personal crisis and not feeling God's presence in prayer, the director will not say, "I'm *sure* you must be feeling *something*." Instead, the director will listen patiently to the person's experience and accompany him or her. The director might pray that the directee has an experience of God's presence, but during the direction session the focus is on accompaniment, not rebutting or explaining away whatever experience is occurring.

Second, the focus is on the directee's *experience*, not ideas. Again, if someone is going through a rocky time and speaks about their anger at God, a director will be attentive to that rather than speaking about the theology of suffering: "You know, St. Thomas Aquinas defines suffering as . . ." The directee might naturally ask theological questions, and at times the director might respond, but a spiritual director is focused less on theological education and more on the directee's experience of God. As Karl Rahner said, "Knowing God is more important than knowing about God."

Finally, the experience is viewed as part of an *ongoing* relationship with God. This is similar to the case of someone who visits a pastoral counselor to talk about an argument with a spouse, an issue that is then considered within the context of the marriage. It's not about helping the person understand fighting or conflicts in general, but about this argument in the context of a specific real-life relationship. Likewise, the spiritual director looks at what is discussed in the session as part of the story of God's relationship with the directee.

These rules are not ironclad. A director might occasionally offer some advice and at various moments speak about Christian theology. But the spiritual director is there primarily to listen and help the directee notice where God already is. "Direction," then, is something of a misnomer. A spiritual director doesn't direct as much as listen and notice, and help the directee listen and notice.

A good spiritual direction session, say Barry and Connolly, should include: empathetic listening, paying attention, affirming, assisting in clarification, raising questions when the directee wants them, and helping the directee to recognize the affective attitudes that influence his or her attitude toward God. But regardless of the particular technique, the emphasis always remains on the directee's situation, where the individual finds himself or herself in relation to God.

Barry offers a superb summary of spiritual direction in *God and You*:

> He or she [the spiritual director] would be interested in your actual experience of God, not your speculations about God. So the director would want you to talk about your experience and would patiently help you to do this. We almost have to invent a language to talk about our actual experience of God because we are so unused to speaking about it. The director will ask you questions like these: "What happens when you pray?" "What is God like for you?" "What do you want or desire from God when you pray?" At first such questions may puzzle or even scare you, but gradually, if the director is patient and really interested in your experience, you will find yourself able to articulate more and more of what you experience in prayer.[2]

Joyce Rupp, in her book *Prayer*, also astutely notes that a good spiritual director is necessary to counteract our own judgments of our prayer, which are often negative:

> We have our own preconceived notions about how we ought to pray and about whether our growth is, or is not, happening. Thus, we cannot stand outside our self to see the truth clearly. An objective person listens and encourages us to remain faithful in the midst of prayer's diverse rhythms.[3]

We're not always the best judge of our prayer. That is precisely why Thomas Merton says, "Humility and docile acceptance of sound advice are very necessary in the life of prayer."[4]

That may sound sensible, but what does it mean *in practice*? What does spiritual direction look like? What can one expect?

Typically, a spiritual director meets with a person on a regular basis, usually monthly, for roughly an hour. The director will want to know what has been happening in a person's prayer (similar to the things we've been discussing in this book) and daily life. A good director will do more listening than talking. And a good directee will be as honest as possible with the director and be open to being questioned and challenged.

Spiritual direction is different from psychotherapy, which is mainly concerned with exploring the roots of psychological problems and need not be religious at all; it is different from pastoral counseling, in which trained men and women from a religious background offer one-on-one counseling; and it is different from simply giving advice to someone going through a tough time.

Although there may be elements of all these practices in spiritual direction sessions—psychological problems may arise, difficult situations need to be looked at in a pastoral setting, and advice is sometimes requested and given—none of those elements is the focus of spiritual direction. The focus is on God's activity in the directee's life.

Thus, one of the most common questions from directees, "What do you think I should do?" is often answered with the question, "Have you brought that question to God in prayer?" The emphasis is not on what the director thinks (as it might be in psychotherapy, pastoral counseling, or advice giving), but on God's activity. As Barry and Connolly say, "In terms of the director and the directee, both are united in a purpose: to help the directee deepen his or her relationship with God."[5]

Spiritual direction is also different from a "spiritual friendship," in which two people discuss their prayer lives together. This has an ancient history in the church and is often found in the lives of the saints—two holy people sharing their experiences—St. Benedict and St. Scholastica, St. Francis of Assisi and St. Clare, among them.

Certainly these people were qualified to give spiritual direction! But that model—two people speaking on an equal plane with one another—is not precisely spiritual direction.

By contrast, in spiritual direction there is a director, who is *trained* to help the other notice where God is, and a directee, who is attentive to where the director is leading. The Holy Spirit is in charge, but the director guides the conversation in a way that does not usually happen when two people are speaking more or less as equals, as in "spiritual conversations." Optimally, people well acclimated to the prayer life will do both: speak with a director about their spiritual life and speak with close friends as well.

Being trained in spiritual direction means not only learning to listen carefully and being attentive to what the other person is saying, but also understanding the various ways that people pray, that God works with them, and that people live out their spiritual lives. As well, they are trained to ask probing questions to help individuals see their relationship with God in a new light and to challenge them to look at something they might be avoiding. They are also trained to accompany people in dark times, through the dry moments of prayer and difficult moments of life, always trying to help them notice God's gracious activity. Mainly, they are trained to notice.

This training happens in formal settings—college and university programs, courses sponsored by dioceses and religious orders, or retreat and spirituality centers. It's never a good idea to have a spiritual director who hasn't been professionally trained.

Indeed, for many years I puzzled over St. Teresa of Ávila's famous comment that if she had to choose between a spiritual director who was wise and one who was holy, she would choose one who was wise. Never did I understand that comment until I had someone who was not trained as a director.

This director, an elderly priest, now deceased, was one of the holiest people I had ever met. He seemed a natural fit to be my director during a short period in my Jesuit formation. However, he had never been trained as a spiritual director. The first time we met, I poured out my experiences and told him where I thought God was present and not present in my prayer and daily life. In response, he said, "That sounds great. You're doing a great job. Keep it up!"

His style was more like encouragement than direction. I would often ask, "Do you have suggestions for my prayer?" He'd say, "No, you're doing fine." It was encouraging, but it didn't help my prayer life and taught me to seek out trained directors.

What is the responsibility of the directee? First, to *pray*. Second, to *meet regularly* with the director. And third to *be honest* with the director. For spiritual direction to work, directees need to be open with the director about everything going on in their spiritual life, in the way that patients are open with physicians about all aspects of their physical life.

In one of my first spiritual direction sessions in the Jesuit novitiate, my spiritual director asked me about a particularly painful part of my life—the fact that my parents were separated (eventually they reunited). I balked and told David that I didn't want to speak about it. I said, "It's not really part of my spiritual life anyway, is it?"

"Jim," he said, "it's all part of your spiritual life. You can't just put that part of your life in a box and stick it on the shelf of a closet and not look at it. You have to take it down and open it up. And let God look at it with you."

The director and directee also trust that the real guide in the conversation is the Holy Spirit. Both rely on the presence of the Holy Spirit in the conversation to help the director direct and the directee take direction.

Spiritual directors work in a variety of settings: parishes or retreat houses, college or university campus ministry settings, or even their own homes. There are many guidelines and rules for ministry as a director that relate to being paid (usually there is a fee, because many directors make their living from that practice), where to do it (in a more formal setting, like an office in a parish or retreat house, or a less formal one, like a home office), and how often to do it (monthly usually, though if a person is in crisis it may be done much more frequently).

Barry and Connolly's book is comprehensive. Anyone wanting a fuller explanation of spiritual direction and even a bit of training could fruitfully consult it. For the purposes of this chapter, which does not aim to be exhaustive, perhaps the best short way of describing direction is to recount what happens in a typical session.

This brief interchange is not based on one person, but includes many common topics I have seen come up in spiritual direction since I started almost thirty years ago.

I'll call a single man in his thirties Joe and the spiritual director Cathy. They are meeting in Cathy's office at a retreat house.

CATHY: Hi, Joe. Come on in. Nice to see you!

JOE: Boy, am I glad to see *you*! We have a lot to talk about since last month.

CATHY: Well, I'm looking forward to hearing what's been going on. But let's start with a prayer. Do you mind if I pray, Joe?

JOE: I'd love it.

CATHY: Let's take a moment and remember that we're in the presence of God. [Pauses.] Loving God, we thank you for bringing us together, and we thank you for the gift of your Spirit in our lives. We ask you to be with us as we talk about the ways that you've been at work in Joe's prayer and daily life over these last few weeks. Give us a spirit of wisdom and discernment like the one you gave St. Ignatius Loyola. We ask all this in your holy name. Amen.

JOE: Amen. I really needed that prayer.

CATHY: Oh, we all need prayer! So what's been going on between you and God?

JOE: Well, I don't even know where to start, to be honest. Things have been pretty rough lately.

CATHY: You can start wherever you like, Joe.

JOE: Maybe I'll just get right to the point. I lost my job! I got fired, basically. And I'm pretty worried about money right now. I can't believe this is happening. [Gets choked up and pauses.]

CATHY: I'm so sorry to hear that, Joe. That sounds very upsetting. Can you tell me what happened?

JOE: Well, nothing all that interesting, really. Just downsizing. But it came out of the blue. I mean, I was doing well, and my manager gave me a good performance review last year. You remember all the traveling I was doing? Well, they liked that. But then things went south with our budget, and since I was one of the newer hires, they just let me go. It was pretty awful too. You know, now they have to march you out of the office with a guard next to you. I couldn't believe it.

CATHY: That sounds humiliating.

JOE: Yes! Humiliating! That's exactly it—humiliating. It was awful. I've never been treated like that in my whole life! I'm embarrassed to say this, but . . .

CATHY: Go ahead.

JOE: I almost felt like crying. I almost *did* cry as they were walking me through the hallway past all my friends. Can you believe that? It was so frustrating and embarrassing. In front of all my friends. Like I was a criminal or something! Even though I hadn't done anything wrong. I've never felt like that before.

CATHY: Yes, that sounds really hard.

JOE: It was. Awful.

CATHY: Have you been able to pray about this, Joe?

JOE: Well, yes, sort of. It took me a while before I could get over my anger and pray about it at all.

CATHY: Can you say more about that, Joe? Why did you feel you needed to get over your anger before you talked to God?

JOE: I don't know. I guess I'm embarrassed to be angry in front of God. Like I'm ungrateful or something. I mean, shouldn't I be grateful?

CATHY: Do you think God might want to be with you when you're angry?

JOE: I know you've said that before, but I guess this is the first time that I've really been angry enough not to pray. I couldn't even concentrate.

CATHY: God's been handling people's anger for a long time.

JOE: Okay, I guess I was bottling it up when I was praying.

CATHY: And how did that make you feel?

JOE: Like I was holding something back from God, to be honest. I really wanted to talk about all this in prayer, but I didn't know how. It seemed like I was ignoring it or shoving it aside.

CATHY: I see.

JOE: So instead I just asked Jesus to be with me.

CATHY: You mean instead of talking to God the Father, you went to Jesus?

JOE: Yeah. I just feel more comfortable with him.

CATHY: Can you tell me what that was like?

JOE: After I calmed down, I was able to imagine myself sitting next to Jesus. You remember I told you that I liked to imagine myself with him at a campfire?

CATHY: Yes, in a place that you enjoyed when you were younger. Is that right?

JOE: Yeah, my dad and I always had this spot where we would sit and talk together. I haven't been there in years, but that's where I like to meet Jesus.

CATHY: What happened when you were with Jesus?

JOE: Not a whole lot, actually. No words or anything. You know how hard that is for me, right? I can talk to Jesus, but having him talk to me seems forced. But I got this feeling of calm when I was with him.

CATHY: That sounds like a gift in the midst of a tough time.

JOE: Actually, it was really peaceful. I almost forgot about that until now, to be honest. Things have been so crazy. But I was sitting with him, next to the campfire, and I just sort of exhaled and he exhaled and we both sat there, and I felt this wave of peace. Like I could just give him my problems and worries or maybe put them into the fire. I wasn't sure if I was supposed to just throw them into the fire or just sit with Jesus. It wasn't clear exactly what was going on, so in the end I just sat with Jesus, next to him on the ground. But I definitely felt calmer. And I felt calmer after the prayer. Do you think that was for real?

CATHY: Did it feel real to you?

JOE: Yes, definitely.

CATHY: And that makes sense too. It's what Jesus would want to give you at a time like this, isn't it?

JOE: So you think that Jesus was really giving me that calm?

CATHY: What do you think?

JOE: Yes, I do.

CATHY: It sounds like Jesus really comforted you.

JOE: Yes, he did. So now what?

CATHY: How would you feel about sharing your feelings of anger and humiliation with him?

JOE: I guess he would understand that, wouldn't he?

CATHY: Yes.

JOE: Jesus didn't do anything wrong, but he was marched through the streets on Good Friday, right?

CATHY: Right.

JOE: You know, sitting here talking about it, I have this weird feeling that I want to tell Jesus how I feel. Realizing that he would know how it felt to be marched out—isn't that what they did to him before the Crucifixion?—makes me want to talk with him. It's weird. Sitting here now makes me want to talk with him.

CATHY: Yes, that does describe the Crucifixion. And that was part of his life, Joe. Perhaps it's an invitation to be with Jesus in his suffering. And for him to be with you in yours.

JOE: What, this feeling right now? That's an invitation?

CATHY: How else would God encourage you to come closer to his Son?

JOE: Wow. Yeah. I guess I will. Next time I pray I'll try to share some of my anger with God. Or with Jesus, I guess. I'll let you know what happens.

CATHY: I'll be looking forward to it.

Cathy and Joe's session would usually last longer than this brief interchange. It would also focus on where Joe felt signs of God's presence (and perhaps calm) in his daily life—not just in his prayer. Perhaps a co-worker called him to console him after his embarrassing firing, and Joe found God's comfort in that. These are the kinds of things that he would also share with Cathy.

Let's notice a few things about this conversation, which will help us understand spiritual direction. First, Cathy does not try to solve Joe's problems. She does not offer advice on how to look for a new job or give him tips on writing a résumé. Nor does she tell him to "get over it" or "look on the bright side." Instead, Cathy focuses on Joe's *experience of God*. Even if Cathy were to be surprised by what she hears in his prayer (for example, if she had never heard of an image of Jesus at a campfire), she tries to accompany him.

Far less does Cathy try to psychoanalyze Joe by investigating the psychological reasons behind his weeping (memories from his youth that may have made him feel his humiliation more intensely). Again, psychotherapy, pastoral counseling, and advice can be an immense help, particularly as ways of finding freedom from unhealthy patterns of behavior, but that is not the task of the spiritual director. Besides, Cathy may not have much background in psychology, so it would be counterproductive (even dangerous) for her to act as Joe's psychiatrist or psychologist.

Also, notice that Cathy doesn't do much "theologizing." She doesn't tell Joe that this is all "part of God's plan," which under the circumstances would be a particularly cruel thing to say, since Joe might hear that comment as saying, "God wants you to lose your job." She may hope that God has good things in store for Joe, but she is mainly concerned with helping Joe notice God's activity in his prayer and his daily life. This is her main task. Besides, she had better be careful in predicting good things. She has no idea what will happen in Joe's life. All God promises is that God will be with us; God does not promise to solve all the problems in our lives, including Joe's.

Cathy also gently encourages Joe to open more to God and to share some of his feelings of anger when he is ready. This is the "directing" part of direction; that is, she's offering him some guidance, saying, in essence, "Why not go here?"

Now let's look at Joe's part in this session. Joe is open with Cathy, sharing not only his frustration, but something potentially embarrassing: feeling on the edge of tears as he was led out of the office. Being honest with your director is essential. If Joe had not shared that he was near tears, Cathy might not have picked up on the depth of his feeling, his frustration and anger. That helped her to accompany him more compassionately.

Also, even though Joe is unclear about exactly what happened in prayer, he still tries to recount it. He couldn't explain, or even tell, if he was being invited to throw his problems into the fire or simply sit next to Jesus. Experiences in prayer are often hard to describe. A good spiritual director knows that just because you can't explain it doesn't mean it's not real and will allow directees to explain their spiritual experiences as best they can.

Joe and Cathy are also open to something happening in the spiritual direction session *itself*. When Cathy invites him to be more open about his anger, Joe feels a desire to do so. That is common in spiritual direction. The session can prompt a spiritual experience—an emotion, insight, memory, desire, and so on. The director needs to be open to that possibility and provide a welcoming space for Joe to talk about it.

At some point in their conversation, Cathy would invite Joe to speak not only about his prayer, but about where he felt God in his daily life. Cathy might ask the following questions: "Where did you experience God outside of prayer? Were there any moments when you felt God's presence, perhaps in a kind word from a friend, an email that lifted your spirits, or a chance encounter in nature?" Often in difficult times, people may focus so much on what's happening in prayer that they forget to look to their daily life for signs of God. (The opposite happens as well.)

At the end of the session, directors often sum up what was discussed, reviewing any insights the directee has noticed and offering them to the directee. In this case Cathy might say something like:

> Joe, before we close with a prayer, I would just like to reflect back some of what I heard about your prayer. It sounds like Jesus was offering you some calm in the midst of a turbulent time in your life. We also talked about your desire to be more open about your anger the next time you're with Jesus in prayer. Overall, it sounds like you're being invited into a deeper relationship with Jesus.

Cathy might be even more specific about places to go in prayer and recommend some Bible passages for Joe.

Over time Cathy would come to know how God is at work in Joe's daily life and prayer. Cathy might become one of the people Joe relies on most to help him with his spiritual life.

By contrast, if your director seems not to be helping, it may be time for a change. Mark Thibodeaux is blunt about this in his book *Armchair Mystic*. He says that if you sense that the director doesn't understand you, that he or she talks too much or too little, that the advice given is unhelpful, or that "for some unknown reason" the two of you "simply do not fit," then you should tell the director and, if the problems persist, look for another director.[6]

In my own life spiritual direction is essential. I've seen directors regularly, once a month, ever since I entered the Jesuit novitiate. (In fact, in the novitiate we saw them weekly.) They have helped me through some of the most difficult times in my life as well as in some key moments of discernment. And I've also had some great directors during my annual retreats, which brings us to the next important facet of the spiritual life.

Retreats

Increasing numbers of corporations (as well as schools and other organizations) are inviting employees on "corporate retreats." A corporate retreat allows a group of employees to spend time away from the daily grind of the office, often at a separate location and usually over one or two days, to focus on strategic planning, generate creative ideas, and enjoy one another's company in team-building activities. But the origins of the retreat are not to be found in the business world. The retreat began among religious communities and has had a long history as a spiritual practice.

A retreat is a period of time spent away from one's normal activities to focus intentionally on one's relationship with God in prayer. Usually retreats happen at facilities known as retreat houses or retreat centers and sometimes include meetings with a retreat director. Let's unpack that definition.

First, a retreat is time spent away from one's normal activities. Any retreat includes an element of "withdrawing," as the Gospels say that Jesus did from time to time. If it's not possible for that "withdrawing" to take the form of another location for health or financial reasons, a retreat can be done at home, but this should be something of a last resort. Sometimes in Jesuit communities, if a member is too old or infirm to go on a retreat outside the house, he will stay in the house, setting aside his daily tasks and perhaps eating his meals in silence separately from the community.

The nonnegotiable aspect of "withdrawing," however, is time. You must set aside a designated period of time, whatever its length. A retreat means taking time out for God. As with prayer in general, during a retreat we are implicitly saying to God, "This time is yours," or "This time is for you and me."

Is it possible to spend time with God in your daily life, going about your daily tasks? Yes! That's one reason for the Daily Examen—to notice times when you were especially able to see God's presence. But during a retreat we focus entirely on God in prayer for an extended period of time. So you carve out a day, a weekend, or a week.

A retreat is also intentional. The reason you "do" or "go on" or "make" a retreat (the terminology varies) is to be with God. It may require some effort on your part to secure the time away, which may include making sacrifices or tradeoffs in your schedule and possibly even some financial outlay. But you do this because you are intentional about your retreat plans—you are consciously giving over your time to God.

Also, the focus is on God. I have nothing against corporate retreats, but ultimately they're aimed at the bottom line, not God. In the end, the goal of all effort in the corporate world is the financial success of the company. An actual retreat, that is, a spiritual one, is focused on one's relationship to God.

And it is the practice of prayer that forms the operative basis for a retreat. You can take time off to read books on spirituality or theology, but if all you do is read, to my mind, it's not a retreat. It's a few days spent reading.

Finally, those on retreat usually (but not always) meet with a retreat director, who is essentially a spiritual director for the duration of the retreat. They meet once a day, perhaps for thirty minutes, to discuss how praying is going.

Retreats happen in a variety of places, most often in a retreat house, a place designed to accommodate large groups of retreatants. They can also happen at monasteries, colleges, and universities and in many other settings, especially if they are shorter in length. (A daylong retreat in a parish church, for example, is not uncommon.)

But the traditional setting is in a retreat house. At least in the Catholic world, these are places built specifically for that purpose or older buildings (schools, convents, mansions, residences for religious orders) that have been converted. Most have a large number of simple rooms, several places to pray, and a dining room. They will usually (but not always) be located in a secluded area, in the midst of great natural beauty.

Retreats can last anywhere from a day to a month. The full Spiritual Exercises of St. Ignatius Loyola, a retreat that follows a specific plan designed by Ignatius, lasts a full month. Most people make weekend retreats or weeklong (or eight-day) retreats. Often they begin with shorter retreats and work their way up to longer ones.

Let's look at the main types of retreats. (As with prayer, there are often many terms for the same thing, varying from organization to organization.) Normally one is with a group of people, either a group that you come with (say, a church group) or others who have signed up for the retreat on their own (a group of people whom you may not know). Typically retreats are done in silence, though not always.

Preached Retreats

Especially popular before the Second Vatican Council, preached retreats focus, as their name suggests, on the preaching or lecturing done by one person or a group of people to the retreatants. Often a weekend preached retreat might feature a particular theme, say, "Jesus and Women." The director or directors might offer a lecture on Friday night after dinner, two or three on Saturday, and then perhaps one or two on Sunday. Preached retreats are usually content-heavy, with plenty of time for taking in information. In a Catholic setting, Daily Mass and perhaps other opportunities for communal prayer are usually included. There may be less emphasis on silence.

Generally speaking, on a preached retreat there is also some time for private prayer. On a Catholic retreat there may be time for one meeting with a spiritual director and with a priest for confession. These retreats are very popular with large groups, and in many parts of the world men's preached retreats and women's preached retreats are a staple of retreat houses. The main benefit is not only the time away, but also the input from the preacher. The main drawback is that there is not as much time for personal prayer and time with a director.

Directed Retreats

Presentations on a preached retreat might be organized for the group, but directed retreats are more tailored to the individual. In directed retreats, which became more popular in the wake of Vatican II, the primary focus is on the private prayer of the retreatant, who has daily meetings with a spiritual director. There are usually no presentations save for the homilies at Daily Mass. Silence is the norm, and retreatants have minimal interaction with others outside communal worship services. The main benefit is long stretches of uninterrupted prayer. Depending on the retreatants, there may be as many as four or five periods of prayer per day, perhaps lasting as long as an hour. Retreatants are encouraged to write down the fruits of their prayer in order to remember them and discuss them with their director.

Often on a directed retreat the director provides Bible passages for retreatants to use for their prayer and will fit them to each person's life. The retreat may begin with a simple prayer of rest (Isaiah 55: "Come to the waters") and then move to a prayer reflective of where the retreatants are in daily life. Someone thinking about changing direction in life may be given a Gospel passage that relates to a call from Jesus. In determining where retreatants will move next in prayer, the director will be attentive to what they are experiencing. If a person's prayer seems especially deep on one passage, the director may suggest remaining there for one or two more days.

Guided Retreats

A guided retreat is a hybrid between a preached retreat and a directed retreat. It usually has fewer presentations than a preached retreat, perhaps one or two a day, sometimes with an opportunity for brief spiritual direction. Again, Masses and other forms of communal prayer are possible in a guided retreat, which is usually done in a group. Guided retreats can be silent, but don't have to be. (The terms "guided retreat" and "directed retreat" are sometimes used interchangeably.)

Private Retreats

A private retreat is done by a single individual, with a spiritual director, not in conjunction with a group, perhaps for a shorter period of time (a day or a weekend) at a retreat house or in another setting. This may be an annual retreat or a retreat to address a particular problem or crisis. As with directed retreats, various Scripture passages are often tailored to the person's needs. Many people have benefited from doing a private retreat during a time of discernment. Someone looking to change careers, grieving a loss, or hoping for a quiet period during a stressful time might find a private retreat well suited to their needs.

The Spiritual Exercises

There are also more programmatic retreats. The Spiritual Exercises are one of the most well-known and popular. Based on the manual of the same name, written by St. Ignatius Loyola, the Spiritual Exercises is a four-week retreat that invites people to use Ignatian contemplation to meditate, step by step, on the life of Christ and their response to Christ's call.

The first week focuses on the way God has blessed us, our sinful history (since we're all sinners), and the recognition that we are "loved sinners." Gratitude for this leads to the second week, in which we learn to know Jesus in order to love him and follow him more closely. During these days, we also imagine ourselves in the life of Jesus's public ministry. The third week focuses on the Passion and death of Jesus, through which we gain an understanding of the ways that our own sinfulness contributes to a sinful world. Finally, the fourth week looks at the Resurrection and our response to God's love. Here we ask to experience Jesus's joy and consolation. Along the way are individual meditations on humility, choosing good over evil, making good decisions, and other topics.

The Exercises are a more organized or formalized retreat, unlike other models that follow a looser form. For example, on a directed retreat the Bible passages offered will vary widely, depending on the person. In the Exercises, however, the plan is more highly structured. The Exercises can also be done outside of a retreat house setting, on a looser time period, in a retreat called the 19th Annotation Retreat, also known as the Exercises in Daily Life.[7]

Other Retreats

The variety of retreats is endless and depends on the individuals or groups participating. There are retreats for students, parish groups, women's groups, young adult groups, people in Alcoholics Anonymous, and so on. Often group retreats tailored for a stable group (a parish, for example) have an emphasis on building community. High-school and college campus ministry groups also offer retreats geared toward the needs and desires of young people. Kairos retreats and Emmaus retreats, with set schedules that involve faith sharing and often the reading of letters from parents and relatives, are also popular with students. But overall, the focus of every kind of retreat, from preached retreats to private retreats to guided retreats, is the same—taking time out from one's schedule to connect with God.

Retreats have become more difficult for many people to do these days, not only for reasons of a busier life overall, but primarily because of the influence of technology. More time online and more time checking your phone for text messages mean not only less time for private prayer, but also a diminished sense of the importance of solitude. If you feel guilty for not being reachable, you may feel guilty about privacy itself. These days, even when people spend time at retreat houses for the explicit purpose of prayer, not checking texts and emails seems almost anathema.

Silence, a key aspect of most retreats, can be a shock to people who are not used to it. Almost twenty years ago, I helped to direct a weekend retreat for a group of young adults from a parish in New York City. The retreat house was in a bucolic setting north of the city. On Friday night, as is the custom for most weekend retreats, I gave a brief introduction to the next few days. There would be four presentations during the weekend, meals in common, a great deal of time for prayer, Mass, and an opportunity for spiritual direction with me or the other retreat director.

"And of course," I said, "we'll all be in silence."

Like deer sensing danger, they perked up their ears.

"Silence?" said one. "What do you mean?"

"Well, silence," I said. "That means no talking, and no loud noises like radios and so on."

"Not even at meals?"

"No, not even at meals." I briefly explained the reasons. Almost all the retreatants looked shocked.

"What if there's an emergency?!" said one young man.

I explained that if the house were burning down, then they could certainly yell, "Fire!" but short of that there probably wouldn't be any need for talking. They looked at me, dumbfounded.

"I didn't know this would be . . . *silent*," one man said, as if having heard someone pronounce a curse on the weekend.

After the presentation, I walked into the kitchen where the group was chatting away merrily.

"Silence, remember?" I said, as gently as possible.

"You mean now?!" one said.

"Yes," I said.

Even with these reservations, the retreatants—to a person—were in the end grateful for the silence. One recent college graduate said that he didn't think he had ever been quiet in that way before. This was not his fault, but rather the inevitable byproduct of the world in which he lived. He simply had had no opportunity for that kind of communion with God.

Especially with such pressures against solitude and silence, retreats are an important way for people to come to know God.

Faith Sharing

On the first full day of our novitiate, after our families and friends had dropped us off the day before, we new Jesuits were introduced to our weekly *ordo*, or schedule. A few things on the *ordo* needed explanation. But even though it was in English (with a little Latin), there was one item I didn't understand—"faith sharing," which was scheduled every Sunday evening. It sounded weird.

In fact, it turned out to be one of the most enjoyable parts of the novitiate and a practice that I have continued ever since. I wish more people knew how wonderful—and how easy—it is.

In faith sharing a group of people speak to one another about their experiences of God in their prayer and daily life. That definition may sound like spiritual direction, and it's not surprising; the content of the sharing is the same, that is, where God has been found in prayer or in life. But faith sharing is different from spiritual direction, because you are sharing with a group, not an individual, and no one is in charge or directing.

Faith sharing seems to work best with roughly four to six people. I've done faith sharing in groups of as many as fifty people, but smaller groups generally work best.

Usually someone begins with a prayer, and then the group waits until someone feels moved to begin sharing. Depending on the size of the group, each person might spend five or ten minutes talking about his or her experience of God in prayer and in daily life. Also depending on the group, someone might be more or less inclined to share personal aspects of their life. In a setting where people know one another well, the sharing will inevitably be deeper and more personal. But, as in spiritual direction, it is focused on individuals' experiences of God.

The group continues until all participants have shared their experiences, and the session usually ends with another prayer. As a general rule, particularly in larger groups, it is better if listeners don't respond or offer only very short responses to the speaker. It is more important for speakers to share their faith than to receive a response. Why? Because often those listening, if they are unfamiliar

with faith sharing, will good-naturedly want to offer support or advice. If someone says, "I've been going through a dry period in my
prayer," often another will be tempted to say, "Don't worry! It will
pass, I'm sure!"

Faith sharing is not meant to be group counseling or group therapy. The purpose is not to try to solve one another's problems—and
unless everyone is a trained counselor, it's best not to try. Besides,
introducing long responses into the practice means that those whose
experiences do not garner many comments will feel as if their sharing was somehow lacking.

Groups meet regularly, perhaps once a month or several times a
year. One of the most extraordinary benefits of faith sharing is seeing the Holy Spirit at work in other people. And that can be life-
changing. Other than spiritual directors, spouses, and spiritual
friends, most people do not get to see the way that the Spirit works
so intimately in another person's life. But in faith sharing you can
see it *clearly*. And it's stunning to see how the Holy Spirit works so
uniquely with each person.

For the past few years, for example, I have been helping to lead
groups of around a hundred people on pilgrimage to the Holy
Land. We visit places associated with Jesus's life, death, and resurrection, from the Sea of Galilee in the north to Jerusalem in the
south. Our pilgrimage is structured more like a retreat than a tour,
which means not only a more leisurely pace but also the opportunity for prayer, reflection, and Daily Mass as well as faith sharing
at the close of the day.

On the first evening of our pilgrimage, after our first full day, when
we are divided into two groups of roughly fifty people, pilgrims are
reluctant to share. But it's necessary. So much that happens on pilgrimage is overwhelming, and people need a place to process it—and
a place to hear that what they're experiencing is normal. They need

to know that they're not crazy if they weep when they see a certain place—and also not crazy if they feel nothing at all.

Most people are abashed when they hear, "We're now going to share our experiences of God," so instead I start off by saying something less threatening, like "I'll ask you to share something meaningful, significant, or interesting that happened today." This naturally leads people into talking about God.

The sharing is usually powerful for the pilgrims, not only because it may be the first time they've ever spoken about their faith publicly or heard others do so, but because they may not have previously seen the amazing ways that the Holy Spirit deals with people individually. For example, one person on the pilgrimage might be moved by hearing a Bible passage read aloud at a holy site. Another pilgrim might have heard a historical tidbit from a tour guide that unlocks an insight. Another might have had a conversation with another pilgrim that provides unexpected healing. And yet another might be moved simply by gazing at the Sea of Galilee.

Thus, they see how the Holy Spirit deals with people in unique, tailored, and personal ways. Spiritual directors are fortunate to see this all the time. But for someone unused to that recognition, it can be life-changing. I often say, "It's the *same* Holy Spirit dealing with each of us one-on-one." When people realize that this is the same Holy Spirit that was with Jesus, not some "other" spirit or some "portion" of the Spirit, it can be revelatory, or at least eye-opening. As Jesus said in the Gospel of John, "He gives the Spirit without measure."[8]

By the end of the pilgrimage people invariably say that faith sharing was among their favorite things. A few years ago when I suggested to a group of pilgrims that we might have to skip it one day because of a tight schedule, they shouted in unison, "No!"

No matter how you do it, faith sharing enables you to see the Holy

Spirit at work in other people, and this can support your own faith. Even if your faith feels weak, you can see it in another and say, "The Spirit is still there!"

Journaling

In spiritual circles, journaling refers to writing about your prayer or about God. Mark Thibodeaux calls his journal "a diary of the spiritual movements of my life."[9]

There are many reasons to journal. The most important is to record our experiences of God in prayer—to guard against forgetting them. Why do we forget? In addition to the normal human process of forgetting (you don't have to be a neuroscientist to know that the older you get, the more you forget) comes our equally human tendency to focus on the negative. If you have a moving experience in prayer in which you feel God's consolation, it's natural to forget that feeling the next time a tough situation presents itself.

All the more reason to record your experiences. St. Ignatius Loyola counsels that we should store up the consolations we receive as a defense against the times when we are feeling low, like a squirrel storing up nuts for the winter.

Another, subtler reason to journal, and so have our meaningful prayer experiences available to us to recall and reflect upon, is because that is exactly what the evil spirit, or the spirit that moves us away from God, *does not want* us to do. From time to time I invite my spiritual directees to try to think as the evil spirit would, in order to anticipate and protect themselves from its onslaughts. When they have experienced a particularly fruitful insight, emotion, or feeling in prayer, I sometimes ask them, "What's the last thing the evil spirit would want you to do with this experience in prayer?" And they'll say, "Remember it."

So the evil spirit uses whatever it can—our tendency to focus on the negative, our laziness in writing it down, our unwillingness to put the fruits of prayer into action—to get us to forget, ignore, or set aside our experiences in prayer.

Or deny them. One common experience for someone who has finished a retreat or a pilgrimage, during which they have had some deep experience of God, is that afterward they start to doubt or deny that anything happened. They are often tempted to think, "I was just being emotional," or "What happened in that prayer was just something I made up," or "I was just highly suggestable thanks to the environment (or spiritual director, or other retreatants)." The temptation to doubt or deny happens so often, so predictably, that I usually tell people who are finishing a retreat or pilgrimage to expect it.

Journaling guards against both kinds of forgetting: the more natural kind and the kind intensified by the evil spirit. It's hard to deny, downplay, or ignore something if you have written evidence of your experience.

Journaling also counters the tendency to forget the *details* of a prayer experience, without which it may have less of an impact. Let's say that you are praying about Jesus's entry into Jerusalem on Palm Sunday. In the middle of your prayer, you imagine walking alongside Jesus as he enters the Holy City to the shouts of the crowd. You can easily picture the cheering crowds as he makes his way through the winding narrow streets. You imagine having a conversation with Jesus, in which you talk about not only Palm Sunday, when the crowds were adoring him, but also Good Friday, when many in the crowd will turn against him.

You start to understand how he was able to navigate the tension between being loved and being hated, and you start to realize that he didn't need the crowd's affirmation and that he was also detached from the need to have the authorities approve of him. Certainly the crowd's hosannas on Palm Sunday encouraged him and certainly the jeering crowds on Good Friday disappointed him, but he didn't need the crowd's response in either case. This helps you to reflect more deeply on your own need for approval or admiration. All this comes from your prayer.

If you journal about this experience—what you noticed in your prayer, your conversation with Jesus—then in the coming weeks, months, and years, you will have this experience to return to. It will serve as a treasure trove of advice and counsel from God.

But if you *don't* write these things down, in the months and years to come you may remember only the vaguest outlines of this prayer. You were with Jesus and felt something about him on Palm Sunday, but can't remember what it was. Or was it Easter? The opportunity for you to return to this rich prayer experience is gone. Months or years later, if you are struggling with the need for approval, insights from God on that particular topic will be harder for you to access.

Many ordinary reasons keep people from journaling. They're too busy; they're tired after a long day (or after prayer, if they're on retreat); or, more commonly, they don't like to write. But, again, imagine if Jesus walked through the door right now and gave you a message. You'd surely write it down, wouldn't you?

It's also helpful to read your journals over an extended period of time to see where you started, how far you have progressed, and how things have changed. When I read the journals from my retreats as a novice, I am astounded to see someone who was a bundle of anxieties and fears. I still have a few anxieties and fears, but seeing how much God has helped me to grow is itself a grace.

Sometimes I'll invite directees or retreatants to review long stretches of their journals, as a kind of extended examen. The end of the year, the end of a job, or the end of a time spent in one place is a good time to review your journal as a way of appreciating what God has done for you in that time or place. Often these reviews become deeply moving experiences. With distance the graces become even more evident.

Writing down the fruits of prayer is also helpful when it comes to spiritual direction. To communicate effectively with your spiritual director, it is important to remember what precisely happened in prayer. To use an analogy, imagine going to your physician about a problem and not being able to describe it. Often a small detail may escape your notice, and your spiritual director can help you see why it might be important.

Finally, the writing down of prayer experiences can *itself* be like prayer in the results it can produce. Sometimes on retreat, writing down the fruits of prayer can prompt a new insight that you were unaware of during the actual prayer. The ability to reflect on the prayer in writing, with a little distance, can help you to see it in a new way.

Journaling, however, doesn't have to be limited to the fruits of prayer. It's important to journal about how God has been at work in your daily life as well. Margaret Silf suggests other things to record in your journal, including incidents or special objects that catch your attention, places where you might have felt at ease or close to God, special insights, significant dreams that spoke to you, names of people who have been wisdom figures either in the past or today, moments when God has "touched" you, and times when you have felt truly loved, encouraged, and enlivened.[10]

Journaling can also refer to the practice of writing contemplatively. This type of journaling does not focus on the fruits of prayer; rather, the journaling itself becomes a prayer. Some people "process" what is going on inside them by writing it out. They might want to write a letter to God, or to their past selves, or to a saint or a deceased friend or relative. Writing a letter to God, for example, can help unblock prayer and enable some people to speak more freely.

Overall, I find journaling essential. Sometimes when directees tell me of a profound experience in prayer or in their daily life, I'll listen and discuss it with them, and then ask, "Have you written it down?"

More often than I would like, they'll shake their heads.

And I'll practically shout, "Why not?"

17

Topics in Prayer

DISTRACTIONS, DRYNESS, EXPECTATIONS, AND THE OVERALL UPS AND DOWNS OF THE SPIRITUAL LIFE

Like any other part of life, the spiritual life is filled with natural ups and downs. Often this surprises newcomers to prayer. It's similar to the situation of a newly married couple who discover that wedded life is sometimes a challenge. An older couple might nod knowingly and say, "Of course! It goes with the territory." As it goes with the territory of prayer.

In this chapter, I would like to look more carefully at the most common challenges of those who have come to me for spiritual direction.

Distractions

The most common complaint about prayer is being distracted. I have never met anyone who was not distracted at some point in his or her prayer—by noises, a physical ailment, something going on in his or her life, concerns about the prayer itself. And although prayer can be done anywhere, some measure of silence is important for prayer. Thomas Green writes, "The first thing we need in prayer too, if we are going to hear God, is to come to quiet."[1] By this he means interior silence, but exterior silence is important too. And sometimes that's hard to find.

As you know by now, one of my favorite places to pray is the Eastern Point Retreat House in Gloucester, Massachusetts. The sprawling complex is situated right on the Atlantic Ocean; you can hear the waves crashing on the rocky shoreline from almost any place in the house. It's also a place, as they often say there, "known for its silence."

On the first night of most retreats the directors, after going over the basics of the house, will turn to the topic of silence. "Silence is a gift we give to ourselves and to other people," they will say. "Please be mindful of not disturbing those who are praying. No talking during the retreat, unless it's with your spiritual director or unless it's an emergency. If you have to use your cell phone, leave the house and take it to your car or far away from the retreat house."

Almost everyone is grateful for those announcements. Anyone who has been on retreat knows how frustrating it is to have someone sitting next to you in a chapel making a distracting noise. Sometimes when I am directing, I'll add something more specific: "Here's a reminder for anyone who is new. If you would like to use the chapel, remember that it's a place for praying. Not for sipping your coffee, tapping something out on your phone or computer, flipping through the pages of the book, scribbling in your journal, or even knitting. But praying. All those other things to do are fine if you'd like to do them, but please do them in your room."

Invariably someone will come up to me afterward and whisper,

"Thank you so much!" I can tell it's someone who was once distracted by a noisy retreatant!

Even with that encouragement, people can unintentionally distract. A few years ago at Eastern Point, I was praying in one of my favorite places, the Mary Chapel, a former solarium (the building was once an elegant summer house for a Gatsby-era tycoon from Boston) with a perfect view of the ocean. If you crane your neck, you can sometimes see seals sunning themselves on the rocks below. There are chairs and cushions to encourage contemplation, and in the middle of the room stands a beautiful wooden statue of the Virgin Mary; slim and elegant, she holds the Infant Jesus, with a placid expression on her face. I can't imagine a setting more conducive to contemplation.

After breakfast on the first day, I happily made my way from the dining room to the Mary Chapel. There was no one there, and I sat down contentedly on one of the cushions, positioning myself to see the ocean, sparkling in the sun. After I got comfortable, I thought, *This is going to be a great retreat!*

A few minutes later someone entered the chapel. She sat down and took a deep breath. Then she stirred a spoon in a coffee mug, which produced a loud tinkling noise. Then she took a loud sip of her coffee, smacked her lips, and said, "Ahhhh."

So I thought, *Well, that's not so bad. Now that she's had her coffee, she'll pray.*

Wrong. Taking out her Bible, she flipped through its pages until she found the passage she apparently wanted. Then she was silent for a few more moments. So I thought—notice that I'm not praying now, just paying attention to my fellow retreatant—*Well, now that she's found the right passage, she'll surely start to pray.*

Wrong again. She started to clear her throat, something she would do for the next hour. "Eh *hem*. Eh *hem*. Eh HEM!" She took out her journal, flipped through its pages, and started writing. I thought to myself, *How could she have anything to write? She's hardly prayed.* Then she set down her journal, picked up her Bible again, flipped through it, put it down again, took a sip of coffee, said "Ahhhh," took out her journal again, sighed heavily, flipped it open, started writing, and cleared her throat, "Eh HEM!"

As you can tell, I was getting distracted. What's more, as often happens on a retreat, I was not only distracted, but I was angry that I was distracted and then, on top of that, angry that I was angry. *I should be more relaxed about this*, I thought. *I should be more detached, and not care about all this.* But the coffee sipping, page turning, and throat clearing lasted for another half hour.

Try as I might, I couldn't pray. So I stood up and left the chapel, searched for another place to pray—unsuccessfully—and finally retreated to my room, disappointed. The next two prayer periods, one after lunch and one after dinner, were repeat performances: she showed up a few minutes after I did, Bible, journal, coffee mug, spoon, and all.

The next morning I decided to pray at a different time. Normally I find that the period after meals is a natural time for prayer: the postmeal torpor makes it easier to sit still. Perhaps the throat-clearer liked to pray at the same time. So I would pray an hour later: at 9:00 instead of 8:00. She was there anyway, sipping coffee, flipping pages, and clearing her throat. (Yes, she may have had some medical problem, but it was still distracting.)

A few hours later, I met with my spiritual director, Joe, who had directed me through many retreats, the first when I was a Jesuit novice. When I told him of my frustration and even repeated her throat clearing, he chuckled.

"It happens to all of us," he said. "Why not just pray in your room?"

It was an obvious solution that I had been ignoring. So intent was I on having my big moment, my transformative prayer, my mystical experience in my favorite place that I was getting angry just by being distracted. Of course the retreat went fine, and there was nothing magical about the Mary Chapel. God was able to meet me in my room too.

For the rest of the retreat, every time Joe passed me in the hallway, he would catch my eye and say, softly, "Eh hem!"

Types of Distractions

Why did I tell you the story of my distraction in the Mary Chapel? Not for sympathy. Being distracted at a beautiful retreat house on the seashore is far down on the list of problems in the world! Rather, it's to let you know that even after three decades as a Jesuit, I often get distracted. So does everyone else. As Thomas Merton wrote, "If you have never had any distractions, you don't know how to pray."[2]

A large number of distractions come from your surroundings, what is happening around you. Some of us may not be able simply to go to another room. Maybe there is only one room in our house or apartment to pray in. Maybe all the rooms are noisy. If you're trying to pray with small children in the house, you may hear nothing but kids running around, shouting at one another, or, if they're young enough, crying. If you live in a big city, you may hear nothing but sirens blaring, cars honking, and trucks backing up (*beep beep beep*). If you are in an apartment with noisy neighbors, you may hear nothing but what sounds like elephants bowling upstairs. There may be an awful smell coming from outside, or some delicious ones may be wafting in from the kitchen.

Your distractions may also be physical, coming from your own body. Perhaps you have back pain, and it is uncomfortable to sit on certain chairs or sofas. Or you are suffering from a sore throat, and you find that every time you swallow, it feels like needles are going down your throat. Or you have a headache. Physical problems can be extremely distracting.

Mental distractions could be numerous. You are worried about financial problems. You are nervous about a situation with your boss. You are upset about a fight you had with your spouse. On a less fraught level, you are thinking about a project you have at work or are worried about a busy day. Or you can have sexual distractions: you're thinking about an attractive person or something you've seen that has aroused you. All these things are part of the human condition.

How to Handle Distractions in Prayer

What do you do about distractions?

First, *don't get angry at yourself.* It's nothing that you did—it's human and natural to encounter distractions. But we shouldn't let *the fact that* we have distractions disturb us.

A few months ago a woman who sees me for spiritual direction explained it as follows. For the past few weeks during the summer, she had been trying to declutter her apartment. She decided to go through all her old books and take the ones she no longer wanted to a used bookstore. She cleared out her shelves, but realized she couldn't take them to the bookstore right then, because it was blisteringly hot outside. Then she had a revelation. It was similar to her efforts to declutter her prayer from distractions. In the same way that she didn't get mad at herself for not immediately dispensing with her unwanted books, she shouldn't get mad at herself for not getting rid of her distractions in prayer. She was doing her best, but some things were out of her control.

Second, *let go of whatever you can, and don't worry about what you can't let go of.* If you are distracted by a simple matter that doesn't trouble you too much—like "I wonder what I should make for dinner"—it may be easy to let it go. You may just have to say to yourself, "I really don't need to be thinking about this right now."

But often, for every thought we can dispense with easily, another pops into its place. Our minds do not like to be empty; they keep refilling with thought after thought. How can we deal with those?

Some people use visualization techniques. They might use the image of clouds floating by to represent distractions simply passing by. "Birds, balloons, and bubbles," said one spiritual director to me, chuckling. He admitted it was hokey, but it worked for him. He imagined his distractions as birds flying in and out of his field of vision, balloons floating up and away, or bubbles lightly rising to the surface and finally popping.

Margaret Silf describes it as driving a car. On the way to your destination, all sorts of things may distract you: a rainstorm, children squabbling in the back seat, an annoying song on the car radio, even a road block. You notice them but press on, and when you reach your destination, you barely remember them.[3]

Sometimes you can use techniques from centering prayer, such as returning to a prayer word like "Jesus," "God," or "love." A friend of mine, when distractions come into his consciousness, says to himself, "Who cares?" Or you could pray the prayer that my friend Barbara Lee, author of *God Isn't Finished with Me Yet: Discovering the Spiritual Graces of Later Life*, a book on the spiritual life for older adults, shared with me once: "Lord, return me to my prayer!"

But many distractions are not as easy to let go of. You have wrenched your back and are in serious pain. You have a major paper due in a course that you are failing. Sometimes it's hard to let go of these distractions, no matter how "Zen" you try to be.

Third, then, *try to pray while distracted*. So much fruitless energy is spent on trying to rid ourselves of distractions when that may be impossible. We have bodies and minds and concerns that are part of us. Sometimes these distractions can be put out of mind, but often they cannot. In those cases I suggest to directees that they simply accept the distractions and pray while distracted. And remind themselves that it's okay to be distracted.

In other words, do your best to let distractions go, but if you cannot, acknowledge them and pray one of my favorite prayers, "God, I'm distracted, but I'm here with you." Acknowledging distractions can be a relief; often the mere acceptance of distractions can offset their severity. Distractions cease to be something that you are obsessed with letting go of and become more like background noise.

Gerard Hughes compares this to the beginning of salvation history as recounted in the Book of Genesis. In a beautiful phrase he suggests showing God your "scattered mind and distracted heart" and letting the Spirit of God hover over your "inner chaos."[4]

On a more down-to-earth level, let's return to the model of a personal relationship. Imagine that you are going to dinner with a friend. Before the dinner begins, you admit that you are distracted by something that is weighing on you. You might say, "Look, I'm so happy to see you, but forgive me if I seem distracted. I have a big test coming up tomorrow."

What would your friend say? Most likely, "That's okay! Don't worry about it. We all get distracted. I'm just glad that you're here."

If your friends, with all their limitations, can be with you in your distractions, how much more can God be with you? God wants our attention, but God can also accompany us in our distractions. Overall, then, let go of what you can let go of. Let whatever distractions remain be part of the person you bring before God.

When a Distraction Is Not a Distraction

When it comes to distractions, however, an important consideration is distinguishing between *unimportant* and *important* ones. Unimportant distractions remain just that: distractions. But an important distraction may be something that God is asking you to look at. That is, God may be bringing up a particular issue, so that you can attend to it. It's the difference between thinking about what to make for dinner, which you can let go of, and something that may be a matter for prayer. Gerard Hughes reminds us that such distractions can become the "substance" of prayer.[5]

A few years ago, a Jesuit said to me in a direction session that he was bothered by something that kept coming up in prayer—someone in his community he'd had an argument with. "Every time I start to pray, he comes into my mind. It's such a distraction. And it makes it hard for me to pray about anything."

Maybe it wasn't a distraction, I suggested, but something that God was raising up for his attention. Even if it wasn't something God was bringing up, it was still something that was bothering him, so why not talk to God about it? In time, he was able to bring his relationship with the other person before God, pray about it, ask for healing, and then reconcile. His distraction turned out to be an invitation.

Often people think that any strong emotion in prayer is a distraction, when, again, it may be something that God is raising up for them to look at. Mark Thibodeaux's book on that topic, *God, I Have Issues*, looks not only at emotions but also states of life, chapter by chapter, for example, "God, I'm Afraid, "God, I'm Angry," "God, I'm Angry at You." His book offers prayer suggestions based on emotional states and reminds readers that it's more than okay to feel these things and bring them to prayer. The subtitle of his book is a reminder of this essential insight in the spiritual life: *50 Ways to Pray No Matter How You Feel.*

How can you determine the difference between important and unimportant distractions, between what God is raising up and what you can just ignore?

Sometimes it may be a case of asking God for some insight. "Is this something that you want me to look at?" Even physical problems that seem on the surface to be a distraction may warrant a look in prayer. If you are worried about some upcoming surgery, upset that you have a serious illness, or concerned about a potential physical problem, perhaps this is something to share in prayer. If you are constantly upset or frustrated about your job and angry at your boss, perhaps you need to discuss this with God. Ask yourself if the distraction you're considering is important or unimportant.

Sometimes it's a question of ego. If it is a distraction about a relationship ("I'm sorry I was mean to that person today") and not about you ("My neck is bothering me"), chances are that you are being asked to look at that in prayer with God. But not all the time. Constantly praying about a boss whom you dislike may indeed be distracting you from some other parts of your life where God may be waiting to meet you.

In time, with more experience or a little spiritual direction, you will be able to tell the difference between what you can let go of and what you can't, between what's important and what's not. And you may find that, because of this discernment, distractions won't bother you as much. Even the odd "eh hem" won't matter as much.

Dryness in Prayer

The second most common complaint about prayer is: "Nothing happens." This is often referred to as dryness. "I close my eyes and nothing seems to happen." "I don't feel anything when I read this passage from the Bible." "I don't feel God's presence at all." "I don't feel a thing." "Sort of dry." "Not much." I have heard these reports—and experienced these same things—for many years.

The first thing to say about dryness is that it's natural. As with distractions, I do not know one person who has not faced dryness in prayer. Also, as with distractions, the fact that we experience dryness should not disturb us. "There will be days, and maybe long stretches," says Joyce Rupp bluntly, "when the experience of praying is mostly miserable, dreary, and undesirable."[6]

My own daily prayer life usually goes as follows. Every morning I wake up and pray for an hour. Before doing anything else, before the gym, before showering, before turning on my phone, I pray. I use the daily prayer for priests (called the breviary); I read the Gospel passage for the day and try some Ignatian contemplation to put myself in the Gospel story. Later in the day is Daily Mass, which in our community is at 5:45 p.m., and then the Daily Examen at the end of the day. But my main contemplative prayer is in the morning.

Here is what sometimes happens in the morning: *nothing*. At least that's what it feels like. I read the Gospel passage and try to see where God is inviting me to spend time. Then I spend time there, and my mind drifts. Sometimes even when I call myself back to prayer and I'm able to focus and turn that passage over in my mind, nothing comes. No emotions, no desires, no memories, no insights, no images, no words, no nothing. Instead, I simply sit in God's presence. And even then I sometimes don't feel anything: no calm, no comfort, no consolation.

On an intellectual level, it is a comfort to know that I am in God's presence and that transformation is happening on a deep level; at other times I am just grateful for some quiet. But if I were to tell a spiritual director what happened in my prayer, I might say, "Not much."

This is part of the spiritual life. Not every prayer can be rich or moving or consoling or wonderful or challenging. Knowing that dryness is a natural part of prayer can help you relax. Simply being in God's presence, even if it feels like "nothing is happening," is transformative.

It is, therefore, not a sign that God is somehow angry or disappointed with you. Mark Thibodeaux notes that it is not a matter of "God's anger or wrath." God is not punishing you with dryness. "The Father of love does not play those games."[7]

It's also a potent reminder of an essential truth in the spiritual life: you're not in charge. Some time ago a college student came to see me for spiritual direction during exams, a stressful period for anyone. At the very moment that she felt that she needed God's presence the most, she couldn't feel it. Worse, she felt that she had somehow failed by being too distracted by studies, thus frustrating God's ability to "break in." So she was in a funk, feeling not only abandoned by God, but also saddened by her apparent inability to pray.

We talked about the invitation not only to accept the occasional periods of dryness in prayer, still trusting that God is with us, but also to recognize that God does everything: instill in us the desire to pray, enable us to pray, and give us the fruits of prayer. So these kinds of experiences are invitations to humility.

By contrast, when this happened to me in the novitiate, I used to worry a great deal. I thought I must be praying wrong or that God had somehow withdrawn his graces from me. But it was part of the normal ups and downs of prayer.

In the novitiate I once told my spiritual director that the dry periods seemed a waste of time. He challenged me to see the craziness of that statement and asked, rhetorically, "Being in the presence of God is a waste of time?" Then he told me that one of his favorite definitions of prayer was "wasting time with God."

Think of it this way. Imagine if, somehow, you had never had the flu before and had never met anyone who had had it. One day you wake up achy and feverish, and for the rest of the day you feel terrible. You can't imagine what is wrong with you, so it's frightening. Then you visit the doctor and he allays your fears: "It's just the flu. It happens to everyone from time to time." The next time you get the flu, while it's just as unpleasant, it isn't as worrisome or frightening. Dryness in prayer is similar. It happens to everyone.

In addition to accepting it, there are a few ways to respond. St.

Ignatius suggests trying to pray more (to act against the normal tendency to pray less in these situations); perhaps doing some physical penances (say, giving up certain foods or refraining from a persistent bad habit) in order to sharpen our appetite for God; and then reminding ourselves that God is in charge.

The silence of dryness itself can be an invitation to a deeper relationship with God and an invitation to faith. In *Encounters with Silence* Karl Rahner writes: "I know why You are silent: Your silence is the framework of my faith, the boundless space where my love finds the strength to believe in Your Love."[8]

Barry and Connolly note that when prayer is dry, it is often because "the level of dialogue on which the prayer has been taking place has broken down, and the person is being invited to another level." They suggest that the new level will be "less general, less abstract, more deeply personal."[9]

Often in situations of dryness, before reaching that deeper level, it may help to try a different kind of prayer. If you have been spending time mainly in Ignatian contemplation, it may help to switch to *lectio divina*. If you've been doing nature prayer, it helps to move to centering prayer. Trying new ways to pray—even if you are happy with the ones you know—can help you encounter God in a new way, and newness can be helpful in times of dryness.

A few years ago on my annual retreat in Gloucester, I felt stuck. My prayer was dry, and I felt flat. In response, my retreat director suggested, "Why don't you go on a walk with Jesus?"

"You mean in my imagination, sitting in the chapel?" I asked.

"No, I mean, literally walk down the road and imagine he is with you."

"You know," I said, "I've never been able to do that. I can imagine walking with him, but when I walk, I get distracted."

"Try it," he said.

So I left the retreat house and started walking over one of the most beautiful roads I know, next to a large freshwater pond that leads to the town of Gloucester. At the beginning I tried to imagine Jesus walking next to me and waited for something to pop into my head. Would he speak to me? Nothing happened. I walked around aimlessly.

A few hours later I tried again. This time I more consciously imagined Jesus next to me, really visualizing him, and in the process walked much more slowly, paying attention to him. Suddenly I felt a kind of presence, as if he were physically there.

At the time, I was thinking about the reaction to a book that I had written, which had occasioned a good deal of controversy. And as we walked, I thought, "Why not speak to Jesus about it?" So I said to Jesus in prayer, "What do you think about that book?"

In response, in my imagination, he suddenly embraced me and kissed me on the cheek. It was such a surprise! I had never experienced anything remotely like that before. A mile down the road, I sat on a stone bench overlooking the pond. I imagined Jesus sitting next to me. As I did, a swan silently glided past me, only a few feet away. And I said, "I'm a little worried about all the pushback."

"Does it matter?" I heard him say.

"No," I said.

It was an extraordinary prayer period, one of the richest I had had in years. And it came only because I was willing (after being pushed) to try something new.

The Seven Ds

But what about a more protracted problem with prayer? What if it's not just dryness but something more serious, say, the "dark night," which you might have heard about?

One challenge for pray-ers is to distinguish between *darkness, dryness, desolation, doubt, disbelief, depression,* and *despair*—what you could call the "Seven Ds" of the spiritual life. The Seven Ds, however, are distinct from each other, and Christian spiritual masters have long used specific terms to refer to them.

One may experience dryness without depression (for example, during a retreat when one suspects that the period of dryness in prayer is temporary). One may encounter darkness without disbelief (as did St. Thérèse of Lisieux, the French Carmelite who continued to believe despite spiritual aridity at the end of her life). Darkness can lead to occasional doubt. And depression can lead, as even atheists and agnostics know, to despair.

Darkness has been an important theme in Christian spirituality since at least St. Gregory of Nyssa in the fourth century. Perhaps the most often quoted source on the topic is St. John of the Cross, a Spanish mystic. Ironically, he may be the most misquoted as well, as illustrated by frequent references to the "dark night of the soul." His original sixteenth-century poem is called simply *Noche Oscura*, "Dark Night."

"Dark night," however, is only one way of describing a state of feeling isolated from God. Around the same time St. John was writing, St. Ignatius Loyola wrote of "desolation" in his *Spiritual Exercises*. Thus, even the most educated Christians can be forgiven for wondering if the two phenomena the saints are talking about are the same, similar, or different.

To add to the confusion, where one spiritual director uses "darkness," another uses "dryness" to describe the same experience. Perhaps the confusion stems not only from an imprecise, overlapping, and shifting use of terms, but also from a failure to recognize that everyone who prays will at some point encounter many of these states.

What are these states? How do they affect our relationship with God? What follows is a brief description. But remember, they may overlap. The important thing is not to lose heart in experiencing any of them.

1. *Darkness* is a feeling of God's absence after having developed a personal relationship with God. For St. John of the Cross, there were two types of dark nights. The "dark night of the senses" is an experience of one's own limitations and the removal of attachments to the consolation felt in prayer. "The dark night is an inflowing of God into the soul which cleanses it of its ignorances and imperfections," wrote St. John.[10] At a later stage, some experience the "dark night of the spirit," a more profound challenge to faith. But St. John saw both as steps toward deeper union with God, when old ways of prayer and relating to God fall away.

2. *Dryness* is a limited period of feeling emptiness in prayer. Dryness is more temporary than darkness. Anyone who prays will at times feel dryness in prayer, when nothing seems to be happening. There is little in the way of "sensible consolation," Father Barry once told me.

The experience of dryness, a natural part of the spiritual life, can increase our appreciation for richer moments. We never know what kind of inner change occurs during dry times, and being with the Living God in prayer is always transformative. Much as even a close friendship goes through some quiet or dull times, so our relationship with God will go through dry patches. But being with a friend in such times is necessary, if the friendship is to be sustained and grow in intimacy.

3. *Desolation* is feeling God's absence coupled with a sense of hopelessness. St. Ignatius describes it as an "obtuseness of soul, turmoil within it, an impulsive motion toward low and earthly things, or disquiet from various agitations and temptations."[11] It is more than feeling dejected or sad. Desolation is often confused with simply feeling bad, says Bill Barry. It is a feeling of estrangement from God.

Desolation is distinct from St. John's dark night. In desolation, writes St. Ignatius, one is moved toward a lack of faith and is left without hope and love. In the dark night the opposite is happening, as one moves toward complete abandonment to God.

The desolation Ignatius describes may seem removed from the lives of average Christians. But it is a common, painful state experienced by many people, coupled as it is with feelings of "gnawing anxiety," as Ignatius puts it. He counsels that in these times we should, among other things, redouble our efforts in prayer, remember times when God seemed more present, or remind ourselves that this state will eventually pass. He also reminds us that all the fruits of prayer are gifts from God, which we cannot control.

4. *Doubt* is intellectual indecision about God's existence. Many believers face doubt at some point. Most people are relieved to be able to talk about doubt in spiritual direction, according to Janet Ruffing, RSM, an experienced director. In fact, no one reaches adult faith without doubt. Frequently people encounter doubt and then move toward a faith that is more complex, paradoxical, and ultimately more mature.

5. *Disbelief* is the intellectual state of not accepting the existence of God. Sometimes disbelief is the way believers discard old images of God that no longer work for them. Margaret Silf reflected on her own experience in a conversation with me: "I've been through times when all the old props have fallen away, and have felt that I just couldn't go on believing. So what to do? Bolster this old system, or let things be and see what happens? For me, this finally enabled me to break through to a deeper level of faith, which I would call trust." Disbelief is a serious challenge in the spiritual life. If the journey ends at that point, there will be little space for God. The key is to continue seeking, even in the midst of disbelief.

6. *Depression* is a profound form of sadness. In the medical and psychological community, it has a more technical definition. It's a clinical category that can often be treated medically, says Bill Barry, who is also a psychologist. "We don't want to spiritualize

primarily psychological problems," said Jane Ferdon, OP, who has trained many spiritual directors, in an interview. But today, she adds, we can also psychologize spiritual issues. So it's very important to discern the root causes of depression.

7. *Despair* is a feeling that all is and will remain hopeless. Thomas Merton defined despair as "the ultimate development of a pride so great and so stiff-necked that it selects the absolute misery of eternal damnation rather than accept happiness from the hands of God and thereby acknowledge that He is above us and that we are not capable of fulfilling our destiny by ourselves."[12] The form of despair Merton describes implies that we know better than God does, and what we know is that things can never get any better. Such pride leads to a spiritual dead end: despair.

This may sound harsh. For those living in grinding poverty, facing a life-threatening illness, or confronted with another personal tragedy, despair can seem like a rational response. It can also stem from depression.

You don't need to be a scholar of Christian spirituality to see that disentangling these spiritual strands can be encouraging, clarifying, consoling, and freeing. Understanding that most of these experiences are common can encourage us by reducing anxiety. "These are stages in everyone's spiritual life," says Janet Ruffing. Knowing that these stages are not identical can help us discern the correct responses to these different events in our spiritual lives.

Being able to bring such experiences to prayer can also be consoling, because it can deepen our relationship with God, in the same way that speaking about a thorny problem with a friend can strengthen a friendship and lead to greater intimacy.

Finally, knowing that all these experiences can lead us to God can free us from fear, which can cripple our spiritual lives. The Father by whom Jesus felt abandoned on the cross is the same God who delivered Jesus from death, giving him new life. "My God, my God, why have you forsaken me?" is the beginning of Psalm 22. A few lines later, though, the psalmist sings another song: "[H]e did not hide his face from me, but heard when I cried to him."[13]

Expectations

If you're reading this book, then you're interested in learning to pray, deepening your prayer life, or trying new ways to pray. Along with those desires come some expectations.

Likewise, you may choose to go on a retreat for a weekend, or eight days, or even thirty days. Or you may decide to do a daylong retreat at a parish or participate in a faith-sharing group. Or you may opt to find a spiritual director and begin the practice of direction.

Along with these decisions come expectations as well. What kind? They vary. Your expectations might be:

> If you begin to pray regularly, your prayer will always be rich.
> If you commit yourself to a life of prayer, you will be "rewarded" in life.
> If you go on a retreat, you will have a powerful experience in prayer.

It's entirely natural to expect that if you "put in the time" or, as a friend likes to say, "show up and shut up," then your prayer will reflect your efforts. But that is not necessarily the case.

The fruits of prayer are in the hands of God. So part of the spiritual life is managing your expectations. You may go for days or even months without discernible results in prayer, at least results that you can see. You may go on a retreat without some great epiphany—or no epiphany at all. You may sit down (or kneel or lie down) for your full hour and not feel much of anything.

Why is that the case? The best answer is that God is sometimes hard to understand. Sometimes you feel close to God and filled with grace, and sometimes you do not. Sometimes your prayer feels rich, and sometimes it does not. To compare it to a relationship, as we have been doing throughout this book, it's like not wholly understanding a friend whom you still love. How much more mysterious is God!

Still, in the spiritual life we *do* have control over some things.

First, you have control over *when and how often you pray.* It's like exercise. You can't complain about being out of shape if you never exercise. With prayer, it is up to you to decide to spend time one-on-one with God.

But be reasonable about your expectations of time spent in prayer. Margaret Silf notes wisely, "Be realistic about the time you can actually give to prayer and try to honor that time faithfully. The more of yourself that you give to prayer, the more fruit it will bear in your life. A friend of mine expresses this as an invitation to give 'more of me, rather than more time being given by less of me.'"[14]

Second, you have control over *your attention.* There is a way of being attentive to the workings of God. Sometimes you can plop down in your chair, let your mind wander, not worry about being alert, and then say, "Well, nothing happened."

Third, you have control over *your openness.* You can be open to the new ways, the new insights, the new directions that God wants to take you in prayer. If you're closed to the new things that God wants to show you, you will be closed to God.

So you do have some control over your time, attention, and openness. But the rest of it—the fruits of prayer—are largely outside your control. They are not something to feel guilty about or bad about or even sad about. Well, maybe you can feel sad about them, but it doesn't mean that God dislikes you.

Closely related to the question of expectations is the question of when prayer becomes burdensome. Sometimes prayer itself feels like a series of tasks. Many devout Christians with the best intentions end up overwhelmed by the many things they feel they must do in daily prayer, as if their prayer is a to-do list. For example, in the morning, they start with the Morning Offering prayer, then they read the breviary, then they pray with the Daily Mass readings, then they pray a Rosary for all those people in their life who are sick, then they pray for those who have died recently, and so on.

Each of those practices is laudable, but sometimes people feel overwhelmed by that kind of schedule. Missing in that prayer routine may be some quiet time with God in which they can sit and be in God's presence wordlessly. Sometimes people who have busy prayer routines feel so overwhelmed, burdened, or even unhappy that they come to prayer with a sense of dread rather than anticipation.

In response, I'll tell them to drop one or two of their prayer tasks—to pare down the to-do list—or leave the most burdensome out every other day. Think of it like a friendship. If your relationship with a friend becomes so burdened by things you feel you *have* to talk about every time you're together, spontaneity will be seriously diminished. So if you're burdened with prayer, let go of some things. "Come to me, all you that are weary and are carrying heavy burdens, and I will give you rest," as Jesus says.[15]

Overall, your expectations in the spiritual life, and in the life of prayer, need to be modest, and you must always keep in mind that it is God who gives you the desire to pray, God who enables you to pray, and God who gives you whatever fruits you receive in prayer.

So what *can* you expect in the prayer life? I would say the following. You may not feel it every time you pray, but you can expect that:

God will show up.
You will encounter God.
You will experience God's love.
God will invite you into further conversation.
God will invite you into a deeper relationship.

All these things, even if they happen fleetingly, make prayer more than worthwhile.

18

Now What?

MOVING FROM PRAYER TO ACTION

From our chapter on *lectio divina* you might remember the four-step method as outlined by Daniel Harrington. As we meditate on a Scripture passage, we ask ourselves the following questions:

What does the text say?
What does the text say to me?
What do I want to say to God on the basis of this text?
What difference can this text make in how I act?

As we come to the end of this book, we might ask similar questions about prayer. We might ask those questions about a single prayer experience, a period of prayer, or prayer in general. Perhaps we can reframe Father Harrington's *lectio* questions as follows:

What does my prayer say?
What do I want to say to God about this prayer?
What difference will this prayer make in my life?

The life of prayer is not simply for our own benefit. It is also meant to encourage us to grow, to change, to act—and in the process to become more faithful to God and more loving toward other people. Prayer has a communal effect. Dan's final question, "What difference will this make in how I act?" is tremendously important. Prayer is not simply to help us feel good about ourselves or close to God. It should move us to action. "The surest sign of prayer's genuineness," says Joyce Rupp, "is when it influences what we say and do."[1]

Bill Barry told me recently, "The first thing I would stress here is that relationships develop. Secondly, that we are changed for the better by having good friends, and especially by our friendship with Jesus. So we will be changed by engaging in the relationship."

Incidentally, I'm not denigrating the interior benefits of prayer. It's important to move toward the person you're meant to become and to feel closer to God. But the consolation we receive from prayer is not for us alone. It is meant to move us ahead, to help us serve God and others.

Overall, prayer should change us. To begin with, our days should feel, as Ruth Burrows says, "oriented to prayer." Prayer is "a way of life."[2] It should also change the way we live in the world, and as we pray, we should be aware of this change. "Gradually we begin to realize," Thomas Green writes, "that the experience is in fact transforming us, that we're different in our encounters with people, that we are different in our work, that somehow the experience of God is not just a nice experience, but it is something transforming, something remaking us."[3]

Sometimes this is straightforward. If you are fearful in general and you have been graced with a prayer experience in which God seems to be inviting you to see your fears in a new light, to confront them in a new way, or to set them aside, then it may seem clear what the prayer is meant to do. Or if you are wondering whether you should pay more attention to the poor, and you find that, while in prayer, you are moved by Jesus's attention to the poor and his words "blessed are the poor" bring you close to tears, it may seem clear what is going on.

Sometimes it may not be as straightforward. Perhaps you have felt distant from God and you suddenly have a powerful experience of God's presence. What is God inviting you to do? In this case the action may be a renewed assent to the reality of God, an acceptance of that presence, and a more confident approach to life, with the knowledge that God is with you. But in each case there is something called for, some action, some response.

Prayer is also a preventative against despair. As Johann Baptist Metz writes in *The Courage to Pray*, prayer always moves us to hope, because it reminds us of God's presence alongside us and thus stirs us up to resist what he calls "annihilating hopelessness."[4] It tells us that things can be done.

I don't mean to suggest that after every prayer we have to do something. But over time prayer should move us to act. It's not simply about our relationship with God. It also has to do with the relationship between us and our fellow human beings, our fellow creatures, and the whole rest of creation.

Coming Down off the Mountain

In the middle of Jesus's public ministry, according to the Gospels, comes a unique revelation of Jesus's identity. Of course, all along—at his baptism, during his healing miracles, when demons identified him, and even during the few times that he speaks about himself—the disciples were given clues about who Jesus was: the Messiah, the Son of God, or the Stronger One, "the one who is more powerful," as the Gospel of Mark puts it.[5]

It takes time for the disciples to begin to understand Jesus, and even after witnessing his miracles and hearing him speak about himself, they still don't entirely get it. This is not surprising. How could they have understood something so astounding? Even in the face of Jesus's healings and other revelations of his identity, they remain confused.

One of the most dramatic of these revelatory moments is the Transfiguration, in which three of his closest friends, Peter, James, and John, climb a hill (traditionally Mt. Tabor) with their teacher.[6] When they reach the summit, something astounding happens. Jesus is "transfigured" before their eyes—his clothes turn dazzlingly white (whiter, says the Gospel of Mark in a homey touch, than any bleach could make them), and his appearance becomes radiant. Then, beside Jesus appear Elijah and Moses, conversing with him.

The Transfiguration is an unmistakable sign not only of Jesus's identity as a prophet (he is speaking with Moses and Elijah on a mountain, the traditional place for God's revelation), but something more: his divinity. The disciples are stupefied. Needless to say, no one before had experienced anything remotely like this, except perhaps when the followers of Moses saw his face radiant after he had spoken with God on Mt. Sinai.[7]

Here's the story, in Mark's Gospel, the earliest Gospel written, told with the evangelist's trademark brevity:

> Six days later, Jesus took with him Peter and James and John, and led them up a high mountain apart, by themselves. And he was transfigured before them, and his clothes became dazzling white, such as no one on earth could bleach them. And there appeared to them Elijah with Moses, who were talking with Jesus. Then Peter said to Jesus, "Rabbi, it is good for us to be here; let us make three dwellings, one for you, one for Moses, and one for Elijah." He did not know what to say, for they were terrified. Then a cloud

overshadowed them, and from the cloud there came a voice, "This is my Son, the Beloved; listen to him!" Suddenly when they looked around, they saw no one with them any more, but only Jesus. As they were coming down the mountain, he ordered them to tell no one about what they had seen, until after the Son of Man had risen from the dead.[8]

Some New Testament scholars suggest that this event might be a post-Resurrection narrative retrojected back into the Gospels by the evangelists. In other words, some say that this appearance of Jesus to the disciples happened *after* the Resurrection (thus, it is an appearance by the Risen Christ), and the Gospel writers have placed it earlier in the story.

How are we to understand the language of this story, with its talk of white clothes and bleach and clouds? In the original Greek Jesus himself is described as *metemorphōthē*, having undergone a metamorphosis, a change in his "form."

On the one hand, it may have happened precisely as described: with the brilliant white garments, the enveloping cloud, and the heavenly voice. On the other hand, this narrative may have been the best way of explaining a profound spiritual experience that the disciples had in the language available to them at the time. That is, this extraordinary mystical experience, which surely defied words, was explained in this way by those who were there, then passed on orally, and finally written down and edited by the Gospel writers. (The story appears in all three Synoptic Gospels: Matthew, Mark, and Luke.)

What we read, then, is a story in which the eyewitnesses, and later the oral storytellers, and still later the evangelists are telling an essentially untellable tale. Mystical experiences, as we have discussed, are hard to explain and describe—especially ones involving the Risen Christ. To be clear, I'm not saying the Transfiguration didn't happen; nor am I saying it didn't happen as recorded. Rather, the experience the disciples had was probably hard, if not impossible, to describe fully.

As another example of this, think of how hard it was for the eye-witnesses and evangelists to describe the appearance of the Risen Christ's "glorified body" after the Resurrection. In some passages Jesus seems almost ghostly; in others he is distinctly physical; in some the disciples recognize him immediately; in others it takes them some time.

To sum up, at the Transfiguration the disciples had a deeply mystical encounter with Jesus either during his public ministry or after the Resurrection. Although you and I won't experience the Transfiguration, we will indeed experience God in our prayer and daily life, and we will find ourselves in situations similar to this experience of the disciples, who wondered how to *respond*. They wondered: *Now what?*

In these last few pages, then, I would like to look at that question, which is in essence the question of how our prayer and our spiritual life change us.

Now What?

Let's look at the disciples' response to their own moment of encounter with Jesus and see what it might teach us about how to respond to our experiences of God.

Their first response is *gratitude*. "It is good for us to be here," says Peter, taking the lead.

Peter's response is different from his response to an earlier miracle, when Jesus first called him by the Sea of Galilee. In what is called the Miraculous Catch of Fish, Peter has been fishing all night when Jesus asks him to again "put out into the deep." Though Peter is doubtful, he does so. Thereupon his net is filled to the breaking

point. In the face of this encounter with the divine, Peter is overcome by an awareness of his sinfulness and says, "Go away from
me, Lord."[9] By contrast, at the Transfiguration, Peter, perhaps more
comfortable with his own humanity and with Jesus's identity as Messiah, cannot contain his gratitude: "It is good for us to be here."

Peter has moved from fear to gratitude. This may be something
that you have experienced. Perhaps the first time you had a strong
experience of God in prayer or in daily life, you were afraid. It's not
surprising. As we mentioned at the beginning of this book, the idea
that the Creator of the universe is communicating with you directly
can be overwhelming. But gradually you will move from fear to gratitude, as Peter did.

Gratitude is the most fundamental response to God's gifts. Preceding anything else in the spiritual life is gratitude for what God
has done. Sometimes that's the only possible response, so overwhelming are these gifts.

In this book we have looked at many ways to pray. We have talked
about rote prayer, petitionary prayer, the Daily Examen, *lectio divina*,
nature prayer, Ignatian contemplation, centering prayer, and more.
We've also looked at what happens when you pray, which is perhaps
the most neglected aspect of writings about prayer. We've considered emotions, insights, memories, desires, images, words, feelings,
and mystical experiences.

All these things may happen during the various forms of prayer
that we have discussed, even in the midst of distractions and dryness
and even with varying degrees of expectation. At various points in
our prayer life, something happens. God communicates with us.

There is no better response than gratitude. We can do nothing
without God, least of all pray. After all, it is God who created us,
placed within us a desire for God, calls us to prayer through our
desires, helps us pray, and offers us the fruits of prayer. God is the
beginning, middle, and end of prayer. Our gratitude to God is the

best response for the life of prayer. As Meister Eckhart said, "If you never say any prayer other than 'Thank you,' that's enough." (That certainly would have made this book a lot shorter!) So Peter's first reaction is a perfect response to prayer—gratitude.

His second reaction illustrates an equally common response to prayer: "Let us make three dwellings, one for you, one for Moses, and one for Elijah." What does Peter mean? Well, the "dwellings" (or "booths") would be set up for worship (or may have a connection to the booths used by the Jewish people at the celebration of Sukkot). Peter seems so overcome with what has happened that he wants to stay there and worship. It certainly seems a strange request after a mystical vision. One Gospel writer states, perhaps by way of explaining to his early readers why Peter would make such a request, "He did not know what to say."[10]

Peter is demonstrating a second common response to the fruits of prayer: *confusion*. "He did not know what to say." How like our own experience! Often we have an experience of God in prayer or daily life, and it's difficult for us to know what it means or what to do. Even if it is not a dramatic moment, it might make us wonder: *I'm not sure what this means. I'm not sure if this is real. I'm not sure what to do. I don't know what to say!*

The Gospel says that Peter's confusion came from terror, which is understandable. Some of our own confusion may spring from fear, but just as often it comes from being unable to grasp what the experience may have meant.

But with those same words—"Let us make three dwellings"— Peter also expresses a third common reaction: *the desire to stay.*

How often that is the case for us! The last thing we want to do after a profound prayer experience, a grace-filled time at a retreat, or an experience in daily life of God's love is to "leave." It's wonderful to spend time in prayer and experience God's grace and love. Likewise, it's hard to go from that experience back to the "real world."

Life can be busy and overwhelming. It can be painful and difficult, regardless of our age or situation. So those moments of silent
prayer in which we feel God's gentle touch can provoke gratitude
and confusion, and also make us want to avoid our reality. We don't
want to go back to "real life." (I always smile when people talk about
"real life," as if the life of prayer is not one of the realest things ever.)
If it's a good prayer experience or a wonderful retreat, it's hard to get
up out of that chair or leave that church, retreat house, or place of
encounter with God and get back to the rest of life.

We may experience what Peter did. He doesn't want to return to
the workaday public ministry with Jesus. He wants to stay: "Let us
make three dwellings."

Think for a moment how surprising this is. Think of all the things
Peter had seen during Jesus's public ministry. All the miracles, from
the Miraculous Catch of Fish, to the healing of his mother-in-law,
to the Multiplication of the Loaves and Fishes, to the healing of the
paralyzed man, and on and on. Think, too, of what Peter had heard:
Jesus's preaching of the Beatitudes and his parables explaining the
coming of God's reign. How could Peter not want to return to all
that? Ministry with Jesus was both beautiful and exciting.

But it must have felt especially consoling and affirming to be on
the mountaintop with Jesus and his friends. It was physically away
from the cares of the world, a quiet secluded place in which Peter
and his friends were consoled by the unmistakable signs of God's
presence. In this way, it's similar to some people's experiences on retreat. Mt. Tabor is a good walk up the side of the hill and away from
Jerusalem. It's away, apart, separate.

Again, how like the life of prayer! Sometimes all we want to do
is stay on the mountain. But, critically, this is not what Jesus wants
for Peter, James, and John. Even though worshipping God is essential, that is not what this experience calls them to do. A few lines
later we are told what happens next: "As they were coming down

the mountain, he ordered them to tell no one about what they had seen, until after the Son of Man had risen from the dead."

Notice the words "coming down the mountain." Peter and the disciples follow Jesus off the mountain and return to their daily lives, in this case to the life of following him along the way, through the rest of his public ministry, and ultimately to his Passion, death, and resurrection. They would allow their experience on the mountaintop to guide and inform their future discipleship.

At the end of my first retreat as a Jesuit novice, my spiritual director told me, "Time to come down the mountain!" I didn't know exactly what he meant, but I surmised that it meant, "Come off that peak experience." In fact, he was referring to the Transfiguration. Spiritual experiences are given to us not only for our personal sanctification, but as invitations to action. We are meant to treasure our experiences with God, but also to use them in our active lives.

We can take our cue from the disciples. What did the Transfiguration mean for Peter, James, and John? That's something that only they can answer. But at the very least it was a confirmation of who Jesus was. And this enabled them, in their own ways, to believe in him, to be faithful to him, and to live more wholeheartedly for him.

As they came down the mountain, the disciples had to ask themselves: "Now that we have encountered God in this way, what difference will it make?" In the Gospels they return to following Jesus along the way. Our own lives are different from theirs, in that we don't see God in the same way, but we are nonetheless called to follow along the way.

Now that you have experienced prayer, the same question can be asked of you: "What difference will it make in your life?"

You have a lifetime to answer.

And the answer is your life.

Acknowledgments

First, thanks to God, who makes all things possible.

The people who have taught me the most about prayer have been my spiritual directors over the last thirty years, and so I would like to thank, first, the Jesuits who have been my spiritual directors over extended periods of time, beginning in the novitiate and continuing to today: David Donovan, Ken Hughes, J. J. Bresnahan, Jack Replogle, Dick Anderson, George Drury, George Anderson, Jeff Chojnacki, and Damian O'Connell. Thanks also to David and Paul Fitterer, two Jesuits who led me through the Spiritual Exercises, first in the novitiate and then during my tertianship, the final stage of Jesuit formation.

Also thanks to the women and men who have led me on my annual eight-day retreats, who likewise taught me a great deal about prayer: Ron Mercier, Joe McHugh, Jim Gillon, Phil Shano, Harry Cain, Jim Bowler, Bill Devine, Jim Keegan, Paul Harman, Dick Stanley, John Kierdejus, and Pat Lee (Jesuits all); as well as Gerry Calhoun, Assunta Boyle, RSM, and Maddy Tiberii, SSJ. Thanks to Bill Creed, SJ, and Martha Buser, OSU, who led me through a summerlong training program on the Spiritual Exercises at the Jesuit Spiritual Center in Milford, Ohio; and to Maureen Steeley, SU, and Eleanora Murphy, SU, for their spiritual direction practicum at the Linwood Spiritual Center in Rhinebeck, New York. William A. Barry, SJ, has also been of immense help not only with his books, but with conversations about prayer and about spiritual direction over the years. This book is dedicated to him.

Many thanks to all those men and women, young and old, who have come to see me for spiritual direction over the last thirty years. Thanks to them, I have come to see the varied ways that God interacts with people—tailored to their own lives and circumstances. Also thanks to those who have joined me on pilgrimages to the Holy Land

and participated in faith sharing, again showing me the personal and unique ways that the Spirit works. I learn so much about God from seeing God at work in other people.

Thanks to all my Jesuit brothers who have participated in faith-sharing groups with me over the years, beginning in the novitiate and continuing today. They have helped me in my own spiritual journey and, again, have invited me to see the way that God is at work in their lives.

As for the writing of this book, many thanks to four friends who offered immeasurable help in reading the unedited manuscript and offering their wisdom. Each is a trained spiritual director. So I am grateful to Bill Barry, Martha Buser, Maureen Steeley, and Mark Thibodeaux, SJ. Thanks to Heidi Hill, my indefatigable fact-checker, and Vinita Wright, my longtime and treasured copy editor.

Thanks also to Teresa Donnellan, an O'Hare Fellow at America Media for one year, who patiently combed through my favorite books on prayer for quotes, passages, and insights related to each of this book's chapters. She saved me hours of work, and I'm very grateful for her diligence. After Teresa had finished with her research, I suggested that she was ready to write her own book on prayer! Thanks to my sister, Carolyn Martin Buscarino, for proofreading the final galleys. Also, abundant thanks to Joseph McAuley, an associate editor of *America*, who provides immeasurable help with the editing and inputting of edits for all my books as well as other essential tasks. He is a gem.

Thanks to my friends at HarperOne for their longtime support of my writing, including Mickey Maudlin, Anna Paustenbach, Laina Adler, Chantal Tom, Lisa Zuniga, Makenna Holford, Adrian Morgan, Stephanie Baker, Judith Curr, and so many others. Ann Moru did her usual amazing job with the final edits. Don Cutler, my treasured literary agent with a unique brand of agenting, which also includes helping with the writing of the book, is also an occasion for gratitude.

For Further Exploration

Here are some books that I have found helpful in my own prayer life and in helping others to pray.

How to Pray

There are many good books that, like this one, hope to teach you about the basics of prayer. This category contains more "how-to" books than some of the other selections below. Chief among them would be almost any book by William A. Barry, especially his books *God and You, God's Passionate Desire*, and *A Friendship Like No Other*, all of which develop the analogy between a relationship with God and a friendship. Other excellent books are Thomas H. Green's *Opening to God* and *Experiencing God*, Gerard Hughes's *God of Surprises*, Joyce Rupp's *Prayer*, and Mark Thibodeaux's *Armchair Mystic* and *God, I Have Issues*. That last book focuses on praying during various emotional states (angry, grieving, lonely, etc.). Ruth Burrow's *Guidelines for Mystical Prayer* offers insights into the mystical aspect of the spiritual life; her book *Essence of Prayer* is more of a general introduction to encountering God. Margaret Silf's *Close to the Heart* is a fine invitation to prayer, written in a highly accessible style.

The Daily Examen

Among the good books on the Daily Examen, Jim Manney's *The Prayer That Changes Everything* is a fine place to start. Mark Thibodeaux's *Reimagining the Ignatian Examen* offers a surprising variety of ways to pray the examen, and George Aschenbrenner's brief (thirty pages) *Consciousness Examen* offers his own distinctive take on the classic Jesuit prayer.

Lectio Divina

Two user-friendly and very fine books on *lectio divina* are *Sacred Reading*, by Michael Casey, an Australian Cistercian, and *Lectio Divina*, by M. Basil Pennington, an American Trappist. Both are written by trustworthy and reliable guides.

Centering Prayer

Finding Grace at the Center, by M. Basil Pennington, Thomas Keating, and Thomas E. Clarke, essentially a series of essays by three experts, is to my mind the best introduction to centering prayer. It is also admirably brief.

Nature Prayer

There aren't many books on praying with nature specifically, though Wendell Berry has written many poems on (at least implicitly) finding God in nature, which is close to the same thing. Many of them are gathered under the rubric of "Sabbath Poems." Annie Dillard's book *Pilgrim at Tinker Creek* is a beautiful meditation on the wonders of the natural world. You might also try reading sections of Pope Francis's beautiful encyclical on the environment, *Laudato Si'*. Better yet, take a walk in a forest, along a beach, in the wild, or just look up at the sky.

Spiritual Direction

The classic book on spiritual direction is *The Practice of Spiritual Direction*, by William A. Barry and William J. Connolly. Anthony de Mello wrote several essays on the Spiritual Exercises and on spiritual direction in general, which were collected in a volume called *Seek God Everywhere*, published after his death.

The History of Prayer

Christian Spirituality, by Lawrence S. Cunningham and Keith J. Egan, is an excellent overview of the tradition that focuses not only on prayer, but on the spiritual life more broadly. A book by the same title, equally good, by Richard Woods, focuses on similar themes. *Prayer in the Catholic Tradition*, edited by Robert Wicks, is an impressive compendium of essays on the varieties of prayer within the Catholic tradition, including the various "schools" of prayer (Carmelite, Benedictine, Dominican, Jesuit, etc.). It covers some of the same topics included in this book (e.g., spiritual direction, distractions) and some not covered (e.g., postures in prayer). *The New Dictionary of Catholic Spirituality*, edited by Michael Downey, is an exhaustive look at spiritual topics more broadly, from A to Z, and includes many entries that touch on prayer. Harvey Egan's *Soundings in the Christian Mystical Tradition* is an overview of spiritual masters throughout Christian history from Origen and St. Augustine to Thomas Merton and William Johnston.

Jesuit Prayer and Spirituality

There are many good books on the traditions of Jesuit (or Ignatian) prayer, including Ignatian contemplation. *Inner Compass*, by Margaret Silf, is a popular introduction to Jesuit prayer and spirituality written in an inviting and accessible style. *Eyes to See, Ears to Hear*, by David Lonsdale, is a comprehensive and more scholarly look at Jesuit spirituality. *An Ignatian Spirituality Reader*, a collection of essays edited by George W. Traub, and *The Ignatian Way*, by Charles J. Healey, both look at key aspects of Jesuit spirituality. Kevin O'Brien's book *The Ignatian Adventure* is an invitation to the "19th Annotation Retreat" (doing the Spiritual Exercises "in daily life" over an extended period of time) that can be used profitably by either spiritual directors or individuals. Finally, *Finding God in All Things*, by William A. Barry, looks specifically at the dynamics of the Spiritual Exercises of St. Ignatius Loyola.

The best translation of and commentary on the Exercises is *The Spiritual Exercises of Saint Ignatius*, by George Ganss, though bear in mind that the Exercises can't be "read," but only "done." Still, Father Ganss's book, because it focuses on the Exercises, offers in the process an overview of Ignatian spirituality and includes excellent passages on discerning what in prayer might be coming from God and what might not be.

Contemporary Invitations to Prayer

Rather than serving as strict how-to guides, some books speak more broadly about the spiritual life, touch on spiritual themes, and serve more as invitations to prayer. Karl Rahner's book *The Mystical Way in Everyday Life* expands on his famous dictum that in the future Christians will be mystics or there will be no Christians at all. *The Need and the Blessing of Prayer* is his general introduction to prayer and meditation; his *Encounters with Silence* is a collection of essays written as prayers directed to God. Father Rahner and Johann Baptist Metz wrote an excellent book on topics in prayer (including praying to the saints) in *The Courage to Pray*. Almost all of Thomas Merton's books can be used as invitations to prayer, but my favorites are *New Seeds of Contemplation* and *No Man Is an Island*, which include short essays on spiritual themes (poverty, humility, etc.). Anthony de Mello, one of the most influential spiritual writers of the twentieth century, wrote many popular books of meditations and invitations to prayer, including *Sadhana: A Way to God, Awareness*, and my favorite, *The Song of the Bird*, which offers many parable-like stories as invitations to meditation. *Days of Deepening Friendship*, by Vinita Hampton Wright, is designed for women in particular, but can be used by all who want, as the subtitle says, an "authentic life with God."

A Few Classic Books on Prayer

The list of classic books on Christian prayer would fill many chapters. Let me suggest a few that have helped me and those I have directed. St. Teresa of Ávila's *The Interior Castle* describes the progression of the spiritual life over time. St. John of the Cross's *Dark Night of the Soul* is the most well-known look at spiritual dryness and also describes his movement from dryness to a mystical encounter with God. *The Sacrament of the Present Moment*, by Jean-Pierre de Caussade, focuses on experiencing God in the present. St. Francis de Sales's *Introduction to the Devout Life* is about the Christian spiritual life in general, but also touches on prayer. Finally, Thomas Merton's *Contemplative Prayer* introduces readers to Merton's distinctive approach to the Christian traditions of prayer.

Books of Prayers

Many books of already written prayers are available. *Hearts on Fire*, edited by Michael Harter, is a brief collection written by a variety of Jesuits and is very popular in Jesuit schools. Charles J. Healey's *Praying with the Jesuits* is a newer addition to that genre. Macrina Wiederkehr's *Seven Sacred Pauses* is a marvelous book of short prayers that I often use on retreats. Joyce Rupp's *Prayer Seeds* is a "gathering of blessings, reflections, and poems." Edwina Gateley's *Psalms of a Laywoman* uses the Psalms to great effect and is also a goad to prayer. One book of poems that always moves me to prayer is *Woman Unbent*, by Irene Zimmerman, which vividly recreates various Gospel scenes, as in Ignatian contemplation. Speaking of poetry, I would also recommend almost any poem by Mary Oliver or Denise Levertov as a way of sparking your prayer.

NOTES

1. Everyone Can Pray

1. William A. Barry, SJ, *A Friendship Like No Other: Experiencing God's Amazing Embrace* (Chicago: Loyola, 2008), 94.
2. Karl Rahner, *The Need and the Blessing of Prayer* (Collegeville, MN: Liturgical, 1997), 39.
3. Rahner, *Need and the Blessing of Prayer*, 49.
4. Ruth Burrows, OCD, *Essence of Prayer* (Mahwah, NJ: Hidden-Spring, 2006), 14.
5. Dennis M. Linehan, SJ, also used to say, "A gentleman never needs to give a reason to oppose change."
6. For more on those devotional practices (Adoration, pilgrimage, and others), see *Awake My Soul: Contemporary Catholics on Traditional Devotions* (Chicago: Loyola, 2004). For more on the spirituality and celebration of the Mass, see *Celebrating Good Liturgy: A Guide to the Ministries of the Mass* (Chicago: Loyola, 2005).

2. Walking to School

1. Lk 1:26–38.
2. Ruth Burrows, *Guidelines for Mystical Prayer* (London: Sheed & Ward, 1976), 6.

3. Why Pray?

1. Most likely this is derived from a saying of Rumi, or Jalāl ad-Dīn Muḥammad Balkhī, the thirteenth-century Persian poet and Sufi mystic, who said, "That which you seek is seeking you." I've also seen it attributed to other sources. But there is more than just the seeking involved. The *desire within you* is part of God seeking you. William Barry has also written that the desire of God *for us* creates in us a desire for God.

2. Augustine, *Confessions*, bk. 1.
3. William A. Barry, SJ, *God and You: Prayer as a Personal Relationship* (Mahwah, NJ: Paulist, 1987), 74.
4. Gerard Hughes, *God of Surprises* (Grand Rapids, MI: Eerdmans, 2008), 43.
5. Thomas Merton, *Contemplative Prayer* (New York: Herder & Herder, 1969), 86.
6. Joyce Rupp, *Prayer* (Maryknoll, NY: Orbis Books, 2007), 21.
7. Lawrence S. Cunningham and Keith J. Egan, *Christian Spirituality: Themes from the Tradition* (Mahwah, NJ: Paulist, 1996), 59.

4. Praying Without Knowing It

1. Joyce Rupp, *Prayer* (Maryknoll, NY: Orbis Books, 2007), 13.

5. What Is Prayer?

1. Lawrence S. Cunningham and Keith J. Egan, *Christian Spirituality: Themes from the Tradition* (Mahwah, NJ: Paulist, 1996), 98.
2. *Catechism of the Catholic Church*, #2559.
3. Lam 3:41.
4. Thérèse of Lisieux, *Story of a Soul* (Washington, DC: ICS Publications, 1976), 242.
5. Teresa of Ávila, *The Book of Her Life*, in *The Collected Works of St. Teresa of Ávila*, vol. 1, 2nd ed., trans. Kieran Kavanaugh, OCD, and Otilio Rodriguez, OCD (Washington, DC: ICS Publications, 2019), 67.
6. Mark Thibodeaux, SJ, *Armchair Mystic: Easing into Contemplative Prayer* (Cincinnati, OH: St. Anthony Messenger, 2001), 17–30.
7. Walter Burghardt, SJ, "Contemplation: A Long, Loving Look at the Real," *Church* (Winter 1989): 14–18.
8. Burghardt, "Contemplation."
9. William A. Barry, SJ, *God and You: Prayer as a Personal Relationship* (Mahwah, NJ: Paulist, 1987), 12.
10. Is 55:9.
11. Walter C. Smith, "Immortal, Invisible, God Only Wise" (1867).
12. Ps 139:13, 139:4.
13. Barry, *God and You*, 12.
14. Thomas Green, *Experiencing God: The Three Stages of Prayer* (Notre Dame, IN: Ave Maria, 2010), 1.

6. Beginning a Friendship with God

1. Am 3:3.

2. James Martin, SJ, ed., *How Can I Find God?: The Famous and the Not-So-Famous Consider the Quintessential Question* (Liguori, MO: Triumph, 1997), xiv.

3. Martin, *How Can I Find God?*, 1, 3.

4. Ex 4:10.

5. Martin, *How Can I Find God?*, 130–31.

6. Martin, *How Can I Find God?*, 133.

7. Martin, *How Can I Find God?*, 133.

8. Lk 10:29–37.

9. Lk 13:18–19; Mt 13:24–30; Mt 13:1–9.

10. Lk 15:1–10; Mt 13:47–50; Mt 6:25–34; Lk 15:11–32.

11. Pierre Teilhard de Chardin, *Writings in Time of War* (London: Collins, 1968), 14.

12. Margaret Silf, *Wayfaring: A Gospel Journey in Everyday Life* (Notre Dame, IN: Sorin, 2009), 139.

13. Jb 10:1.

14. Karl Rahner and Johann Baptist Metz, *The Courage to Pray* (New York: Crossroad, 1981), 12.

15. William A. Barry, SJ, *A Friendship Like No Other: Experiencing God's Amazing Embrace* (Chicago: Loyola, 2008), 133.

16. William A. Barry and William J. Connolly, *The Practice of Spiritual Direction*, 2nd ed. (San Francisco: HarperOne, 2009), 39.

17. Mark Thibodeaux, *God, I Have Issues: 50 Ways to Pray No Matter How You Feel* (Cincinnati, OH: Franciscan Media, 2005), 163.

18. Thibodeaux, *God, I Have Issues,* 164.

19. Katherine Marie Dyckman, Mary Garvin, and Elizabeth Liebert, *The Spiritual Exercises Reclaimed: Uncovering Liberating Possibilities for Women* (Mahwah, NJ: Paulist, 2001), 131.

20. Vinita Hampton Wright, *Days of Deepening Friendship: For the Woman Who Wants Authentic Life with God* (Chicago: Loyola, 2009), 48.

21. Gerard Hughes, *God of Surprises* (Grand Rapids, MI: Eerdmans, 2008), 36.

22. Guy Consolmagno, SJ, *God's Mechanics: How Scientists and Engineers Make Sense of Religion* (San Francisco: Jossey-Bass, 2008), 72.

23. Barry, *Friendship Like No Other*, 99.

24. Elizabeth A. Johnson, *She Who Is: The Mystery of God in Feminist Theological Discourse* (New York: Crossroad, 2002).

25. Ws 8:1.

26. C. S. Lewis, *A Grief Observed* (San Francisco: HarperOne, 2001), 78.

27. Jer 29:11.

28. Hughes, *God of Surprises*.

29. Mark Thibodeaux, *Armchair Mystic: Easing into Contemplative Prayer* (Cincinnati, OH: St. Anthony Messenger, 2001), 27.

30. Carlos G. Valles, SJ, *Sketches of God* (Chicago: Loyola, 1987), 168.

31. Barry and Connolly, *Practice of Spiritual Direction*, 93.

32. Anthony de Mello, SJ, *Seek God Everywhere: Reflections on the Spiritual Exercises of St. Ignatius* (New York: Image/Doubleday, 2010), 3.

33. 1 Kgs 19:12 (King James Version).

7. Everyone Needs Help

1. Karl Rahner, *The Need and the Blessing of Prayer* (Collegeville, MN: Liturgical, 1997), 48.

2. Gn 18:23–33.

3. Nm 14:19.

4. 1 Sm 1:11.

5. 1 Chr 17:23.

6. 1 Kgs 17:17–24.

7. Pss 86:1, 143:1, 13:1, 13:3, 65:2.

8. Lk 18:1–8.

9. Lk 11:8–9.

10. Lk 22:42.

11. Acts 1:24–25.

12. 1 Thes 3:10.

13. Rom 15:30–31.

14. 2 Cor 12:8–9.

15. Dennis Olkhom, "Prayer," in *Evangelical Dictionary of Biblical Theology*, ed. Daniel J. Treier and Walter A. Elwell, 3rd ed. (Grand Rapids, MI: Baker Academic, 2017).

16. Mt 18:3.

17. Ps 137:9.

18. Carroll Stuhlmueller, "Psalms," in *HarperCollins Bible Commentary*, ed. James L. Mays, rev. ed. (San Francisco: HarperOne, 2000), 442.

19. Augustine, *Expositions on the Book of Psalms*, Ps 137.

20. Lester K. Little, *Benedictine Maledictions: Liturgical Cursing in Romanesque France* (Ithaca, NY: Cornell Univ. Press, 1993), 36.

21. Mk 9:17–22.

22. Margaret Silf, *Close to the Heart: A Practical Approach to Personal Prayer* (Chicago: Loyola, 2003), 73.

23. Rahner, *Need and the Blessing of Prayer*, 49.

24. Mt 7:7–11.

25. For more on the historicity and the story of the Church of the Holy Sepulchre, see *Jesus: A Pilgrimage* (San Francisco: Harper-One, 2014).

26. Rahner, *Need and the Blessing of Prayer*, 101.

27. Rahner, *Need and the Blessing of Prayer*, 48–59.

28. Mk 14:36; Jn 11:42; Lk 22:42.

29. Rahner, *Need and the Blessing of Prayer*, 56–57.

8. Now I Lay Me Down to Sleep

1. Charles J. Healey, SJ, *The Ignatian Way: Key Aspects of Jesuit Spirituality* (Mahwah, NJ: Paulist, 2009), 55.

2. Thomas Merton, *Thoughts in Solitude* (New York: Farrar, Straus & Giroux, 1981), 79.

3. Karl Rahner and Johann Baptist Metz, *The Courage to Pray* (New York: Crossroad, 1981), 9.

4. Some other good collections include Phyllis Tickle's *The Divine Hours*, based on the Episcopal lectionary and the Book of Common Prayer, and *Hearts on Fire*, a treasury of prayers by Jesuits compiled by Michael Harter, SJ. Also, there are easy-to-carry books such as *A Catholic Book of Hours and Other Devotions* by William Storey. Online searches for "prayers for hard times" or other descriptions or for prayers of specific saints, for example, "prayers of St. Teresa of Ávila," will yield decent collections. Good resources can also be found on the websites of religious orders such as the Franciscans, Carmelites, Benedictines, and so forth.

5. Lawrence S. Cunningham and Keith J. Egan, *Christian Spirituality: Themes from the Tradition* (Mahwah, NJ: Paulist, 1996), 79; Mt 6:7.

9. I Am Here

1. Ignatius of Loyola, *The Spiritual Exercises of Saint Ignatius*, trans. George E. Ganss, SJ (Chicago: Loyola, 1992), 153 (#23).

2. George Aschenbrenner, *Consciousness Examen* (Chicago: Loyola, 2007), 2.

3. Thomas Green, *Experiencing God: The Three Stages of Prayer* (Notre Dame, IN: Ave Maria, 2010), 28.

4. Jim Manney, *The Prayer That Changes Everything* (Chicago: Loyola, 2011), 1.

5. Mark Thibodeaux, *Reimagining the Ignatian Examen: Fresh Ways to Pray from Your Day* (Chicago: Loyola, 2015), xxi.

6. Ignatius of Loyola, *Letters of St. Ignatius Loyola*, trans. William Young, SJ (Chicago: Loyola, 1959), 55.

7. Aschenbrenner, *Consciousness Examen*, 9–10.

8. Manney, *Prayer That Changes Everything*, 36.

9. Manney, *Prayer That Changes Everything*, 52.

10. Aschenbrenner, *Consciousness Examen*, 14.

11. Aschenbrenner, *Consciousness Examen*, 18.

12. Karl Rahner, *Meditations on Hope and Love* (New York: Seabury Press, 1977), 48.

13. James Martin, SJ, ed., *How Can I Find God?: The Famous and the Not-So-Famous Consider the Quintessential Question* (Liguori, MO: Triumph, 1997), 181–82.

14. See Thibodeaux, *Reimagining the Ignatian Examen*; Aschenbrenner, *Consciousness Examen*.

15. Margaret Silf, *Inner Compass: An Invitation to Ignatian Spirituality* (Chicago: Loyola, 1999), 38–41.

16. Manney, *Prayer That Changes Everything*, 5.

17. Manney, *Prayer That Changes Everything*, 16.

10. What Happens When You Pray?

1. Ex 3:13–14.

2. Mark Thibodeaux, SJ, *Reimagining the Ignatian Examen: Fresh Ways to Pray from Your Day* (Chicago: Loyola, 2015), 14.

3. Universal language is usually not coming from God, if it is expressed negatively: "*No one* loves me." "*Everyone* has it better than I do." "I *never* get what I want." "*None* of my friends ever call me." Be careful about such universal language. It can inaccurately (and profoundly) affect how we perceive life.

4. Richard Leonard, *Preaching to the Converted: On Sundays and Feast Days Throughout the Year* (Mahwah, NJ: Paulist, 2006), 85.

5. Ps 13:1.

6. Mk 2:1–12.

7. "At its simplest the parable is a metaphor or simile drawn from nature or common life, arresting the hearer by its vividness or strangeness, and leaving the mind in sufficient doubt about its precise application to tease it into active thought" (C. H. Dodd, *Parables of the Kingdom* [New York: Scribner, 1961], vii).

8. For more on discernment and the ways that one can prayerfully come to a decision, see *The Jesuit Guide to (Almost) Everything: A Spirituality for Real Life* (San Francisco: HarperOne, 2010).

9. Gerard Hughes, *God of Surprises* (Grand Rapids, MI: Eerdmans, 2008), 87.

10. Ignatius of Loyola, *The Spiritual Exercises of Saint Ignatius*, trans. George E. Ganss, SJ (Chicago: Loyola, 1992), 91 (#221).

11. Mk 10:46–52.

12. Jn 4:1–42.

13. In recent years some people who are blind have challenged traditional interpretations of this story, questioning whether it helps to consider blindness something that always needs healing. Likewise, many take issue with the Gospels' frequent equation of physical and spiritual blindness. (Often in the Gospels, a story about a physical cure of blindness is placed side by side with Jesus's arguing with his critics, who are shown to be "blind.") These are fair critiques that must be heard from the blind community. But it's also important to note that Jesus first asks Bartimaeus what he wants, and that Bartimaeus, at least as the Gospels recount the story, *asks* to see. In the first century, blindness was almost a guarantee of poverty and social exclusion. Thus, he may have wanted and needed healing for both physical and financial reasons. So here, at least as I read the story, Jesus is listening carefully to Bartimaeus's explicit desires.

14. Augustine, *Confessions*, bk. 1.

15. Ignatius of Loyola, *A Pilgrim's Testament: The Memoirs of Saint Ignatius of Loyola*, trans. P. Divarkar and L. G. da Camara (St. Louis, MO: Institute of Jesuit Sources, 1995), 8.

16. Mt 14:14–21.

17. For more on the history of Lourdes and the pilgrimages, see *Lourdes Diary: Seven Days at the Grotto of Massabieille* (Chicago: Loyola, 2006).

18. Vinita Hampton Wright, *Days of Deepening Friendship: For the Woman Who Wants Authentic Life with God* (Chicago: Loyola, 2009), 48.

19. Lk 4:16–30.

20. Ignatius of Loyola, *Personal Writings*, trans. and ed. Joseph A. Munitiz and Philip Endean (London: Penguin Books, 1996), 77.

21. Ignatius, *Personal Writings*, 86.

22. Ruth Burrows, *Guidelines for Mystical Prayer* (London: Sheed & Ward, 1976), 6.

23. See Karl Rahner, *The Mystical Way in Everyday Life* (Maryknoll, NY: Orbis Books, 2010).

24. Burrows, *Guidelines for Mystical Prayer*, 10.

25. C. S. Lewis, *Surprised by Joy: The Shape of My Early Life* (San Francisco: HarperOne, 2017), 17.

26. Abraham Joshua Heschel, *God in Search of Man: A Philosophy of Judaism* (New York: Farrar, Straus & Giroux, 1976), 74–75.

27. Joyce Rupp, *Prayer* (Maryknoll, NY: Orbis Books, 2007), 77–78.

28. Rupp, *Prayer*, 77.

29. Burrows, *Guidelines for Mystical Prayer*, 51.

11. How Do I Know It's God?

1. This is not the normal situation for martyrs. Usually martyrs are either killed outright by hostile forces or given the choice between denying the faith or dying themselves—rather than seeing others harmed. But fashioning the "choice" to include others was one way Endō dramatized Rodrigues's plight.

2. Ex 33:20.

3. Mt 16:13–20; also Mk 8:27–30; Lk 9:18–20.

4. Mk 1:11.

5. Some may ascribe the message I received from the elderly retreatant to "coincidence," so let me put a word in for coincidence as a way that God reaches out to us. Not every coincidence should be interpreted in this way, and we have to be on guard for superstitious beliefs ("If I see a bird, that means I'm supposed to leave my job"). But some coincidences seem inescapably clear signs of God's presence.

As I was writing this book, I was struggling to remember a poem that I had heard on the retreat mentioned in order to include it in the chapter on centering prayer. I was sitting in front of my computer, racking my brain, flipping through various books, unsuccessfully trying to recall the name of the poet, when an email popped up. It was from my retreat director, who said, "I just used that poem that you liked on retreat, and it made me think of you." I was thunderstruck. At the precise moment that I was searching for it, an email came from someone I hadn't heard from in months, about a poem we'd read on a retreat six years ago. Could this be anything other than God's playful reaching out? That poem, "Beckoner," now appears in Chapter 14.

6. William A. Barry, SJ, "How Do I Know It's God?," *America* 186, no. 17 (May 20, 2002): 12–15.
7. C. S. Lewis, *Apostle to the Skeptics* (Oregon: Wipf & Stock, 2008), 82.
8. Barry, "How Do I Know It's God?," 13.
9. Ignatius of Loyola, *The Spiritual Exercises of Saint Ignatius*, trans. George E. Ganss, SJ (Chicago: Loyola, 1992), 127 (#335).
10. George Aschenbrenner, *Consciousness Examen* (Chicago: Loyola, 2007), 20.
11. Ignatius, *Spiritual Exercises*, 127 (#335).
12. Barry, "How Do I Know It's God?," 13–14.
13. Barry, "How Do I Know It's God?," 15.
14. Mt 14:13–21; Lk 9:12–17; Jn 6:1–14.
15. Ignatius, *Spiritual Exercises*, 121 (#315).
16. Ignatius, *Spiritual Exercises*, 121 (#315).
17. Mt 7:15–20.
18. Thomas Green, *Experiencing God: The Three Stages of Prayer* (Notre Dame, IN: Ave Maria, 2010), 79.
19. Margaret Silf, *Close to the Heart: A Practical Approach to Personal Prayer* (Chicago: Loyola, 2003), 132–33.
20. Jn 10:3–5.

12. The Gift of Imagination

1. William A. Barry, SJ, *God and You: Prayer as a Personal Relationship* (Mahwah, NJ: Paulist, 1987), 45.
2. Barry, *God and You*, 25.
3. Bonaventure, *The Life of St. Francis*, chap. 10, #7.
4. David L. Fleming, SJ, *What Is Ignatian Spirituality?* (Chicago: Loyola, 2008), 55.
5. Ignatius of Loyola, *The Spiritual Exercises of Saint Ignatius*, trans. George E. Ganss, SJ (Chicago: Loyola, 1992), 40 (#47).
6. Ignatius, *Spiritual Exercises*, 98 (#112).
7. Jodi Magness, *Stone and Dung, Oil and Spit: Jewish Daily Life in the Time of Jesus* (Grand Rapids, MI: Eerdmans, 2011), 130.

8. Lk 2:1–7.

9. Charles J. Healey, SJ, *The Ignatian Way: Key Aspects of Jesuit Spirituality* (Mahwah, NJ: Paulist, 2009), 44.

10. Mt 1:18–25, 2:1–23; Lk 2:1–7.

11. Joan Taylor, *What Did Jesus Look Like?* (London: Bloomsbury T&T Clark, 2018).

12. Joseph A. Tetlow, SJ, *Making Choices in Christ: The Foundations of Ignatian Spirituality* (Chicago: Loyola, 2008), 72.

13. Mk 4:41.

14. Irene Zimmerman, *Incarnation: New and Selected Poems for Spiritual Reflection* (Lanham, MD: Cowley, 2004). A favorite of mine is "The Healing of the Paralytic," 53–54.

15. Rom 8:26–27.

16. Gerard Hughes, *God of Surprises* (Grand Rapids, MI: Eerdmans, 2008), 52.

17. Barry, *God and You*, 42.

18. Ignatius, *Spiritual Exercises*, 46 (#53).

13. Praying with Sacred Texts

1. Kevin Irwin, "*Lectio Divina*," in *The New Dictionary of Catholic Spirituality*, ed. Michael Downey (Collegeville, MN: Liturgical, 1993), 596.

2. Irwin, "*Lectio Divina*," 596.

3. Now the Boston College School of Theology and Ministry.

4. James Martin, SJ, ed., *How Can I Find God?: The Famous and the Not-So-Famous Consider the Quintessential Question* (Liguori, MO: Triumph, 1997), 130.

5. Mt 8:22.

6. My favorites: *The New Collegeville Bible Commentary* (for general readers), *HarperCollins Bible Commentary* and *HarperCollins Bible Dictionary* (slightly more scholarly), and *The New Jerome Biblical Commentary* (very scholarly). Also the *Sacra Pagina* series, which looks at the individual books of the New Testament one by one, is superb. That is my favorite resource for the understanding of the Gospels. For specific Jewish practices, try *The Jewish Annotated New Testament*, which explains the Jewish-related words, places, and events as well as the Jewish practices that underlie the words and deeds of Jesus as recorded in the Gospels.

7. Ps 137:1–2.

8. Thomas Merton, *New Seeds of Contemplation* (New York: New Directions, 1961), 34–36.

9. Merton, *New Seeds of Contemplation*, 31.

14. Finding God at the Center

1. Harvey Egan, SJ, "Negative Way," in *The New Dictionary of Catholic Spirituality*, ed. Michael Downey (Collegeville, MN: Liturgical, 1993), 700–703.

2. Ex 20:21, 24:15.

3. Egan, "Negative Way," 700.

4. Egan, "Negative Way," 701.

5. Jn 14:9.

6. Egan, "Negative Way," 701.

7. Ignatius of Loyola, *The Spiritual Exercises of Saint Ignatius*, trans. George E. Ganss, SJ (Chicago: Loyola, 1992), 100 (#258).

8. M. Basil Pennington, OCSO, Thomas Keating, OCSO, and Thomas E. Clarke, SJ, *Finding Grace at the Center: The Beginning of Centering Prayer* (Woodstock, VT: SkyLight Paths, 2007), 80.

9. 1 Cor 6:19; Rom. 8:11.

10. Augustine, *Confessions*, 3.6.11.

11. Pennington, Keating, and Clarke, *Finding Grace at the Center*, 31.

12. Pennington, Keating, and Clarke, *Finding Grace at the Center*, 32.

13. Pennington, Keating, and Clarke, *Finding Grace at the Center*, 38.

14. Johnston, William, trans. and ed. *The Cloud of Unknowing* (New York: Random House, 2012), 80.

15. Pennington, Keating, and Clarke, *Finding Grace at the Center*, 40.

16. Ignatius of Loyola, *Personal Writings*, trans. and ed. Joseph A. Munitiz and Philip Endean (London: Penguin Books, 1996), 107.

17. Pennington, Keating, and Clarke, *Finding Grace at the Center*, 51.

18. Quoted in James Martin, SJ, *The Jesuit Guide to (Almost) Everything: A Spirituality for Real Life* (San Francisco: HarperOne, 2010), 167.

19. Joyce Rupp, *Fragments of Your Ancient Name: 365 Glimpses of the Divine for Daily Meditation* (Notre Dame, IN: Sorin, 2011), 50.

20. Pennington, Keating, and Clarke, *Finding Grace at the Center*, 60.

15. Discovering God in Creation

1. Pope Francis, *Laudato Si'*, 97.

2. C. H. Dodd, *Parables of the Kingdom* (New York: Scribner, 1961), 16.

3. Mk 4:30–32; Mt 13:31–32.

4. Ps 19:1.

5. Ps 95:3–5.

6. Ps 8:3–4.

7. Gerard Manley Hopkins, "God's Grandeur," line 1.

8. Caoimhe Twohig-Bennett and Andy Jones, "The Health Benefits of the Great Outdoors: A Systematic Review and Meta-Analysis of Greenspace Exposures and Health Outcomes," *Environmental Research* 166 (October 2018): 628–37.

9. Mary Oliver, *Devotions: The Selected Poems of Mary Oliver* (New York: Penguin, 2017), 131.

10. William A. Barry, SJ, *God and You: Prayer as a Personal Relationship* (Mahwah, NJ: Paulist, 1987), 20.

11. Ps 42:7.

12. Rachel Carson, *The Sea Around Us* (New York: Oxford Univ. Press, 1961), 29.

13. Ignatius of Loyola, *The Spiritual Exercises of Saint Ignatius*, trans. George E. Ganss, SJ (Chicago: Loyola, 1992), 95 (#235).

14. Ignatius, *Spiritual Exercises*, 95 (#236).

15. Ignatius, *Spiritual Exercises*, 95 (#236).

16. Pope Francis, *Laudato Si'*, 84.

17. Pope Francis, *Laudato Si'*, 67.

18. William Souder, *On a Farther Shore* (New York: Broadway, 2012).

19. Pope Francis, *Laudato Si'*, 84.

16. Talking About Prayer

1. William A. Barry and William J. Connolly, *The Practice of Spiritual Direction*, 2nd ed. (San Francisco: HarperOne, 2009), 8–9.

2. William A. Barry, SJ, *God and You: Prayer as a Personal Relationship* (Mahwah, NJ: Paulist, 1987), 76.

3. Joyce Rupp, *Prayer* (Maryknoll, NY: Orbis Books, 2007), 53.

4. Thomas Merton, *Contemplative Prayer* (New York: Herder & Herder, 1969), 41.

5. Barry and Connolly, *Practice of Spiritual Direction*, 11.

6. Mark Thibodeaux, *Armchair Mystic: Easing into Contemplative Prayer* (Cincinnati, OH: St. Anthony Messenger, 2001), 116.

7. The "19th Annotation Retreats" are so called because the idea is taken from one annotation in a series that St. Ignatius made

to the text of the *Spiritual Exercises*. The 19th concerns people who are unable to take part in the full four weeks of the Spiritual Exercises mainly for reasons of time (which these days is most people). More about the Spiritual Exercises can be found in *The Jesuit Guide to (Almost) Everything: A Spirituality for Real Life* (San Francisco: HarperOne, 2010).

8. Jn 3:34.
9. Thibodeaux, *Armchair Mystic*, 68.
10. Margaret Silf, *Close to the Heart: A Practical Approach to Personal Prayer* (Chicago: Loyola, 2003), 211–12.

17. Topics in Prayer

1. Thomas Green, *Experiencing God: The Three Stages of Prayer* (Notre Dame, IN: Ave Maria, 2010), 18.
2. Thomas Merton, *New Seeds of Contemplation* (New York: New Directions, 1961), 224.
3. Margaret Silf, *Close to the Heart: A Practical Approach to Personal Prayer* (Chicago: Loyola, 2003), 180.
4. Gerard Hughes, *God of Surprises* (Grand Rapids, MI: Eerdmans, 2008), 81–82.
5. Hughes, *God of Surprises*, 49.
6. Joyce Rupp, *Prayer* (Maryknoll, NY: Orbis Books, 2007), 85–86.
7. Mark Thibodeaux, *Armchair Mystic: Easing into Contemplative Prayer* (Cincinnati, OH: St. Anthony Messenger, 2001), 132.
8. Karl Rahner, *Encounters with Silence* (South Bend, IN: St. Augustine's Press, 1999), 56.
9. William A. Barry and William J. Connolly, *The Practice of Spiritual Direction*, 2nd ed. (San Francisco: HarperOne, 2009), 71.
10. *The Collected Works of St. John of the Cross*, trans. David Lewis (New York: Cosimo, 2007), 121.
11. Ignatius of Loyola, *The Spiritual Exercises of Saint Ignatius*, trans. George E. Ganss, SJ (Chicago: Loyola, 1992), 122 (#317).
12. Merton, *New Seeds of Contemplation*, 180.
13. Ps 22:24. For more on the Seven Ds, including ways to respond to them, see my article "Shadows in Prayer: The Seven Ds of the Spiritual Life," *America* 198, no. 9 (March 17, 2008): 19–24.
14. Margaret Silf, *Wayfaring: A Gospel Journey in Everyday Life* (Notre Dame, IN: Sorin, 2009), 64.
15. Mt 11:28.

18. Now What?

1. Joyce Rupp, *Prayer* (Maryknoll, NY: Orbis Books, 2007), 109.
2. Ruth Burrows, OCD, *Essence of Prayer* (Mahwah, NJ: Hidden-Spring, 2006), 31.
3. Thomas Green, *Experiencing God: The Three Stages of Prayer* (Notre Dame, IN: Ave Maria, 2010), 84.
4. Karl Rahner and Johann Baptist Metz, *The Courage to Pray* (New York: Crossroad, 1981), 28.
5. Mk 1:7.
6. Mt 17:1; Mk 9:2; Lk 9:28.
7. Ex 34:29–35.
8. Mk 9:2–9.
9. Lk 5:4–8.
10. Mk 9:6.